WRITERS DREAMING

WRITERS
DREAMING

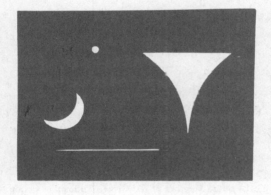

Naomi Epel

Carol Southern Books

New York

Photo Credits: Jerry Bauer: pages 93, 119, 160, 237, 270; Doyle Bush: 106; Chris Callis: 229; Nancy Crampton: 43, 74, 244; Evergreen Studios: 188; Rosina Fleming: 167; Robert Foothorap: 281; Kristina Ford: 54; Rosemary Herbert: 59; Brigitte Jouxtel: 31; Gigi Kaeser: 255; Tabitha King: 133; Joan Leonard: 144; Marcia Lieberman: 7; Will & Deni McIntyre © 1992: 200; Robert Marshak: 219; Leonard Michaels: 152; John Nichols: 178; Karen O'Brien: 209; Nancy Robinson: 25.

Grateful acknowledgment is made to William Morrow and Co., Inc. for permission to reprint from "Seismosaurus" from *Tyrannosaurus Was a Beast* by Jack Prelutsky, copyright © 1988 by Jack Prelutsky, and from "Ballad of a boneless chicken," "The day they sent Sam to the grocery story," "We're fearless flying hot dogs," "Today I shall powder my elephant's ears" all from *Something Big Has Been Here* by Jack Prelutsky, copyright © 1990 by Jack Prelutsky.

Published by Carol Southern Books, 201 East 50th Street, New York, New York 10022. Member of the Crown Publishing Group.

Random House, Inc. New York, Toronto, London, Sydney, Auckland

CAROL SOUTHERN BOOKS and colophon are trademarks of Crown Publishers, Inc.

Manufactured in the United States of America

Design by Iris Weinstein

Library of Congress Cataloging-in-Publication Data

Writers dreaming / [interviewed] by Naomi Epel.—1st ed.

1. Authors, American—20th century—Interviews. 2. Creativity (Literary, artistic, etc.) 3. Authors—Psychology. 4. Creative ability. 5. Authorship. 6. Dreams. I. Epel, Naomi.

PS129.W74 1993

810.9'0054—dc20   92-43862   CIP

ISBN 0-517-58982-6

10 9 8 7 6 5 4 3 2 1

First Edition

To my mother, Beatrice, who taught me how to ask
questions, and my father, Joseph, who gave me
the courage to do so.

ACKNOWLEDGMENTS

It is with deep gratitude that I acknowledge the generosity of the writers who have contributed their time, thoughts and dreams to this book. By talking with me about their most private thoughts and recounting their dreams and personal ways of working, they have made an enormous contribution to an understanding of the creative process. Their fascinating narrative will provide powerful inspiration to writers, dreamers and literature lovers.

I would also like to thank the many friends, teachers and allies who have helped make this book a reality.

Susan Page set this book in motion the day she phoned and suggested I become a literary escort. She then introduced me to Joyce Cole, who launched me in the business; to Dorothy Wall, who, along with Desmond Morris and Darryl Brock, helped me to define the parameters of this project; and finally to Sandra

Dijkstra, the world's greatest literary agent. Each of these people deserves profound thanks.

Sandra Dijkstra has been a wise counselor and a powerful advocate. Her associates Rita Holm and Kathy Saideman have been a terrific support team.

Carol Southern has been a dream of an editor. She has loved this book from the beginning and guided it with a gentle hand. Eliza Scott has also been a delight to work with. I am grateful to Morgan Molthrop for his early interest in the manuscript, and to Marty Asher for his encouragement.

Jeremy Taylor, Harriet Sage and Phyllis Murphy Szerekeo have been important teachers, introducing me to the power and beauty of dreams. Sue Taylor, Midge Lester, and Melody Ermachild helped me to learn the art of interviewing, building on the example my mother provided with her insightful postlecture inquiries.

I had to slow down and "clear my plate" before the idea for this book could emerge. Lee Glickstien and Jennifer Freeman taught me how to do that.

Some of the interviews in this book began as conversations produced for radio. Robert Siegel of NPR didn't know the impact he was having when he suggested I get myself a tape recorder and learn to use it. Leo C. Lee of Western Public Radio and Lynn Chadwick of NFCB generously taught me basic radio production and encouraged my work. "DreamTalk" first aired on KALX in Berkeley thanks to Charles Runnette, Sandra Wasson and Hendrika Davis. The production quality was enhanced by the artistry of Pliny Keep and Michael Johnson. Dan Margolis, Yusef Sabour and Gordy Polatnik engineered some of the first interviews. Daniel Del Solar, Bill Helgeson and Alan Farley provided a new audience for later interviews at KALW in San Francisco.

Melissa McCampbell helped me see what I had on tape by transcribing some of the earliest interviews. Lowell Keller of Resistance Repair saved the William Styron interview from mechanical oblivion.

This book would not have happened without the help of my publicist friends Pamela Henstell, Tammy Richards, Marie Coolman, Hilary Bass, Janet Schnol, Mi-ho Cha. Rose Carrano, Jane Beirn, Diana Faust and Pamela Duevel. Thanks also to Craig Herman, Paul Slovak, Annette Swanberg, Kathleen Krebs, Nancy David, Kurt Aldag, Jo Beaton and, of course, Greg Mowery. Deepest thanks to Shirley Sonderegger, Sue Quiroz and Dan Epel for their efforts in securing key interviews.

Victoria Shoemaker, Elaine Petrocelli, Neal Sofman, Dick Lamb, John Landrigan, Paul Shanahan. Herb Bivins, Adine Korns and Andy Ross contributed valuable guidance. Thank God for great booksellers!

My friends Michael Mercil and Stephen Thewlis not only listened as I obsessed over minute word changes, they fed me while I worked. Also helpful were Peter DeGoey, Sue Halpern, Barbara Dickey, Robert Harris and Sydney Goldstein of City Arts and Lectures. Further thanks are due the staffs at the Graduate Theological Union library. the Highland Dell Inn and the North Branch of the Berkeley Public Library.

Sue Mittelman and my sister Julia Sherry were especially important friends while the book was gestating. I am also grateful to Jo Mohrbach, Sue Bender, Lura Dolas, Linda Applewhite, Dan Winkler, Julie Andelman, Jeff Straal, Andrea Pettigrew, Debby Kelman, Jeff Wildfogel, Catherine Linesch, Brenda Helm, Minou Henon, Sheridan Adams, Pat Macias, Todd Hodson, Allen Williams, Josh Epel, Dena Korda, Katie Blood, Mitch Tyler, Dedra Buchwald, Jan Weinberg, Barbara Lebow, Bob Cowart and my wonderful parents, Joe and Bea Epel.

Thank you all for your help, love, time and support.

CONTENTS

INTRODUCTION

ONE MORNING in the spring of 1974, William Styron woke
to the lingering image of a woman he had known in his early
twenties. He could see her standing in a hallway, her arms full
of books, the blue numbers of a tattoo visible beneath her sleeve.
Suddenly he knew it was time to abandon the book over which
he'd been laboring to tell this woman's story. He went directly
to his studio and wrote the opening paragraphs of what was to
become *Sophie's Choice*.

Styron's experience is one that is echoed throughout the
pages of this book as writers describe the ways they have been
inspired and aided by forces beyond consciousness, while lying
in their beds, asleep.

When I began asking writers about their dreams I had no
idea a book was in the making. I was simply engaging in conversation with the passengers in my red LeBaron convertible as we

traveled the streets of San Francisco. As a literary escort, it was my job to make sure that visiting writers, promoting their books in Northern California, got to their appointments relaxed and on time. It was not infrequent that curious authors, bored with talking about themselves or their books, would inquire about my life outside the car. Upon learning that I worked with dreams—leading workshops to help people tap into their hidden creativity—many of my often tired authors seemed to perk up, eager to share a dream or relate a nightmare. Driving along in my automobile I heard tales of dreams that inspired art and dreams that predicted the future, of childhood nightmares that had never been forgotten and dreams that changed ways of working and ways of seeing the world.

I was so excited by what I was hearing that I began inviting authors to the studio at KALX, Berkeley, where we taped our conversations for my weekly radio program, "DreamTalk."

Still, it wasn't until *I* had a dream that this book began to become a reality.

In the dream I was standing in a doorway watching an artist working in a basement room. I somehow knew that this was a man who didn't like to be disturbed. But, because I was very quiet, he let me stay. When, the following morning, I told this dream to a friend, he asked me just one question: "How did it feel?" Amazingly I found myself in tears. I realized how good it had felt to be accepted without having to *do* anything. I didn't have to impress this person, I simply had to be still.

Now, this dream came at a time when I was doing far too much. Not only was I running the escort business, I was also teaching dreamwork classes, seeing clients and hosting a weekly radio show. My friend suggested I "honor" the dream and simply do nothing for two full weeks. Just keep quiet and sit with the artist in my basement. Following this advice, I canceled the dream workshop I had been planning, leaving hundreds of flyers—printed, stamped and labeled—unmailed, and simply sat. I found myself drawn to the computer, where my fingers flew across the keyboard as I described all that I had learned about dreams and writing while sitting in my car. The artist in my basement had been working silently for years and I hadn't even known it.

Weeks later, while driving writer Desmond Morris, I mentioned the project I had begun, interweaving the stories I'd collected with my own thoughts on the meaning and purpose of dreams. It was his suggestion that I "get out of the way" and simply let the authors speak for themselves. Thus evolved the format for this book, which now consists of lightly edited transcripts of taped conversations, my questions having been deleted to aid the flow. (These were generally one sentence, open-ended questions followed by lots of head nodding, "mmmhmming" and follow-up questions like "what do you mean?" and "how about an example?") Occasionally I have added a word or two for clarification, but mostly what you hear are the writers' thoughts, verbatim.

It was interesting when, a year later, the book nearly completed, a friend pointed out that Morris's message to get out of the way had been embedded all along in the imagery of the dream. The dream picture said stay quiet and let the artists do the work.

Once I realized a book was evolving I decided to focus on writers of fiction and set out to contact my favorites. Many writers were delighted to talk while others declined, saying they never remembered their dreams. Still others didn't want to give away "trade secrets" or risk losing the magic stuff that fueled their art.

It took almost a year and four painstakingly crafted letters to get an interview with Stephen King. I called so often that a friendship formed between King's personal assistant and myself. It was she who slipped my letters to the top of the pile until he found the time to talk.

A combination of luck and legwork brought another favorite writer to the project. My brother Dan called one day to ask if I had heard of the incredible woman with whom he'd spent the last five hours flying from Atlanta—Maya Angelou. I was able to glean the information that she was in the area visiting her son and I set about to track her down. When I finally found her she consented to talk, but was unimpressed when I mentioned that she had been number one on my wish list of authors. "I assume" she said, "that is because my name begins with A."

The interviews were fairly free-form. I usually began by asking "Have you ever had a dream that influenced your work?" and let it go from there. I asked about nightmares and recurrent themes, personal insights and precognitive dreams. Sometimes I asked if their characters ever visited them in the middle of the night, or how they thought dreams functioned.

It was not unusual for a writer to begin by saying that he or she seldom remembered any dreams. "Most people tell me that," was my standard reply and, after a bit of gentle probing, the floodgates would spring open.

Murder, sex, torture and pursuit, flying, falling and visits from the dead were among the adventures recounted during these conversations. Anxiety, pleasure, fear and triumph were all expressed in story form. And very often dream images directly affected the writer's art.

Horror writer Clive Barker told how he turned a sexual dream, charged with the odor of rotting fruit, into the story "The Age of Desire," about an aphrodisiac out of control. Children's poet Jack Prelutsky revealed how he found the punchline for his "Ballad of a Boneless Chicken" in a dream of scrambled eggs. And Bharati Mukherjee described how characters have visited her dreams, urging her to alter the endings to their stories.

In exploring the ways these writers transformed their dreams into art, the discussion turned to tools, techniques and craft. So, we have Elmore Leonard talking about writing exposition, Gloria Naylor on finding the proper point of view and Sue Grafton on plotting a mystery.

By revealing the questions raised by an image, several writ-

ers provided insight into their creative process. When Charles
Johnson, three years into the writing of *Middle Passage*, dreamt
of a mysterious crate he questioned what it might contain. "Is
it animal, vegetable or mineral?" he asked, and was surprised to
discover its contents were none of the above.

Writers Dreaming is not only about writing, it is also about
the affects dreams have on a writer's personal life. A series of
dreams in which a murdered friend taught her to fly and face her
fears helped Amy Tan find confidence in her waking life. A new
ending to a recurrent nightmare helped Isabel Allende notice the
man who later became her husband.

Elmore Leonard's early dreams not only illustrate his pre-
success anxieties but give us an insight into the metaphorical
language of dreams. During the twenty years Leonard was writing without public recognition he frequently dreamt of climbing rickety ladders and falling down flights of stairs. "It was
never a hit" was the phrase he used when describing the moments just before his abrupt awakenings. But with success, these
dreams vanished. So did his recurrent nightmare of being back
at work in an ad agency office stocked with food to last a
lifetime.

It is important to note that I never offer interpretations to
dreams that are told to me. I believe that only the dreamer can
tell what a given image means. A cow to a butcher means
something entirely different than what it might mean to a
Hindu or to a woman about to give birth. I only ask questions
and let the dreamers discover meaning for themselves. It is
often amazing to see the cleverness with which a dream communicates.

In the pages that follow you will meet some of today's most
important writers in a way few people have ever encountered
them before. In talking about their dreams, they reveal a very
private part of themselves and of their working process. Here
you have the opportunity to discover the raw materials—the
fears, desires and anxieties—with which these writers create

their art. I hope that this intimate glimpse behind the scenes into these writers' minds will be both enlightening and inspiring—granting you fresh insight into the creative process, increased understanding of your own dreams and a rich relationship with the artist in *your* basement.

—Naomi Epel
October 1, 1992

ISABEL ALLENDE

ISABEL ALLENDE has, in the words of *The Times* of London, "the rare ability to blend fantasy and legend with political fact . . . to produce an enchanted world unlike anything else in contemporary fiction."

Born in Lima, Peru, in 1942, Isabel Allende was raised in Chile. She fled Chile in 1975 after the bloody coup that resulted in the death of her uncle, Salvador Allende. She spent thirteen years in exile in Venezuela where she raised her two children and worked as a journalist.

In 1982 Allende published her first novel, *House of the Spirits*, which, along with each of her subsequent books, received international acclaim. The book began as a series of unmailed letters to her grandfather, written as he approached his hundredth year. The novel was Allende's attempt to keep the memories of her family and country alive. Her second novel, *Love and Shadows* was followed by *Eva Luna* in 1987 and *The Stories of Eva Luna* in 1990. Each book was written in Spanish and translated by others.

A woman of grace and elegance, Allende lives in a beautiful home overlooking the San Francisco Bay with her American husband, Willi.

———

I WRITE in a very organic way. Books don't happen in my mind, they happen somewhere in my belly. It's like a long elephant pregnancy that can last two years. And then, when I'm ready to give birth, I sit down. I wait for January 8th, which is my special date, and then, that day, I begin the book that has been growing inside me.

Often when I sit that day and turn on my computer or my typewriter and write the first sentence, I don't know what I'm going to write about because it has not yet made the trip from the belly to the mind. It is somewhere hidden in a very somber and secret place where I don't have any access yet. It is something that I've been feeling but which has no shape, no name, no tone, no voice. So I write the first sentence—which usually is the first sentence of the book. That is the only thing that really stays. Then the story starts unfolding itself, slowly, in a long process. By the time I've finished the first draft I know what the book is about. But not before.

Somehow inside me—I can say this after having written five books—I know that I know where I am going. I know that I know the end of the book even though I don't know it. It's so difficult to explain. It is as if I have this terrible confidence that something that is beyond myself knows why I'm writing this book. And what the end of the book will be. And how the book will develop. But if you ask me what the book is about or where I am going I can't tell you. I can't tell anybody. I can't even tell myself. But I have the certainty that I would not have started the book without knowing why I'm writing it.

In a very superstitious way, it is as if I trust that there are voices outside myself, that talk through me. So the voices know. And sooner or later I will listen to the whole message. For the time being, I only have a particle of it.

With *House of the Spirits*, my first novel, I knew how the book would end, I knew what I wanted to say and I knew why I had written it. Still, I had written the last fifteen pages more than ten times and I could never get it right. It was solemn, preachy—too political, melodramatic. I couldn't get the tone. One night, at three o'clock in the morning, I woke up with a dream. In the dream my grandfather was lying on his bed.

Now, my grandfather died at a very old age. He was nearly one hundred years old. When my grandmother had died, he mourned her for a very long time. He dressed entirely in black. The tie, the suit, the shoes, everything. He painted the furniture black. There were no flowers in the house and no radio and no parties and no dessert. Nothing that would remind us of the happiness or the joy of life. It was a very long mourning.

In the dream I saw my grandfather dressed in black on his black bed. Everything was black in the room except the white sheets. I was sitting on a black chair, dressed in black, and I was telling him that I had written this book and what the book was about. So, when I woke up from the dream, I realized that I had been telling this story to my grandfather all the time. The tone of the whole book was his voice and my voice talking. And I realized then that the end of the book, naturally, would be that the grandfather has died and the granddaughter is waiting for dawn to bury him. So the epilogue has the tone of a person sitting beside her grandfather, who is dead, sitting by his bed, telling the story very simply. The dream gave me that.

When I begin a book, very rapidly I get into the story and it becomes the real world for me. That is, when I'm driving the car, I'm not looking at this landscape, I'm in the landscape of the book. I try not to have any social life, or very little. I try not to travel. Because everything that distracts me from the world of the book annoys me, and bores me terribly. I'm a social person, but when I'm writing I'm not. It's a very schizophrenic life. I want to be with my husband—I'm very close with him—and when I'm writing I'm even closer because he's the only person who shares this strange state of mind. So although I operate in a normal state and I can feed my grandson and buy the groceries, my mind is detached. Everything that happens to me that I can use in the story becomes interesting. And everything that I cannot use in the story is eliminated automatically. My mind becomes very selective. If we go to the movies and I see in a movie a sentence, an expression, a color, a little incident that I can transform or somehow use, I want to see the movie again. If I realize that I'm in *Terminator 2* and there's absolutely nothing I can use, I get bored and leave.

With people it happens that same way. Someone all of a sudden says something and that sentence opens a new dimension I had never thought of before. This happened yesterday. I'm finishing another book and in this book I have a person who has a dream. This person has been in the war and he has a nightmare that comes to him all the time. In the nightmare the person is on the top of a mountain. It's misty or foggy. Everything happens in black and white except for sparkles of red, the blood. This person is on top of the mountain and the enemies come in black pyjamas. He shoots but he doesn't hear any sound. And the enemies still walk toward him. The bullets pass through them as if they were made of shadows. That is the dream. He dreams this several times during the book.

The dream is like a beating that is there all the time. I don't know why it is this dream and not another dream but I asked my husband, Do you have any explanation for the dream? Why would he dream this? And he said, Well, it's obvious. He feels that he's attacked and he can't defend himself. He's threatened and he's helpless and—I said, Yeah, but there is something else that I just can't explain. Why is it that he can't stop these guys? What is this? Why is this so terribly threatening for a man who has seen so much, who has had such a hard time? So yesterday, we were watching a movie and somebody was talking about faces—about what you see in other people's faces and why you feel threatened by people of other races—and all of a sudden I had the explanation of the dream. The guy never sees the face of the enemy, but when he forces himself to look he realizes that all those shadows have his own face. He's shooting at himself. So he's aware for the first time that the enemy is within himself. I have been writing this book for two years and I still didn't have an explanation for the dream until this person, yesterday, said this, and I could put both things together. The dream now seems perfectly logical and it's the glue for the whole book.

If you can identify with the enemy's face, and you can see yourself in the enemy, there is no enemy. You realize that war is just so stupid because you are part of the same humanity. You are shooting this guy because he looks different but it's you. It's always you.

My dreams are totally different. My nightmares are very precise. I have only two nightmares. They recur all the time. I know what they mean and I know perfectly well why I have them.

In the longest nightmare, which has been with me all my life, I dream of a very disorganized and messy house. I know that the house is me. This house has rooms, closed rooms, and I know that behind one door there is a mess. It's not a threatening mess. It's not that something is growing inside the room like a beast or anything menacing. No. It's just furniture, old stuff, dust, darkness, unexplored corners. Things that I have to clean up and organize. Sometimes, in the dream, I open a door and clean up the room and then it's white, spic-and-span, perfect. But I know that there's another door over there. I know that behind that door there will be another one and this is a never-ending, never-ending dream. Because there is always another room. Sometimes the whole house is a mess and sometimes I enter the house and it looks great and all of a sudden there's the door, the closed door. So, I know that that's me and all the hidden parts that I have inside me that I have not been able to reach. And I will never be able to reach.

Maybe I'm a writer because I'm desperately trying to clean up my mess. Other people go into therapy or become psychiatrists just to clean up the mess. Well, I couldn't afford therapy at the time I needed it the most, so I started writing. And now I know that the writing helps me a little because, Why do I write about these things? Why do I choose those characters? Why am I so desperate to tell that story? Because there's something inside of me that is bothering me, that gives me a lot of pain and that I need to solve. And by exploring it through writing about other people's lives, I might reach a particle of truth. Maybe. If I'm lucky. That's the whole meaning of writing. So, the dream about the messy house—I know it's my dream. It's me.

Very often I wake up very anxious with a terrible headache. The headache lasts until I can identify what is bothering me the most. Many things bother me in the messy house but often it's one thing in my real life that I've not been able to solve and am postponing. I'm saying, It will be solved tomorrow or it will be solved by itself or somebody else will intervene. But I know that as long as it's there, I will be having the dream every night and I will have the headache. So finally I am forced, organically forced, to face it and talk about it and solve it.

My husband is wonderful at that because he was in therapy for five years. So, though it was many years ago, he still has very clear concepts that help a person like myself. Every time I have this dream I tell him I've had it again, so we sit down and we talk. What is bothering me so much that I had the dream? And if we can talk about it, usually it doesn't come back so often.

The other recurring dream I have is always very violent and has to do with the military. These dreams began after the military coup in Chile, so I know that they are related to that period of my life. It's a wound that is healed but has left a scar. I'm willing to live with that. It's the least that I can do after what happened in Chile.

It comes back when I see a violent movie in the afternoon, especially violence in any form related to abuse of a weak person—say that it's a child who is abused or it's about Nazis or people marching in uniform. The dream isn't always exactly the same, but it always has to do with the military, with people marching or shooting. It's a bloody cream. I'm always without any escape. It's a dream about being trapped.

The night I met my husband I had a dream that I still remember. It was a very strange dream because I was on a lecture tour. I had divorced my ex-husband after twenty-nine years of marriage. We were on very friendly terms but I had to get out of Venezuela for a while because I wanted to get away from the pain and the children. So I went on a lecture tour and ended up in the United States. My husband and I met in San Jose where he went because he knew I was lecturing. After the lecture there was a dinner party in an Italian restaurant with a group of people and he was part of the group. I was tired after two months of travelling. He was just another person at the table. There was nothing peculiar or glamorous about him. Nothing whatsoever. The only thing that made him different was that he spoke Spanish. He didn't even say that he had read my book. So we talked for a while, not much, and then he said, If you come to San Francisco I would like to show you the Bay Area. And I said, Yeah, I'm coming to San Francisco tomorrow. He said, Well, if you have time give me a call.

That night I had the dream of the military again. This time it was in a kind of golf course. I was hiding in the bushes and this long column of soldiers was marching in the middle of the golf course and I knew that when they reached a certain golf hole, it was time for me to die. I was trying desperately to prevent them from reaching that point. When I realized that it was impossible, that I couldn't move the hole or divert the column, I tried to hide in the bushes. But there was no real protection. Then I saw a man, dressed like an Arab with a white tunic, coming to me. Somehow he knew that I was in the bushes there. He came and covered me with his white tunic, and he walked in front of the military with me hidden in his clothes. When I looked at him I saw he had Willi's face.

I told this dream to a very nice gentleman who had gone to hear me talk. We met for breakfast in the dining room and I told him this strange dream because I was upset, very upset, as I always am when I dream of the military. And the man said, Well, maybe this dream means that you want to be protected by this man. So the next day when I went to San Francisco, I called Willi and he invited me to Mount Tam to see the bay. It was a beautiful autumn day, very clear, so it was a lovely sight. Then he invited me to his house for dinner. When I reached his house I realized that his house was the nightmare that I had always had. The messy house. You can't imagine the mess! It was just awful. I couldn't get out of the car because there was so much dog shit in the garage. I couldn't open the door. Inside, there were clothes and toys. There had been a fire on Christmas and the furniture, what there was of it, was burned. There was a broken window. It was awful. And so when finally he took me back to the hotel that night I thought, Oh my God, I hope I will never ever in my life find myself again in a place like that. You see how life is? A week later I was living with him in that mess! It was so messy that we just couldn't clean up. We had to move. So now we are living here. It was a strange dream. Maybe it was a sort of premonition because, in many ways, Willi saved me from the past and from myself and from all the threats of the past. He gave me a country, roots, a home. Many things that I didn't have. I had been drifting for a long time. So that was good.

At times I get misled because I believe that dreams can predict the future. Sometimes I have a terrible dream and I think it will happen so I get very upset and then it doesn't happen. Let me

give you one example. Three and a half years ago my husband
and I were on our honeymoon in Lake Como. It was a beautiful
place. A fantastic hotel, a beautiful full moon, but instead of
making love I had this awful dream that my son, who was
visiting Chile, had been taken by the police and was going to be
tortured. I woke up with the feeling that it was a premonition
and that I had to get my son out of the country no matter what.
I tried desperately to get in touch with him and tell him to leave
the country immediately. The telephone would ring and ring
and nobody would pick it up. I was so, so distressed I couldn't
go back to sleep. My husband tried to reason with me. He tried
to tell me that these were all ghosts from the past and that I had
to think clearly and wait for the morning. With the light and the
sun and the beautiful landscape of the lake I would realize that
it was just a dream. I couldn't get out of the dream. I was so
upset that finally at dawn we called my parents' house and I
learned that my son was up in the mountains skiing. So it wasn't
at all a premonition and when I told him that he had to get out
of the country, he wouldn't listen. He stayed and had a
wonderful vacation. If he had left, we would have never known
if the dream was true or not. So now I'm more cautious about
really making a decision because of a dream.

My grandmother is the model for Clara in *The House of the
Spirits*. My grandmother was just like her. Or maybe she wasn't
and I have made up everything. But I based the character on the
stories I heard about my grandmother, who was a funny,
wonderful, clairvoyant character. She died when I was very little
but I remember her very well.

Sometimes in my dreams she is writing and I read what she's
writing over her shoulder. She's always young in the dreams
although I never knew her when she was young. She was in her
late forties when she died. But when I see her I see her like a
picture that I always have with me. She was nineteen years old
in the picture. I always see her very young and always dressed
in old-fashioned clothes. So I know it's her.

I don't remember the words she is writing in these dreams. Sometimes I remember that she's writing with colored ink or she's writing in a notebook or at the bottom of a photograph. That kind of thing. But I don't remember what she's writing. It's a very soothing dream. When she comes in the dreams it's because I'm really doing well. I'm writing, I'm happy. She always represents, for me, protection.

Her powers are exaggerated in the book. She couldn't move the piano with her mind or play Chopin with the lid on, but they say she could move the salt. I remember when I was little they had these séances on Thursdays at home. I didn't participate, but I watched. There was nothing spooky about it. It was just part of life. It was taken in a very natural way. My grandmother had three very good friends, sisters. In real life they were called the Morla sisters. They were very well-known in Chile. This sisterhood was experimenting, for the first time in Chile, openly, with telepathy, with spiritism and all of these things that now are studied in universities here. But at that time it was forbidden by the Catholic church. So my grandmother was very rebellious in that sense. She was defying everything, the patriarchal authority, the Church.

My grandfather, who was a pragmatic Basque, never paid any attention to any of these things. He thought it was just bullshit, and he never believed in any of it, because she couldn't prove it. It was not scientific. But then, late in her life, my grandmother started saying maybe it was not the souls of the dead that moved the three-legged table but extraterrestrials. Then my grandfather got interested because he thought that was scientific.

I come from a very strange family. With that family you don't need to invent anything. It's given to you.

I don't know where to trace the line between reality and fantasy. Once I said this in a lecture and a person in the audience said I needed therapy. I said, if I go into therapy what will I write about? Without my demons what will I write about? It's true.

Sometimes I don't know what has really happened in my life and what I wrote that I thought happened and maybe it never did.

Who cares! You make up everything anyhow. Memory is so selective. If you tell the same story three times there are different angles. For example, my husband, who is a lawyer, is very careful with words and with the truth. He thinks that the truth exists, and it's something that is beyond questioning, which I think is totally absurd. I have several versions of how we met and how wonderful he was and all that. At least twenty. And I'm sure that they are all true. He has one. And I'm positive that it's not true. It didn't happen that way in my mind. Maybe that is his angle. He says that he read my second novel and fell in love with the book. He felt that the book was telling him something. There was something in the book—he couldn't identify what it was—but he wrote a note to the person who had given him the book, a professor of Latin American literature at the university in San Jose. He wrote her a note saying this woman understands love the way I do. He said that he was interested in that aspect of it. He was not at all impressed by me. People usually expect someone taller with bigger breasts and some clear ideas, I suppose, so he was really disappointed.

My mother used to have a very terrible dream. She separated from my father when I was very little. She was left alone with three kids. She was not prepared to work. She was very young, in a very conservative society where women were not supposed to be in that situation, so she went back to live in her parents' house and started working, trying to make a living.

She would dream that she was in a boat in the middle of the ocean and there was a tempest. The boat sank and she had to save the kids. She could only save one. And she had three. She would be swimming from one kid to the other trying to keep them above the water. But she knew that she would have to make up her mind and save only one. That was her recurrent dream.

I had a similar dream for a while that I had to save one of

my two kids. Fortunately the dream is gone. The worst year in my life was probably 1978. I usually say that it was 1973, because that was the year of the military coup but the consequences of that event were apparent to me only in 1978. In 1978 I realized that all my life had been destroyed. I thought at that time that I wouldn't have another opportunity. I'd been struggling all those years to survive and then, in 1978, I gave up.

I wanted to die. And so I started having that dream—my mother's dream—the dream that I had to save one of my kids. I had to make a choice. And in the dream I was tempted to die in order not to make that choice. I would rather drown myself and let everybody drown so that I wouldn't be forced to make the choice of saving one of them. I would wake up with this terrible feeling of oppression and death, of terrible, indescribable anxiety. Sweating and crying and sometimes nauseated. I tried to analyze the dream. Each time I had it, I wrote it down. Sometimes the children were drowning, sometimes they were in a plane, we were in different situations, but it was always the choice. And in my thinking of the dream and writing the dream over and over again I realized that I was trying to escape from the responsibility of bringing up my kids. I was so distressed because I didn't have anything. I had lost my job, my country. My family was living in exile. I had lost my love too, because I didn't love my husband any more. I felt terribly lonely. I felt that the only thing that really tied me to this world was the kids. And I didn't have the strength to fight for both of them. Or for either of them, really. So my temptation was to die. To kill myself so that I wouldn't have to face it. By thinking about the dream and writing about the dream I realized that I was escaping from them and from everything. It helped me a lot. I could start again. I got a job and I started working because I'd decided that my only goal was to educate my children. By the time they would be out of the university, I would be free to do whatever I wanted. So I postponed any suicidal ideas or anything about my own life—happiness, love, marriage, everything—until I finished with both my kids. That was wonderful because it saved me from myself, from despair.

They say that if you don't dream you go mad. That even dogs, animals dream. I don't know. I think that it's wonderful that one can dream. The first thing my husband and I do in the morning when we wake up is tell each other what we dreamt. It's not that we sit there and analyze our dreams at all. We don't have time for that. But we learn a lot about each other in this way.

In Chile dreaming of losing teeth means that you or somebody else is going to die. If it's painful, somebody very close will die and if it's without pain, then you will hear of somebody's death. And if you lose all your teeth, *you* will die.

Dreaming of snakes in Chile means money. I have had that dream twice and I'm not a gambler. I hate gambling. The first time, all the family, all the tribe, was spending some vacation time on the beach in Chile before the military coup, and I had this dream that nineteen snakes were crawling up my brother-in-law's legs. So the next day I said, "You should go to the casino and gamble because you will get a lot of money playing nineteen." And he said, "No, I'm terrible at that." I said, "Well let's split whatever it is, whatever you lose or gain." So we went to the casino. I bought a comic book and I sat outside to read while he went in. After a while he came out and he said, "I lost everything. Your dream was the shits." And I said, "But did you play nineteen?" And he said, "No. You didn't say that." I said, "I did say that. There were nineteen snakes!" And so we went back together and he played nineteen and he won! We were so surprised and so appalled at the same time that we started yelling and screaming. We left all the money there and it came up a nineteen again. So we had a basket full of bills, which of course with the inflation is nothing, but at that time we could invite the whole tribe, thirteen people, for dinner in the

best restaurant in town. And then I won three hundred bucks in
a casino in Aruba with my stepfather after I dreamt that snakes
were crawling up his body also.

One dream that is always prophetic for me is pregnancy. I knew
with my two children when I was pregnant before there was any
sign. And I knew what the sex of the child would be. I always
see the boy or the girl in the dream. It's the same with my
grandchildren. So when my son came to visit with his wife, I
said you will have a boy. I saw the boy and I saw exactly the boy
that they have now. I saw both my kids as well. I never had to
think of a name because they already had names in the dream.
Names that I would never have chosen because nobody in my
family has those names. So now I know that my daughter-in-law
very soon will be pregnant and she will have a girl. I know.

I have a space in my computer where I write my dreams. I keep
a little notepad near my bed and if I wake up with a dream in
the middle of the night I go silently to the bathroom—because
I don't want to wake up my husband—and I write it down
because I will forget afterwards. Later I write it in the computer.
I know that many of them don't have any meaning. Sometimes
I think they're wonderful and that I can use them in the writing
and the next day I read them and they are terrible. I can't use
a word of them. But that state of semiconsciousness that you
have when you just wake up from a dream—it's dawn and
everything is silent and you are still half asleep and half
awake—in that moment I think that one can listen.

    It is as if one has a storage room where you have infor-
mation that you can't reach when you're awake. Information
that you get through different channels that you're not aware of
during the day. Something you heard, something you saw,
something that happened to somebody. A smell. A color. A
texture. And you grab it. And you store it. And you're not aware
of it at all. Then, in that dreamy state, somehow you can reach
in the darkness and find something like a treasure that is hidden

in this storage room. And that is what your dream is about. It's bringing back information to your conscious mind that has always been there because you wouldn't dream about it if you didn't have it already within you. So it's yours. You're not dreaming anybody else's dream. You just have to get there.

Sometimes I reach back into that storage room and bring out some information, write about it and then it becomes true. And I think that it's like a premonition. But if I try to explain it I would say that the information was in the air. It was always there, somehow, in the collective memory like some sort of radio emission and I tune into it.

For example, in *Love and Shadows* I wanted to symbolize somehow, in a very strong way, the feelings of the people about the military. So I wrote that when the protests began in this country, the people went out into the streets dragging a pig dressed up as a general. They humiliated the pig in the middle of the street until the soldiers came and shot him in order to rescue the emblems of the military. I think that I had a dream about it and then I wrote about it. I went to Spain for the publication of the book. I think it was October. I was in the hotel the first day I got there and I saw in a Spanish newspaper that in Chile the people had dragged a pig into the middle of the street with the emblems of the military. The soldiers had to kill him in order to rescue the cap and the cape. I was so shocked because my book had not been published yet. Nobody had read the book except my mother, the publishers and my agent. I hadn't even seen a copy. How did I get the idea? Maybe so many people were thinking about it that I could just listen, hear. That could be also. I'm sure this is not the only case, many many people do that.

I don't believe that there are independent spirits of the dead that come to you to pull your legs when you're asleep. No. I think that we are all particles of some sort of universal spirit. If we can get over this idea of our little bodies, our little selfishness and greed, this idea that we are something individual, just forget

about it and tune into the wonderful, peaceful idea that we are
just part of something that is there and is whole and that when
you die you will go back to that thing that is whole and is part
of your grandson and part of the flowers and part of everything
that surrounds you and will prevail, then the spirit has a sense.
Because it's not you. It's everywhere. You're just a particle of
something that's beyond you. Then you understand the legends,
the myths. You understand why so many people at a certain
point do the same thing or dream the same thing or hope for the
same thing or fear the same thing. Because you're just part of
that wholeness. When you reach that point, then you believe, as
I do, that my grandmother lives in me and in my grandson and
in my future great-grandchildren. And that when I need her I
don't have to sit at a three-legged table with a candle and use
tarot cards to bring her to me. I just have to listen. I have to ask.

If I am in a very confused situation in which I really need to
make a decision, I always ask myself what my grandmother
would do. My grandmother was a wonderful human being and
she always has an answer. The answer usually has absolutely no
common sense. It's always a very generous answer and there is
some sort of hidden wisdom in it. But no common sense. I know
that it's what nobody else would do. But somehow it works.

Like for example asking when I met Willi. I thought to
myself: This man's life is a mess. He has children addicted to
drugs, a hyperactive child who is also a mess, he has debts. I
don't like the United States. I don't want to live speaking in
English. I have to forget about him. And then I thought, What
would my grandmother do? She would pack a few things in a
very small handbag, leave and run after him. That's what I did.
And it worked fine. When I told my mother what I was going
to do she thought I was totally out of my mind. And the only
person who really supported me, because he thought that I
would get out of it, was my son who said, Yeah, go and spend
a week with him and get him out of your system. So I came. And
I never left.

When I'm scared—and I'm always scared when I have to

face an audience, when I have to read a review, when I publish a book, every time I have a mammogram I'm scared because I already had surgery once—then I think of my grandfather. My grandfather was this strong, tough Basque who would never bend. So, when I think of him, his spirit lifts in me and I say, Well, what would he do? Well, he would go ahead, close his eyes and drive forward. And it works. You do it and the spirit that is within you, that part that you have received and that is still living in me and in my children and in my mother and in everybody else, is there.

Sometimes I think, what would I do if my mother dies? She is the longest and most important relationship in my life. More than any man that I've ever had. More than my own children and my grandchildren. Because she was with me before I was born and she has been with me always with unconditional love. All the other loves that I have had are conditional. I want to love my children if they love me. I want to love my husband if he gives me all that I demand.

With my mother it doesn't work that way. Even if I killed the Pope she would love me. So what will I do when she's not here? She also corrects my books so this is the end of my literary career if she dies or turns senile. The other day I told this, joking, to my publisher. I said, Well, this is probably my last book because my mother is seventy, you know. And he laughed. And I said, Yeah, because if something happens to her mind or she dies I won't be able to write. And he said, You're kidding! Your mother is inside you already. So even if she dies she's always with you. I realized that he's right. Absolutely right. I will always be able to say, Okay, here I have a terrible sentence, how does this thing work? And my mother will come back to me. So that's what it is about. And I hope that when I die I will have been able to, during my life, plant little seeds in the souls of my children and my grandchildren so that when they need something from me I will always be available. That's the way I believe the spirit works.

I believe that I have a spiritual connection with my husband that is beyond any explanation. We are two absolutely totally different people that come from different backgrounds, different cultures, races, language, everything. And yet I feel him inside me. We won't part, I know. I know positively that nothing will separate us. Ever. Because we've found something that is very spiritual and has nothing to do with being sick or in good health, young or not. Poor or rich. No. It works on another level. So, I've relaxed for the first time in my life and I don't care about the tall blondes any more. The world is full of tall blondes.

It's strange the miracles that books will work! If Willi hadn't read my book he would have never gone to that lecture. He would have never met me. You write a book and it's like putting a message in a bottle and throwing it in the ocean. You don't know if it will ever reach any shore. And there, you see, sometimes it falls in the hands of the right person.

MAYA ANGELOU

BORN MARGUERITE JOHNSON in St. Louis, Missouri, Maya Angelou was sent to live with her grandmother in Stamps, Arkansas, at the age of three. After suffering a sexual trauma at age seven she stopped speaking but was brought back to words several years later by a woman who read classic literature aloud to her.

Beginning in the 1950s Angelou supported herself and her small son, Guy, as a singer, dancer and actress. She appeared in the international touring company of *Porgy and Bess,* as well as Jean Anouilh's *Medea* and starred in the New York premiere of Jean Genet's *The Blacks.*

In the early sixties, Angelou became actively involved in the Civil Rights movement. She produced, directed and starred in *Cabaret for Freedom,* a benefit for Martin Luther King's Southern Christian Leadership Conference, and she was appointed the SCLC's Northern Coordinator in 1960–61.

Persuaded by James Baldwin and Kurt Vonnegut to tell her life's story, Angelou published *I Know Why the Caged Bird Sings* in 1970. This best-selling tale of her early childhood was followed by *Gather Together in My Name* in 1974, *Singin' and Swingin' and Gettin' Merry Like Christmas* in 1976, *The Heart of a Woman* in 1981 and *All God's Children Need Traveling Shoes* in 1986—each volume a continuation of her own life's story.

Angelou's volumes of poetry include *Just Give Me a Cool Drink of Water 'Fore I Diiie* (1972), *Oh Pray My Wings Are Gonna Fit Me Well* (1975), *And Still I Rise* (1978), *Shaker, Why Don't You Sing?* (1983) and *I Shall Not Be Moved* (1990).

Maya Angelou's work—in music, theater, poetry, television, film and literature—celebrates not only the black experience, but the universal human power to triumph over adversity.

━━━

THERE IS a dream which I delight in and long for when I'm writing. It means to me that the work is going well. Or will go well. Or that I'm telling the truth and telling it well.

I dream of a very tall building. It's in the process of being built and there are scaffolds and steps. It looks sort of like the inside of the Arc de Triomphe. I'm climbing it with alacrity and joy and laughter. Quite often it's day but it's not very bright because I'm inside the structure going up. I have no sense of dizziness or discomfort or vertigo. I'm just climbing. I can't tell you how delicious that is!

I began, I guess, twenty years ago to notice that when my dream came, it always meant that the work was going well. Whenever I get that dream I know the work is going to be all right for about two or three weeks. So that delights my heart.

There's another dream which also has to do with work. I don't seem to have any just plain delight dreams or dreams about love or anything personal. I seem to only dream when I'm working. Or that's all I remember. But the other dream is also a good dream. That is, when I wake from it, I feel that things are all right. It's not ecstatic, it's not as delicious as the first one is, but it's okay. It has to do with a particular area. I don't know where it is, it seems like a small town with nice, just above modest, houses. I seem to know the area very well and feel quite at home there. As I say, not ecstatic, but comfortable.

And then there are terrifying dreams when the work is really going badly. I don't even want to talk about them. It gives them too much power.

I'm happy to say that generally, the dreams which I remember have to do with the good luck of working well. More than luck, whatever it is, the "that" of working well. Would I have a good dream when the work is going badly? No. No such thing. It just seems they tell the truth.

As an autobiographer I don't seem to have to dream. There's a place I get to that's a little like dreaming. Almost dreaming but I'm awake. It's an enchantment.

You know, from the age of seven and a half to twelve and a half I was a mute. I believed at the time that I could make myself, my whole body, an ear. And I could absorb all sound. Those years I must have done something to my brain, or with it, so that the part of the brain which would have been occupied in the articulation of speech and the creation of sound, those electrical synapses, did something else with themselves. They just reinvented themselves so that I'm able to remember incredible amounts of data. I would say I get along reasonably well in about seven or eight languages. I have spoken as many as twelve. I have taught in three. I seem to have total recall or none at all. And so, when I need to get inside myself, I can do it without going to sleep.

I am an autobiographer as opposed to a fiction writer. In my case I have to remember facts and try to use my talent or my art or my creativity to tell the truth about the facts. I submit that there's a world of difference between truth and fact. Fact tells us the data: the numbers, the places where, the people who and the times when. But facts can obscure the truth. Because I write about a time when real people were alive—I mean, it's not as if that is a time which I can create out of the full complement of my imagination—I have to get back to get the facts. But then I have to do something else in order to tell the truth of the matter.

Sometimes one is obliged to take time out of time and to redefine, to set the time at another time. Or take things out of consequence, out of sequence. They become more consequential when you have the liberty to take them out of sequence.

I know it's strange but, though I have a very commodious, very large house in North Carolina, I keep a hotel room in town. I get up about five A.M., have a bath or a shower, make coffee and take the coffee to this hotel room. Usually, I try to be there by six. Everything has been taken off the walls so that there's nothing to arrest my sight. On the bed I have *Roget's Thesaurus*, a dictionary, a Bible and a deck of playing cards. And I can almost enchant myself back to the time I have to write about. I just suspend everything and go back there.

When I was very young, my grandmother raised me. She was everything to me. And if I acted startled about something that had happened, I'd ask her to explain and she would say, "Sister, that isn't even on my littlest mind." Somehow I decided that there was a small mind and a large mind. Now, when I'm trying to get back, I use the cards to occupy my small mind. In the course of writing a book I will use maybe two or three decks of Bicycle cards before I'm finished. Just playing solitaire. I don't really get down, I don't play the cards. I'm playing at playing. But that's fine. I don't know how this is like dreaming but it is.

I suppose I do get "blocked" sometimes but I don't like to call it that. That seems to give it more power than I want it to have. What I try to do is write. I may write for two weeks "the cat sat on the mat, that is that, not a rat," you know. And it might be just the most boring and awful stuff. But I try. When I'm writing, I write. And then it's as if the muse is convinced that I'm serious and says, "Okay. Okay. I'll come."

To write well, to write so that a reader thinks she's making up the book as she goes along, that's hard. To be in such control of the language! First off, one has to translate what one thinks into words, which is always impossible. And then into such gracious and graceful words that the reader can take it in, almost as a palliative, without even knowing, and be somehow increased as a result. That means that one is offering the reader something twice translated: the reader is going to translate it again. So, to write it so well that you can at least approximate what you mean to say, that's very hard. And to write so that it seems to leap off the page—

I might get two or three sentences that are really graceful but, no matter what, I continue to write and write. And then rewrite. And rewrite. Striking out all extraneous *and*s and *if*s and *too*s and *but*s and *where*s and *therefore*s and *however*s, all that stuff, until it really is clean.

Nathaniel West says, "Easy reading is damned hard writing." It's just hard work, you know?

I do believe dreams have a function. I don't see anything that has no function, not anything that has been created. I may not understand its function or be able to even use it, make it utile, but I believe it has a reason. The brain is so strange and wondrous in its mystery. I think it creates a number of things for itself—it creates launching pads and resting places—and it lets steam off and it reworks itself. It re-creates itself almost every minute.

I remember years ago being told that one can't really learn after one is twenty-five. Or twenty-something. There's a halt, the brain cells die. In my fifties I started studying Japanese. As I reach sixty I'm trying to become proficient in a lot of things, in the sciences. Just because there's so much to be learned. So, the brain—we just don't know anything about it—it creates dreams. Dreams can tell people all sorts of things. It can work out problems. Especially for writing.

Maybe, if a writer is hesitant to get to a depth in a character, to admit that this fictional character does this, or thinks this or has acted this way—or that an event was really this terrifying—the brain says, "Okay, you go on and go to sleep, I'll take care of it. I'll show you where that is."

One sees that the brain allows the dreamer to be more bold than he or she ever would be in real time. The dream allows the person to do things, and think things, and go places and be acted upon. The person, in real time, would never do those things. It may be that's a way the brain has of saying, "Well let me let you come on down and see what really is down here."

There's a phrase in West Africa called "deep talk." When a person is informed about a situation, an older person will often use a parable, an axiom, and then add to the end of the axiom, "Take that as deep talk." Meaning that you will never find the answer. You can continue to go down deeper and deeper. Dreams may be deep talk.

C L I V E   B A R K E R

W HEN I ASKED a friend to characterize the work of
Clive Barker he replied, "Sympathy for the devil." He went
on to explain that in Barker's works of "imaginative fiction"
it is the monsters who are the good guys and the protago-
nists who are often dead.

Born in Liverpool, England, in 1952, Clive Barker grew
up loving monsters. His initial ambition to be a painter was
superseded by an attraction to the theater, where he created
plays such as *Frankenstein in Love, The History of the Devil*
and *The Secret Life of Cartoons*. Eager to portray things that
could not be done on a stage, Barker switched to writing
fiction. In 1984 he published six volumes of short stories
entitled *Books of Blood*. Among the stories in that collection
were "The Midnight Meat Train," about a moving human
abattoir running beneath the city streets; "Rawhead Rex,"

about a baby-devouring monster; and "Sons of Celluloid," the tale of a cancerous growth that spawned ghouls that resembled movie stars.

Barker is not afraid to break taboos. He delights in creating visceral images of sex, death and dismemberment. In his novels—which include *The Damnation Game* (1985), *Weaveworld* (1987), *Cabal* (1988), *The Great and Secret Show* (1989) *Imajica* (1991) and *The Thief of Always* (1992)—he constructs multileveled universes, mixing religious imagery and tales of secret knowledge with horror and humor.

Barker moved to Los Angeles in 1991 to pursue a film-making career. He made his directorial debut with *Nightbreed* and has produced several *Hellraiser* films.

═══

M Y WHOLE FICTION is a fiction which deals with a kind of borderland between what we'll, for the sake of argument, call the real and the unreal. That is, my fiction both on the stage and later on the screen and in books is about a place where the dream life, that is so much a part of our being, invades the real and actually ends up changing it.

What I am doing in my work is drawing upon my own dream life, both waking and sleeping, as a starting place for the nature of those invasions. And making notes daily, nightly, about what images are coming into my head and how they seem to be rooted, on some occasions, in particular psycho-dramas of my own. And how very often, and these are often exciting times, they take off into territories which I can't find any starting place for in myself.

You know my first ambition was to be a painter and that's a craft or an art I still pursue. Very often dreams will give me an image which will be a starting place for a story or for a vision of some kind or other. And it will take sometimes a long time, in a few cases even years, before the narrative, which will be the best bedrock for that image, appears. But normally it comes along eventually. This isn't to say I don't have a backlog of images. I do. I can think of dozens and dozens of things that I want to write about, images I want to make sense of by putting them in a narrative context which I haven't yet found. But I have a kind of faith that that will eventually come along. I'll give you two separate examples—one a very violent visceral image and the other a kind of fantastical one.

The violent image: I've always had very sexual dreams. I think everybody has very sexual dreams. I did a story called "The Age of Desire," which is about a man who becomes the guinea pig, the testee, for an aphrodisiac. Aphrodisiacs hitherto have not worked, but this one—this is the first one that actually works. It goes into his system and it goes wild. Not only does it go wild, it regenerates itself. Instead of being evacuated through the system, and weakening and diluting, it becomes stronger and stronger and stronger. And as the story goes on, this man's world becomes more and more sexualized. Everything becomes, somehow or other, a sexual image. And he ends up exhausted and dying of an excess of pleasure.

The idea of this highly sexual world began one midsummer in London, walking through the markets in Soho. There were fruit peddlers going through strawberries which had rotted. They were throwing away the rotted strawberries and keeping the good ones. The stench was overpowering.

That night I dreamt about this.

The whole place was somehow sexualized by the smell and the sight of these strawberries. And the doors and the windows—I needn't go into the Freudian connotations of the whole thing, it's pretty self-evident. The dream started out with almost a complete retread of what had actually happened that day, and then, in the way dreams do, it became an intensification of the experience.

Out of that dream came a kind of visceral dark image. And out of that scene came a story.

I also wrote a book called *Weaveworld* which is about a world in a carpet. I've often dreamt of puzzles and threads and labyrinths—again a very common image—and in this story I have a world which is literally woven magically into a carpet. Out of that image came, finally, a seven-hundred-page book. Obviously it developed and it developed and it changed but those are two places where images flowered into something.

Something wonderful happens in dreams which I always wished happened in reality more often. I think this is what an artist is trying to do when he or she is writing. You sense the metaphysics, the reasons for being, that underpin something.

In my dream of the rotting strawberries, suddenly what had seemed sensual, but only very, very vaguely sexual when it actually happened, became this extraordinary almost over-powering experience in the dream. And that made great sense to me. I suddenly thought, my God, supposing this were actually to happen! Supposing somebody were to actually be unable to dislocate himself from this intensity of sexual feeling. How scary that would be. How frightening and also how extraor-dinary.

So the dream becomes the starting place for a narrative and then you backtrack from that. You think, Okay, how can I make that work? You think, Ah yes, I'll make him a guinea pig for an aphrodisiac.

I spend most of my working day in some kind of dream state. That is to say, I get up from my bed, I shower, drink my coffee and go to my desk, which is literally ten yards from my bed. I then start, on a normal day, a process which will maybe take me eight or ten hours, writing about something that my inner eye is seeing. It's not like I'm getting up in the morning, as most people do, and stepping out onto the street and being slapped into the solid problem of how I get the car to start. Or whether the subway is crowded. Or how the boss is going to feel about me that morning. None of those things intrude.

I live alone. I don't have anyone to wake me from the reverie into which I've woken when I open my eyes. I don't get a double waking, I only get a single one. And, if I'm lucky, I plug back into this kind of—I'm not saying somnambulence—but I do think that if somebody were to secretly photograph me while I was writing, I'd probably look like a lunatic.

I know, for instance, I talk aloud, because other people have observed that. I know that my blink rate slows, because I can't wear my contact lenses when I'm writing. My eyes are just bang, wide open, staring at the page. I know that, very often, I look up from writing, and can't believe how much time has passed. I don't think these are particularly unusual things, by the way, I think this is true for a lot of writers. But I've deliberately simplified the act of writing. I don't have a computer, I don't have a typewriter. Everything is handwritten. It is the most primitive, and for me the most direct, association I can make between what's going on in my mind's eye, and what's going to appear on the page.

I think writing about an invented world is a dialogue with that invented world. There are clearly tensions which arise between the requirements of a character in terms of his or her natural propensity to want to go off and do his or her own thing and the requirements of the plot. Now I've read lots of writers talking about characters just taking off and doing their own thing—"The character took control of the book," I'm sure you've heard that from writers. That never happens to me. Or, ten books on, it hasn't happened so far. That's because the dialogue that I'm having with characters as an ongoing thing is also a dialogue that I'm having with the shape of the plot.

I think that the major character in the books I write is the shape of the plot.

I value story above all else. I'm talking about my written work—in the movies I value the images—but in the books I value the story. A story has its own meaning. A story has its own significance. And sometimes the characters in that story can almost become transparent. This is true in fairy tales, for instance.

In a fairy tale it isn't important to know the precise significance of why the wicked witch is evil or why the evil queen is evil or why so and so is beautiful and good. They simply are. They have the force of archetypes. And what is important is the nature of their clash, not how they came to be who they are.

In the fiction of the fantastic, that can also sometimes be the case. Particularly toward the end of my books and short stories, characters take on an almost archetypal quality, which I seek out. I want characters to become almost purified by the act of fiction.

Dreams are full of these archetypal forms: people who come in cleansed of their ambiguities, coming in as purely sexual beings or as teachers sometimes. I have my dialogues on the page with those archetypal figures.

D. H. Lawrence said he didn't know what he meant until he wrote it down. I watch myself writing—that is I don't watch myself writing, I can only do it retrospectively. I think if you watch yourself writing probably the magic will have disappeared—but I write these things and I look at them and I think, Aha, that's what happened!

Do I believe the kind of thing that's been described in *The Great and Secret Show:* That our fears can take physical form? I doubt that frankly. At least not in the reality that we're presently occupying. Do I believe however that in certain states of consciousness the body becomes almost redundant and our spirit takes trips, visits states of being which are absolutely as valid as the reality which we are occupying? And that these can be arenas of education and healing? Yes, I absolutely believe that. And do I believe that in such conditions disparate spirits can meet and converge and maybe even learn from each other? Yes, I absolutely believe that.

We are born into this condition, slapped into this condition of the flesh, and it is a very dominant, dominating, domineering condition. It demands attention from us at the time. We get hungry, we have to pass wind, we need to make love, we get headaches and we bruise easily. There are so many facts of the flesh. So many things that the flesh demands of us, demands of our spirits. And, every now and then we are liberated.

Now, we can seek that liberation artificially. I have never been a great advocate of liberation through drugs, feeling perhaps in my own case as though my head was already a balloon on a thin thread and it would be dangerous to set fire to the thread. But I feel there are clearly other ways. Art is one such way. Sex, actually—which begins in the body but ends up in the spirit—can be another way in which we are outside of ourselves. Sleep, under certain conditions, can liberate us into another condition as well. And in those conditions flesh becomes less the fascist that it is. We're not thinking about hunger, and passing wind and the like, we're into a state in which ideas and images and maybe the spiritual presence of others, dead, alive, journeying, are also possibilities, presences.

That combination of images and fellow spirits is something which touches us all at certain times of our lives. And these things have an absolute reality, in the same way that memory has an absolute reality. Not only are they operating, they're actually helping us. Shaping us. Healing us. Making sense of experiences for us. Because experience as we live it moment to moment, day to day, is chaos, is disorder. It's information, most of which is entirely irrelevant to our personal drama, spilling in through our senses. Flooding us. And we have to somehow or other make sense of this.

Now the only way I can make sense of that is to say okay, I'm now going to take from my dreamscape certain images which, I would argue, predate even my birth. Primal things, things which belong to the spirit that I was even before I was even Clive Barker. And take those images and try to find a way that they make sense in this flood of material which is coming at me daily. Trying to find a way that they become islands in this incredible flood.

Writing is actually a means to use this material. I think it's important to say this isn't just crazy stuff which is just going through your head all the time, boiling up. It actually has purpose, it has reason, it has shape. And it's a valid way to understand yourself and the world and your relationship to the world.

I think the fear of insanity touches everybody who works in the imaginative arts, who is really plunging deeply into themselves. We're like people with one foot nailed to the floor. It hurts hugely to pull away from it. And actually, because we're born with a foot nailed to the floor, we're terribly afraid that if we pull too hard we'll either fall over or float away. And who's to say that isn't the case? I think there are dangers involved. Absolutely. Danger that if you pull too hard you will indeed float away and the bedrock of reality, which we have been brought up to believe is the only reality, will no longer be valid, and we'll just be crazies.

There's a balance that has to be absolutely struck, and that's a tough one. I think it's important to confess the fear, confess the anxiety, which I absolutely have—that if I ever let my imagination take over completely I would simply not be a rational individual any longer. That one of the things I value most in all the world, the communication of my vision to other people, would no longer be plausible because I'd be speaking gibberish.

I've never been a big fan of surrealism because the thesis of surrealism is that it should be a naked flowing of the artist's vision onto the canvas, or onto the page, without editorship, without anything coming between the artist and the communicating of that vision. Which seems at first an extremely admirable activity. But in fact what it becomes is an excuse for saying just about anything, painting just about anything. Because the subconscious is also full of a whole bunch of useless stuff. There's a lot of dreck in there which is not useful at all.

There's a lot of flotsam and jetsam floating around in the dream pool and it's a question of actually trying to make and shape the material which is most potent. So what I'm trying to do and which is keeping me—I was going to say sane, and that may not be too far from the truth—is finding the stuff which is genuinely useful to genuinely articulate something. Making sure the shapes that these images take have a narrative function, have a psychological function. And not simply indulging. I've never had a passion for abstract expressionist painting because, well okay so the paint goes all over everything, so what? What's important is that the colors be made to serve the shape and the purpose. Because art is about communication.

The business of art doesn't really begin until the thing is finished. Then the exchange begins. And the exchange is about saying, this is a piece of my mind, this is a part of my dreamscape—does it have any echoes for you, the receiver? Does this make any sense to you? And when, as I do, you take an extremely strange bizarre piece of your personal dreamscape, and put it in front of somebody, and they say, yes, this does make sense, the fear of insanity evaporates immediately. Because then you realize, that in fact this is part of us all. This is not some lonely, terrifying vista. This is part of a panorama that we all wander through. What can be more reassuring than the presence of other people there?

You don't even have to turn dreams into art. For some people the whole idea of turning something into art is going to be a source of anxiety because then you actually have the problem of what art is and whether you can achieve it and so on. But bringing it kicking and squealing into the light and seeing the value of metaphor in your life, talking about the value of metaphor, that's what's important.

So often I think people forget that we live two lives. That we live a physical life—which is about what we have to do during the day—and we live a spiritual life—which can also be very much about the day: the rites of our worship, the rituals of love, our fantasies about love and loss and so on. Those things can very much touch our day but they particularly come to light during the night. What's important is not to deny these things their meaning.

Now, the idea of putting those things into art is an important and interesting issue. But simply to talk about them as things which have meaning, which are intimate self-confessions is, it seems to me, the primary act. The secondary act is the turning it into art. And it may be something that people don't feel predisposed to do. But to simply say I am whispering to myself through the lattice of my consciousness, I am whispering to myself, I am telling myself, What is that thing? What are those many things? And saying, I don't mind what I hear. I don't mind, I forbid myself nothing. I forbid my subconscious and therefore my consciousness, nothing, is the beginning, I think, of great health.

I certainly think you should listen to your dreams, take account of them but don't be bound by "this is the way to interpret or decode your dreams" books. I think there's a whole bunch of books out there teaching people, in almost encyclopedic fashion, the significance of each symbol. I think that's nonsense. Water means a different thing for somebody who doesn't like wine than it does to somebody who almost drowned as a kid. I think you have to look at what it means in your personal scenario.

This is an almost meditative activity, it seems to me. It's a question of sitting quietly with yourself and saying, the only company I have really in all the world is the person I am. And everything else can go away from me, everybody else can go away from me. It is within the bounds of possibility that all the people I love most in the world could be gone tomorrow. I have to be at peace with this myself. And a third of this "myself" is a sleeping self. An important third, perhaps the most important third. So let me be quiet with myself and sit with myself and like myself, and what my subconscious is telling me.

The key thing in my life—and it's taken me a long time to realize this—is that as a child you are given dream time as part of your fictional life. Into your hands go the books of dream travel, Dorothy's dream travel, the Darling family's dream travel in *Peter Pan*, the children of Narnia. You're given books in which children with whom you identify take journeys which are essentially dream journeys. They are to places in which the fantastical not only happens, but is commonplace. Alice falls down a hole, the Darling children take flight, the tornado picks up Dorothy's house. These children are removed and taken to a place which is essentially a place of dreams.

And then, at the age of five or something like that, they start to teach you the gross national product of Chile. And you're left thinking, Wait! What happened to Oz and Never-Never Land and Narnia? Are they no longer relevant? One of the things you're taught is No! they are no longer relevant. They are, as it were, a sweet introduction to the business of living. And now comes the real stuff—so get on with it.

You're going to be taught to compete, very often for spurious reasons. You are going to be taught that the accrual of facts, however unimportant those facts are, will somehow make you better and more able to deal with the world. You're going to be told that the only way the world works is through the waking life in which you get enough money to get a second Porsche. Or indeed a first.

All those things are lies.

It took me until my mid-twenties 'til I realized that I should not be ashamed that I loved Oz more than I loved the gross national product of Chile. And I realized that in doing that I was setting myself up absolutely as a potential idiot, as a potential fool. I realized absolutely that there were going to be an awful lot of people who were going to look at me and say, this guy's a dreamer.

You know the word *dreamer* is pejorative in our culture. The word *fantasy* is pejorative. These are things that we should not be. We should not be dreamers, we should not be fantasists in our culture.

What I realized was that I was not ashamed that I still trip to Never-Never Land. Because I think I come back a better person, a more centered person and a person who could be better in the world. I could be better to my friends; I could be better to my relatives. I could just be a better person.

And so now at dinner parties when people say, "So what's you're favorite part of the world?" and I say, "Never-Never Land" and they choke on their soup, I smile to myself and say, that's cool. I don't mind that. If that's the way it has to be, that's the way it has to be.

Have the confidence of the trip and nobody can ever take it from you. Because it belongs to you from the very word one. It belongs to you.

JOHN BARTH

LITERARY ALLUSIONS, bawdy humor, philosophical ruminations and multilevel puns characterize the highly cerebral comic works of novelist John Barth. Weaving elements of mythology and contemporary concerns into his complex plots, Barth turns literary traditions upside down and inside out to comment on the current state of the narrative arts. As Barth explained in *The Friday Book*, his greatest pleasure is "to take a received melody—an old narrative poem, a classic myth, a shopworn literary convention—and improvising like a jazzman within its constraints, reorchestrate it to its present purpose."

John Barth was born in Cambridge, Maryland, in 1930. He published his first novel, *The Floating Opera*, in 1956. This was followed by *The End of the Road* in 1958 and *The Sot-Weed Factor* in 1960. It wasn't until the mid-sixties that

his work began to gain widespread attention with the publication of *Giles Goat-Boy; or The Revised New Syllabus.*
Nine years after its original publication, *The Floating Opera*
was nominated for a National Book Award. In 1968 *Lost in
the Funhouse; Fiction for Print, Tape, Live Voice* was also
nominated. Barth won the National Book Award in 1973 for
Chimera, a collection of short fiction. In 1990 he published
The Last Voyage of Somebody the Sailor.

Barth lives in Maryland and teaches at Johns Hopkins
University.

—————

LIKE EVERY WRITER'S professional life, mine is spent
doing a kind of dreaming—from the time I sit down at the desk
and pick up my faithful fountain pen until the time I put the stuff
on the Macintosh—which is a kind of waking up. If there is a
law of conservation of dream energy I suspect that we professional storytellers, who are after all kind of professional dreamers, expend so much of that energy in our daily activity that
what's left over for our dreams may be like the shoemaker's
children who are the worst shod. In other words, my dreams are
"shoddy."

So much of what we do in those hours when we're actually
making sentences, inventing characters and feeling our way
through the threads of a plot, is hunch and feel—half unconscious and somewhat autohypnotic. Those rituals of getting
ready to write seem to conduce a kind of trance state.

As soon as I say that I get a little uncomfortable, because I
am a poet of awareness if there ever was one. That's why it
impresses me how much even such a writer as myself—even
such a writer as Henry James, who was the most aware and
self-conscious of our classical American writers—works by
hunch, feel, intuition and by following what might as well be
called a kind of dream pattern.

It is an aspect of that compensatory poverty of dreams that

my literal dreams, as a rule, tend not even to be particularly
verbal. If I were to wake up with a dandy word play in my head
or even an interesting turn of language that came from a dream,
I would be wowed. But it doesn't happen.

There is a kind of dream that plagues me from time to time,
which I think of as an occupational hazard dream. These are the
dreams that are *nothing but* words, no images at all. The dream
is the sleeping equivalent of one of those stock market trans-
luxes or subtitles: words go right across the film of my consciousness, punctuation and all! Can you imagine after writing
all day long, going to bed and dreaming something like "on the
other hand, comma, it might be said . . ." et cetera. Yet literally
I have had dreams that, at least for part of their duration, go on
like that. And I wake up feeling as though I've done an hour's
work. It's not sleep knitting up the raveled sleeve of care at all.
It's just more time at the processor, more time at the desk.

I got in the habit some years ago of dictating my cor-
respondence to a secretary at the university and, because I don't
trust anybody's punctuation except my own, I actually learned
this insidious habit of dictating out loud with punctuation. It
may be the muse's punishment for someone who does that to
another human being: to feed it back to him or her in their sleep.
Those are the dreams that I wake up feeling tired from.

Borges, the great Argentine writer, said that it is written in
the Kabbala that when the words in a dream are loud and
distinct and seem to come from no particular source, these
words are from God. So all I can say is that my god is a god of
punctuation marks and introductory adverbial clauses. And that
it probably serves me right.

It takes me about one presidential term to write a book, about
four years. Maybe one time during that four years I will have
what I would think of as a real novelist's dream—though I've
never been able to use any of them in my novels—one that
actually has a pretty good plot. Usually it's a nineteenth-century
kind of plot with lots of complications and even subplots;

astonishing characters who don't resemble anybody I ever knew; an actually rather coherent narrative line with little surprises and twists. And I wake up thinking, "Not bad." You know, "Not bad—but not for me. This is not Barth the novelist dreaming, but it's not a bad dream there."

Those are the only ones I write down. These Charles Dickens–scale dreams are so rare. I wish I could have one every night. It's like getting another installment in a Dickens novel.

In the history of western literature, particularly in the last couple of centuries, the use of dream passages has been a way for writers to get bravura, quasisurreal effects that they couldn't hack in an ordinary realistic novel. I have the feeling that after Freud we got to know too much about dreams and so it began to seem corny when a writer would bring them off. It's like those terrible movie sequences where you get the soft focus and the violins go tremolo and you go, "Uh-oh, dream sequence."

In my graduate writing workshop, among a hundred other rules that I lay down for beginners is "Don't do dreams." Or if you do a dream, do it out of the full, usually ironic awareness that dreams have been overdone as a device for special effects in fiction. So the dream had better be really surprising. It better not be dreamish in any of the conventional senses.

Deep down in the narrative imagination of every culture is that intimate association between storytelling and dreaming; between the element of the marvelous in storytelling before the invention of realism and the element of dream. The ancients knew that the worst mistake was to make these stories literally dreams, so the ancient narratives like Odysseus's travels, his trying to get home, are very dream*like*. You remember he ends up being brought home asleep in "the dream dark boat" that moves like no other boat in the world, by the very wish of its navigators. Now the Greeks, the ancients, would never have said, "It was all a dream." Only in the nineteenth century with people like Lewis Carroll and *Alice in Wonderland* do you get to the end and read "And it was all a dream." But that's the very materialistic nineteenth century coming onto the scene.

After Freud, after the enormous attention to our sub-conscious and what goes on in our sleep time, we come back to a kind of awareness of the importance of dreams in literary and other artistic imaginations. But it's a super-conscious appreciation of the role of the unconscious. You can't just pull out all the stops and do a dream the way you could in the seventeenth or eighteenth century.

Sleep and dreams play a role in *The Last Voyage of Somebody the Sailor,* despite everything I've just finished saying. I mean what's the use of being a writer if you can't break your own rules? The book is not really about Sindbad, it's about the here and now, but it keeps one foot in the here and now and one foot in the Islamic imaginative past of Scheherazade.

We must remember vis à vis Scheherazade that those tales were told at night. It's the thousand and one *nights,* not the thousand and one tea times or brunches or what have you. The tales are told at night after lovemaking. The ritual in *The Thousand and One Nights* is that the king and Scheherazade make love and then he's restless and she tells her story. She interrupts at the first glimmer of dawn, just before the muezzin cries for the early morning prayer and they spend that short rest of the night in one another's arms. The tales themselves are very dreamish, of course.

Now Sindbad is the Islamic Odysseus. These are the real narratives of medieval Arab voyagers, accreted around a single legendary figure, with the volume turned up on the marvelous so that things become giants and monsters, just as in Odysseus.

In my reorchestration of Scheherazade's version of Sindbad's voyages the element of sleeping and dreaming becomes prominent. As Sindbad is retelling his guests for the umpteenth time the story of his very first voyage, in which he mistakes a sleeping whale for an island, he proclaims, "We who therethrough wander wake such dreamers at our risk." If we reflect that he's not just talking through his hat here, that "a dream long dreamed" does grow a real geography—whether it's a habitual dream that we have in our sleep or a dream in the metaphorical sense of a wish long concealed, which can grow a kind of moss on its back—then Sindbad's lesson is a wise one.

I happen to have a twin sister, and when we were little we were very close indeed, as most twins are. The rest of the world was just there as scenery. Even before we could speak we were enormously close. We valued that closeness. Its touchstone for me was a morning when we began to compare our dreams, as we used to do. We will both swear to this day that there was a night when we dreamt the same dream. Now what makes me a little suspicious of memory here is that neither of us at this remove, this was fifty years ago or more, can remember anything about that dream. And God knows it might have been simply that kids that close want so much to be one person. Some of the myths say all twins are the two halves of what was once a unity. It may be that we improved our own memory of this event a little for the sake of feeling closer to one another. But we will still swear that it happened.

Now is that wandering through another person's dream? Actually it's something a little more subtle than that, I suppose. It's wandering through the same dream. We know that lovers and people "on the same frequency" are wandering through the same dream together. We all make stories of our lives. That's the way in which life resembles the art of storytelling. I don't know which comes first, as a matter of fact, dreaming and storytelling or the notion that our lives have a dramatical shape. But surely that shape, insofar as we see it in our lives and the lives of others, is partly narrative and partly dream.

Maybe the reason why dreams are closer to narrative art than they are even to painting and sculpture is that dreams are linear. In dreams this happens and then this happens and then this happens. Well, that's storytelling. We know of painters,

Paul Klee and Joan Miró and so forth, whose work was enormously influenced by dream images. But their paintings are fixed, whereas our dreams may be discontinuous. They may be jumpy and surreal or quasisurreal, but they are narrative in character, aren't they? It's this and then this. They're hardly ever lyrical in character. Seldom a fixed moment, a poignant moment. It's usually a story. At least my dreams are that way. And most that I hear about.

Once in a long while I have these amazing dreams which are quite objective. Exciting things are happening, but I'm doing this dream as one may read a book or watch a movie without being emotionally, much less physically, involved in the thing at all. These are what I think of as reader's dreams rather than writer's dreams. You're the witness, the observer or registrar of the action of the dream.

But then Prouse tells us in *Remembrance of Things Past*, among many other dreams he records in that epic work, that he remembers as a child dreaming that he was the rivalry between two families. Imagine that you dream you are a rivalry! You're not even a character. It's like saying that I dreamt I was the distance between San Francisco and Oakland. That's high-tech dreaming. A far cry from the famous dream of "I went to the examination and found I didn't have any clothes on."

Like everybody in the world, I've had certain dreams that recur with a kind of frequency that makes you wonder what the beast is trying to tell you.

There are two motifs that're probably embarrassingly obvious. There was one classical flying dream that I had for ages where I was flying by merely flapping my arms. It was always on the street in front of the house where I grew up, and the altitude was never very high, just to the tops of the silver maple trees that used to grow on my street. It was a very pleasant sensation. There was no anxiety about it at all.

So, when I first read in Freud, in the *Interpretation of*

Dreams, that flying dreams are exhibitionist dreams, that didn't wash at all. Nobody was watching, in the first place. I wasn't exposing myself. There was nobody to applaud or say, "Wow, it's Superman."

When I first saw Neil Armstrong and company doing their reduced gravity motions on the moon I knew exactly how it was. Jacques Cousteau said that his flying dreams ceased the first time he put on scuba tanks and experienced weightlessness. He said he knew that that's what he had been dreaming about all the time, without the image. So while I've never been in a weightless space environment, I know exactly what it would be in all my pores.

Its counterpart is what I think of as "the Chicago dream." My wife went to school in that city for a while and we both experienced those days when, down near the lake, you literally can almost not make way against the wind. It's just this enormous effort. Kafka's work is rich in that kind of dream. It's a sort of bogging down of motion so that you realize that you will never get home; that it will take forever to get to the end of the block. Every step is increasing labor. It may be, for all we know, a premonition of old age and its attendant reduced mobility. But in my dreams it's not. In my dreams I'm usually myself, a fairly robust middle-aged person, doing something, but it's as if the mass and the gravity have increased by an order of magnitude.

The obvious symbolism—that life, at that point, must be burdening you down—probably isn't right at all. I don't recall associating that dream with such times of my life, or the exhilarating weightless dream with particularly exhilarating times. I think it's just whatever the old program is ready to do that night.

Another dream is like my punctuation dream. I used to be a jazz musician to pay my way through college. My instrument was the drums, which take longer to set up and longer to take down than the other instruments. It happened more than once that if we were late for a gig, the other guys would have to start playing while I was still assembling my kit. I'd join in on the bass drum while I was still getting the cymbals in line.

I stopped playing twenty-five years ago and yet, as recently as a few months ago, I had, once more, this recurring dream. It was like a sharp recollection of that sensation of "the show's going on." I'm not quite ready, but I will be ready. In the meantime my right foot's going with one rhythm, my left foot with the afterbeat on the highhat cymbals and I will soon have the cymbals ready. The other guys are working all right.

Perhaps it happened because last spring, realizing that I hadn't unpacked my old drums for nearly twenty years, I sold them. And this was a rite of passage. I hated selling these things and so perhaps that was the muse coming back to chasten me a little bit for having done that. "Remember how it was back in the days when you were younger and could keep the beat? And there you were while the other chaps were going and you were going to catch up." I don't like to be analytical about those dreams because I don't take them all that seriously, but being a writer used to examining the significances of what I write, it's not difficult to read all sorts of appropriate messages into that dream.

For example, my public school education was rural and not very good. When I went to university I had a lot of catching up to do. And that business of catching up strikes me as being, I hate the word, but it's what nowadays would be called the subtext of that dream: having to catch up to the other guys, the other people who were a step ahead of you in their preparation. Look, the trumpet player takes his horn out of the case, gives a *toot toot* and blows. But the drummer has got a lot to do. So in life, as well as in music, I was the drummer who had to catch up. I had read almost nothing when I got to college and I had that amateur's feeling, that callow country boy's feeling, that I had to read everything. I had to go to the library and just absorb it. To find it.

Every artist joins a conversation that's been going on for generations, even millennia, before he or she joins the scene.

The art of storytelling, along with cave painting, is the oldest of the arts and so a new young storyteller is entering a medium that's been going on for this intimidating number of generations and millennia before he or she got there. Well, it's not important to know what all your predecessors have done but there are some of us, those of us who started late and are still trying to get our symbols aligned, who may feel a little impulse in that direction. You want to know what the inventory of effects is. You know, what did all the guys and the girls say before you came on? What's been done already? What can you learn from this one and that one and so forth? But you can't learn it all. That's the great liberating truth. So you just pick up hints and cues where you can.

Listening to someone else's dream by itself is not a very interesting discipline. You might as well tell me what you ate three meals ago. Either you're good at telling what you ate or you're not. Or, let's trade love histories. Never mind, unless you're good at telling the story. The material itself I've never found as interesting as the narration.

Now because I am a novelist I maybe am a little more interested in images themselves, particularly if the image is unusual, like something that's the wrong color or that they don't make food like. I would prick up my ears immediately listening to that kind of dream: something that's out of the ordinary in an extraordinary way. All dreams, even humdrum dreams, are somewhat out of the ordinary, but give me the surprising twist or the sensation I remember when I don't remember the plot but I remember the odor. Or I don't remember who the person was but I remember the sort of sound that was made when she did such and such. Those are the things that as a writer I would be inclined to prick up my ears at. That's when I have that feeling that the beast is trying to tell us something. If there is significance, not deep psychological or symbolic significance but a kind of narrative imaginative significance, it would reside in that kind of arresting momentary vividness or incongruity.

Of course icons in general in good fiction, even in realistic fiction, take on sometimes that dreamish voltage. An image that comes back with a kind of buzz on it, like a motif in music that picks up its charge from the fact that it's been there before. Where did we last hear that motif? Or the person that we think we recognize on the street and then, against all odds, see again soon after in another city or an unlikely number of blocks away. The second encounter has a voltage on it because of the first one.

I don't know how dreams work but I know how writers work, and it might not be a bad analogue for the way the imagination works when it's making dreams. The imagination is operating in both instances. When we're making fiction and poetry one of the things we do is monitor what we've done. We play some cards perhaps almost at random and then, like a good card player, we remember what cards we've played and so we work them. I do it actually with little lists and notes. It's like starting out with any six colored yarns and then you make the argyle sock. You see it's time for the blue yarn to come back so now I'm going to cross this with the red one, et cetera.

I wonder if dreams really work that way. They do have that common element of originating in a kind of narrative or quasinarrative imagination. I love Freud's term, the *dreamwork,* because there is a kind of work involved in the making of the dream which is not dissimilar to the making of a story.

RICHARD FORD

RICHARD FORD had unsuccessfully tried a number of jobs when his mother inquired one day about his plans for the future. Hearing himself answer "I'm going to try to be a writer," Ford realized in a flash the nature of his calling. Still, it took eight years before his first story was published— a full five years after it had been seen and praised by the editor who eventually placed it in the *Paris Review*.

Born in Mississippi in 1944, Richard Ford is a writer who rebels against geographical classification. With the publication of his first novel, *A Piece of My Heart,* critics hailed him as an important new Southern writer. Unwilling to be labeled, Ford set subsequent books in Montana, New Jersey and Mexico.

Ford writes in a clean, simple prose about people facing difficult times. His books include *The Ultimate Good Luck;*

The Sportswriter; Rock Springs (stories); *My Mother, in Memory* and *Wildlife*. He lives with his wife, Kristina, in New Orleans.

━━━━

I HAVE NEVER in my life been as bored as I have been by my friends telling me their dreams. So I've thought to myself, I'm not going to do this to anybody else. It's like talking about your work. Tell me something that I can use. Tell me something that will delight me and please me. That will change my life for the better in some way. This is sort of my ethic as a writer. It's what I try to do in my books. I never had anybody tell me a dream where afterwards my life had changed for the better.

Sometimes my wife will ask me, she'll lie in bed in the morning and she'll say, "Did you have any interesting dreams?" And I'll sort of reluctantly plow back into that and say, "Oh, I don't know, let me think . . . You know I always want to forget these as soon as I can." And she'll say, "Well, did you have any?" It's just a sweet way of making conversation in the morning. And, if I ever tell her one, I immediately begin to feel reluctant because I think it's boring. I think it's just solipsism again.

I usually don't, in the same manner, like people to tell me long stories about themselves. Or writers who talk endlessly about their work. Tell me something that you think will be useful to me. Don't just tell me something that you find interesting.

If, in the morning when I wake up, I think to myself, you dreamed something last night, I don't try to remember it if it isn't immediately available. It's a kind of a backward logic really, I think if I forget about it, it will go someplace where I will have some use for it later. Putting it in the bank, you know?

Writers are always scribbling down little things that lance into their minds. Sometimes you don't scribble them down fast enough. Or you think of something you think you'll remember and you quickly find out that you've forgotten it. It always seems like the most important thing in the world to you, the lynchpin in the great novel that you want to write. But what I sometimes think is that, if I forget something, I'll remember it again. Or it'll come back in some other form. Or it'll fuel some little passion which will finally be useful to me in writing a story. I don't think those things get completely lost. I think they come back to you. That's a piece of optimism on my part. I'm not very mystical about these things but I have to believe that if I forget them they don't just go off into space.

As a writer, I don't have ideas for books. I have little bits and pieces of life, little spoken lines and little gestures and settings all represented in language which I then put into a sequence and make into a kind of logic. By the time anything is at the conceptual level it's usually so hard-sided that I don't have any entry to it.

I use the conventions of literature, the conventions of written narrative to make a logic of these bits and pieces. When I'm writing a novel that has something to do with marriage, which, among other things, is an idea, I'm trying to work underneath that level of ideation. I'm trying to write things from which *other* people will make an idea. I'm trying to make something new, every time.

I'm attempting to interest human beings who would be readers in the particulars of life, configured in a way they haven't seen before—to say something different from what convention teaches us, because convention teaches us a lot of things that aren't true. Convention dictates a lot of ways of comporting ourselves which are not useful, but are harmful and sometimes impossible. I'm always trying to write about people surviving and people trying to use affection as the glue that holds them to other people. I'm interested in language as the principal way in which these relationships get formed, one human being to another.

I never try to make metaphors. My flag is staked on the turf of the literal. Metaphors are things people make out of the

literal stuff of life. They are abstractions. They are expressions
in language which unite two otherwise disparate things. Often
they become emblems. And I am always trying to bring literature down to the level below emblem, knowing full well that it
will perhaps become emblematic as soon as it leaves my room.
But I'm trying to cause people to be interested in the particulars
of their lives because I think that that's one thing literature can
do for us. It can say to us: pay attention. Pay closer attention.
Pay stricter attention to what you say to your son. Pay stricter
attention to what you say to someone you love. Isn't it sometimes the case that you say one thing and you mean another? I'm
trying to write stories in which people seem to be trying to gain
dominion over their lives.

I'm always trying to write about the most important things
that people do. The places in their lives where they feel the
greatest stress, the places where they feel the greatest passion
and how they deal with those things and how they survive them
and make their lives go on. Being in love with somebody is one
of those things. It causes huge schisms in life, it causes huge
passions, huge pleasures. It can wreck your life or not.

I don't really know if life, as lived, changes in obvious epical
ways. I think that literature, as a convenience, tries to assert that
it does. You know the last line of Frank O'Connor's wonderful
story "Guests of the Nation"? "And anything that happened me
after I never felt the same about again." Literature says that;
that things occur after which we are different. I think, in our
lives, those forces are much more glacial in effect. They're slow
and they're big and we don't know until years later that those
things have happened. Of course if our parents are wiped out in
an automobile accident . . . If our mother shows up with another
man, we know *something's* happening. But for the most part,
human beings are trying to make their lives seem normal, not
epical. They're trying to make their lives seem not ragged, not
insurmountable. And so those moments get cloaked. They're
cloaked by language, the language of convention, they're
cloaked by secrecy, they're cloaked by lying, they're cloaked by

someone saying everything's fine. And what literature wants to say to us is "You pay attention now. Is that true? Is that true? Is that true?"

I think that a human being finding himself or herself bereft is ordinary. It's what happens to everybody and it's not the most pleasant thing but something good can and in some ways must be made out of it. Once people find they can express bereftness in language, it becomes a fact in their lives and they can get through it.

Language is extremely liberating. That's why telling is good. And I don't mean confessional telling. I don't think it's of much value for me to unburden myself to you. The teller must tell you something which she or he thinks you can use. Not just to let you be the receptacle for all of his ups and downs and sins. That's why I don't like telling dreams. That's why I try to ignore dreams. I can't think of any reason I should tell a dream to anybody that could be anything more to someone else than watching cartoons on Saturday morning.

I don't like thinking that what I write comes from or is synonymous to a dream. I've heard writers speaking about novels as being extended dreams. I don't like that because dreams, to me, mean selfish gestures. I like the other notion that literature is a gift from the writer to the reader.

I have never been able completely to get used to the solipsistic self-regarding embroidery by which people tell their dreams to others. They always seem, when dreams are told to me, to be pointing back towards themselves. And not to me. And I am adamant that when I tell you something it should be *at least* half for your sake. That's why stories seem like gifts to me. And I haven't seen enough gifts which were dreams.

SUE GRAFTON

IT WAS DURING a six-year custody battle with her second ex-husband that Sue Grafton began fantasizing about murder and devised the clever poisoning scheme on which *A Is for Alibi* is based. Published in 1982, this book became the first in a series of alphabet mysteries *(B Is for Burglar, C Is for Corpse . . . H Is for Homicide)* starring Kinsey Millhone, a wisecracking female private investigator.

Born in Louisville, Kentucky, in 1940, Grafton published her first novel *Keziah Dane* in 1967. After writing the film script for *The Lolly Madonna War*, made in 1973, she began writing screenplays for television, collaborating on several of them with her husband, Steven Humphrey.

With the alphabet series Grafton found a way to share her humorous vision of contemporary society while involving readers in the suspense and excitement of hard-boiled detective fiction. Like her protagonist, Kinsey, whom she describes as a younger, thinner, braver version of herself, Grafton is twice divorced, independent and outspoken. Unlike Kinsey, Grafton is married and is the mother of three grown children.

━━━ ━━━

I REACH a point in many of my books, when I'm very heavily engaged in the process of writing, where I have a problem that I can't solve. And as I go to sleep I will give myself the suggestion that a solution will come. Whether this is from a dream state I'm not certain. I know that I will waken and the solution will be there. I attribute it to right brain activity. I don't know the relationship between right brain and dreams but I know when the analytical self, the left brain, finally releases its grip on us and gets out of the way, the creative side of us, which often surfaces in sleep, comes to the fore and in its own playful and whimsical manner will solve many creative problems.

I was working on a novel called *B Is for Burglar,* which is the second in a series, and I had gotten writer's block. I sat at my desk for weeks. There was no way I could get past this block and so I set the book aside. I kept saying to myself, well, instead of calling it *B Is for Burglar* I could call it *B Is for Blackmail, B Is for Burning.* But I have a certain interior writing machine that's very stubborn and dominating and this little machine said, No, ma'am, I'm sorry, this book is called *B Is for Burglar.* So I finally set it aside. I thought, I can't solve the problem, I don't know how to get out of the bind I'm in. Then one night in the wee hours I woke up and a little voice said "I know how to make the story work." I suddenly understood I was to take the same story and tell it from a different angle. So, where I had originally opened the book with the burglar's point of view, I simply shifted off to another character. I could retain all the work I had done but just give it a different form. Now that didn't come out of a dream per se but it came out of the same state that does create our dreams.

A frightening dream is wonderful for me because it re-creates all the physiology that I need in describing my private eye heroine Kinsey Millhone in a dangerous situation. For instance, I remember one night I dreamt that there was a child in a room across the hall playing with a dog. At a certain point, I, in my half-waking state, understood that it was not a dog at all but something very dangerous. And the fear and the horror that rose up in me from the information about this vicious creature in the room with the child created such heart-thumping and sweating that I immediately started cataloguing my physical symptoms so that later, in describing Kinsey in a moment of great terror, I could use that information. I loved it.

I find that it's very possible to remember what's important so I seldom get up and write things down. Occasionally I will have an odd night where, as I go to sleep, many wonderful pieces of information will come to me. Whole lines of dialogue, observations. I will get up and go in the other room and write those down. But I no more than get in bed then another series comes so I'm up and down, up and down. If there is one moment of insight I just trust that in the morning I will still have it.

As I write I keep a journal for each novel that I work on. And many journal entries begin: "R.B. (right brain) told me in the dead of night . . ." That's much of the way I get story twists, plot connection, strange layering of characters. All of that, I think, comes out of that same subconscious or unconscious state.

Generally the journals will run four times the length of a novel, so what I do is log in every day and indicate what's going on in my life. Because my feeling is that, whatever my emotional state, it will come into the writing itself whether I intend for it to or not. If I'm feeling anxious about a day's work and don't own up to that at the beginning of the work day, the work gets tight and anxious. So I will log it in. If my cat is sick or if somebody's coming to town or I think I'm getting a migraine, I will lay that into the journal. Anything right brain has given me in the dead of night goes straight into the journal because often it will send me on whole new pursuits in terms of the writing. I also will, in this journal, indicate the problem I'm working on at the moment. For instance, I have a scene in *H Is for Homicide*, Bibiana Diaz and Kinsey are arrested together. If I'm uneasy about that I will say: this is the scene I'm working on. I'm worried about the pacing. I'm worried about how it would look, what it would sound like, who would say what to whom and then I will solve it there in the journal. I'll then get out of the journal—I work on a word processor—go over to the chapter itself and do the writing. By then the problems have been solved so the writing comes much more easily.

If I am very blocked or very confused or frustrated I will drink coffee late in the day, knowing that it's going to wake me up in the dead of night. So I get to sleep perfectly soundly and then, at three A.M. when left brain is tucked away, not being vigilant, right brain comes out to play and helps me.

The journals are actually done on the word processor and I can switch between the two. I'm finding now that some of the freest writing I do is in the journal because psychologically that feels like playtime. Once I get into the chapter itself it starts feeling too earnest. I think, this is a solemn piece of writing here and I had better not make a mistake, and so I start getting tense. In the journal I can just write down exactly what I'm thinking. Often it's quite lovely writing and I just lift it from one document to the next.

I'm sure I did not invent it but I began to use the journal technique with *B Is for Burglar*. I can't remember the origin of it but I've become more dependent on it as the books proceed. Each book feels impossible. Each time I write a book I think, I surely cannot do this. I have no skill. I have nothing left to say. It's going to be undoable. It will surely defeat me. Which is why I sit and whine throughout these journals. But when a book is

finished and I've tucked the journal away and tucked the
finished draft of the book away and I'm stuck on the next book,
I will often go back and read my journal and I realize that it is
part of the process. That even the feeling of it being beyond my
skills is part of the process. So it's very reassuring to realize
where I was, at this juncture, in the book before.

I write letters to right brain all the time. They're just little notes:

> Dear Right Brain,
>
> Well sweetie, I've asked you for a little help with
> this and I notice you're not forthcoming. I would really
> appreciate it if tonight you would solve this problem.
>
> Your pal,
> Sue

And right brain, who likes to get little notes from me, will often
come through within a day or two.

As I work, I will write in the journal for maybe two or three
weeks. I go through and print out pages and just let them
accumulate. At a certain point, if I'm feeling stuck, I go back
and read the journal with a highlighter and mark everything that
looks interesting. I find that often I have already solved the
problem and it's sitting right there. I've just forgotten it. I have
forgotten that I considered the question and found some possible solutions. And with some distance, when I have already
moved on in the book itself, looking back in the journal, I can
see that right brain, or the elves and the fairies or whoever it is
that helps us with our creative work, has actually done the job
for me. That's what it feels like. So it's a real gift.

My mother used to show up in my dreams. My mother died in
1960 on my twentieth birthday, after a very long bout with
cancer during which they surgically removed her tongue and her
vocal chords. She was a mess when she died. But in the dreams

she would be alive and I would say to her, "I thought you were dead. I had no idea." Or she would be speaking and I would be so amazed that she was able to speak. And I remember very clearly waking and being amazed that she was still with me. I think she *is* still with me actually.

My father, C. W. Grafton, was a full-time attorney who wrote mysteries on the side. He has not shown up in my dreams. His help was while he was still living in the very sound advice he gave me about the process of writing. He always said to me, "It is miracle enough if I have an idea translated into marks on a page and someone else can read those marks and have the same idea appear in their minds." His feeling was that a writer's first obligation was to keep communication clear and simple. He never wanted me to tamper with language or punctuation or spelling because he felt that would muddy the whole process of communication. He also taught me a lot about how to take rejection and how to take editorial criticism. What he gave me were all the tools necessary to survive as a writer. I feel so many people have the ability but they can't withstand the long apprenticeship that every artist must go through. So that if they have the courage or the technique for survival, and they can hang in long enough to learn their craft, they might be fine writers. But often people get discouraged and disheartened and give up way too prematurely. I'm very grateful to my father for teaching me so much about language and the process itself.

Someone once said to me, "Well what was it that you learned from your mother?" And I said, without even thinking, "From my mother I learned all the lessons of the human heart."

Kinsey Millhone is truly an extension of my personality so I'm sure she looks just like me. People who meet me always picture me as Kinsey Millhone though I am older than she by far and I will always be older. By the time I get to the last book, which I think will be called *Z Is for Zero*, Kinsey will be turning forty and I will be sixty-eight years old. She will have totally taken over my personality by then and I may appear in her dreams, not she in mine.

Often situations that I later see her in will appear in my dreams. Anything that's tense or frightening is the best for me. Because often when you describe a character in a tense situation you can't remember where it is in your body. Where is fear in your body? Where is tension in your body? My life is generally quite placid and I live a lot of my day at the machine writing. It's not as though I'm out facing the bad guys or the monsters in the world. So dreams keep me connected to very dark matters. And often very visceral experiences. In my own life I have carefully engineered the world so that I don't have to face these same demons.

I have never seen any particular connection between the circumstances of my life and the dreams themselves. I do believe that often our dreams carry our emotional states, so that you can look at a dream in terms of its overriding emotion. Is it frustration? Is it anger? Is it fearfulness? But I have not been able to see any direct connection between events. Sometimes trivial events will appear in my dreams but I don't feel they're significant.

I think the dreams that are memorable for me are always quite dark. It seems to me I have dreamed that there are people in the house. My dreams, the linking, seems to be the sense of the ominous presence of the other who is after me and that's the one that comes most readily to mind.

My recurring dream is of being in a house where I feel there's danger. There is something outside the house that is coming after me and my job is to see that all the doors and windows are locked. So I go around and there are hooks and there are latches and there are catches. And every time I secure the premises I look back and I see that the walls have slightly separated so that the hook has come out of the latch. The fear begins to accumulate as I work ever more feverishly to secure the premises while "it" is making its attempt on my life and my safety. That dream is one that has haunted me for many years, though not so much lately. I think it comes out of an event in my childhood.

When I was young my father went into the army. He left in about 1943 and came back in '45. During the years he was gone my sister and my mother and I lived in this quite large house, alone. And I can remember once some drunk came to the door and pounded and made a nuisance of himself. I often think that the feeling of jeopardy comes out of some of those nights when I was alone as a child. Even with my mother and sister in the house, the feeling was of being in great jeopardy. I am assuming that's the link.

Often the writing process is filled with a sense of jeopardy because, in essence, with every book I turn myself inside out. One of the things I've learned about this process is that you have to give everything away every single time. You can't hold back. You can't say to yourself, "Oh this is a wonderful idea but I'll save it. I won't put it in this book, I'll keep it for another book." So always there's the sense of consuming yourself. Using yourself up with the worry that you'll never have another book in you. The truth of the matter is that if you give yourself away every single time, you fill up like a well. Always the water replenishes itself. But I'm never sure of that so as I work I am very fearful. Also, nowadays I am getting so much attention that many more people have opinions of my work. So the critics will hump and hurumph. And even praise creates a kind of pressure. Can I be that good again? Can I be that witty? Can I be that clever? So that as I write I am constantly worrying about whether I am measuring up because I have such high standards for myself and I am so determined to make each book different. And to keep the quality up. That general sense of anxiety and fearfulness will translate into heart-stopping dreams that just make the hair rise up on the back of my neck when I wake from a sound sleep.

*   *   *

Generally I begin a book with a title since I am locked into the alphabet for life. With *C Is for Corpse,* I always knew the title of the book. For a while that's all I knew about that book. But originally I thought to myself, I want Kinsey Millhone to work for a dead man. And that was absolutely as much as I knew. The plotting of the book and the generating of that story was a question of sitting with myself alone, day after day, asking various questions. How could it be that someone could work for a dead man? I knew I wanted her to be hired by someone who felt his life was in danger. She takes his money, begins the investigation and he is in fact killed. By then she has formed such an attachment for this kid named Bobby Callahan that she continues the investigation out of honor and her affection for him. But that process of discovering the story by quizzing myself is another way of keeping in touch with the unconscious. Sometimes I believe these books are already written and my job is simply to allow them to come through me. My job is to get out of my own way so that I can let the process take care of me. But that's scary stuff.

Many of the questions I ask myself have to do with who's killed. Why are they killed? Why wouldn't the motive be immediately apparent? If you wanted to kill somebody and hide the body where would you put it? Getting rid of a body is a devilishly hard thing to do. You know you can't leave it on somebody's doorstep, they will quickly discover it. I often put myself in the position of Kinsey Millhone. What would she do in this circumstance? Why wouldn't she call the cops? I personally hate detective stories where you see the detective do something very stupid, especially if it's a woman. You want women to be sensible and you don't want them to go out in the dead of night with just a flashlight when the wolves are howling. The minute I see a character do that I think, why didn't she call the cops? So you need to design a story which will serve your purpose which is to have constant action, jeopardy, excitement, mystery, intrigue, without making your character look foolish or stupid. That takes some doing.

You're honor-bound as a mystery writer to give your reader all the information you have. Actually it's sleight of hand because you certainly don't give them all or you would just publish your journals and they would know as much as you did. But my hope is to tell a story with characters that are engaging so that the reader becomes involved in the story of their fate and truly wants to know "who done it." Then the question is: can we keep the story moving at a pace that will hold the reader's interest? Is there enough balance between pacing, narrative and dialogue to give some variety as the reading progresses?

Once I begin to ask myself questions, an outline will emerge from that process. Little by little I begin to understand what the story is and then I will tell myself a story. *C Is for Corpse* is the story of Bobby Callahan, who believes his life is in danger, and so on. When I can tell myself enough of the story, then I feel confident to begin the writing. Often I don't know all of it and the writing process is one of discovery for me. I will know the beginning. I often know the ending. The middle is the part that makes me sweat bullets night after night.

Part of the construction of a mystery is deciding the order in which you will give information to a reader. For instance, I think of a mystery in three parts. There is what really happened, so the first question is, What really happened? There is what appears to have happened, and then there is the sequence of events whereby the detective pieces together the information. So you really have three layers to the story. My first job is to decide what really happened. Then I need to go back and find a way to disguise the obvious from the reader who is wily and clever.

Mystery readers are fanatics. They read hundreds of mysteries. They know all the tricks. To fool one, which is very satisfying on all sides, requires great ingenuity, because I can't use any of the obvious devices. In a mystery novel the person who looks guilty probably isn't and the person who looks least guilty probably is. But you're always playing with that optical illusion. I feel I'm honor-bound to tell the truth. You can never have the detective pick up the critical clue and tuck it in her pocket without saying what it is. So, in the unfolding of the mystery, once I know what really happened and how I'm going to disguise that fact, then I come back up to the layer in which I talk about the actual sequence of events. And some of that's logic, just the logistics. That's where left brain comes in.

H Is for Homicide is a little bit different. It's not a traditional whodunnit. In this book, a colleague of Kinsey's is found murdered. She knows that it's the proper province of the police to solve the crime so she does not get involved in it. However, she stumbles into another police investigation and the two turn out to be connected. That was a surprise to me. But again it's the process of the journal. When you ask the right questions then you will get the right answer.

The tricky thing in putting together a mystery plot is that sometimes you feel so tenuous or so uncertain you're afraid to ask the critical questions. And yet if you don't ask those questions, even at the risk of your plot falling apart, you don't get to the better solution. With the word processor, if I'm in chapter eighteen and discover that I've left a clue out, all I have to do is get out of that document, whip back over to chapter seven and insert the line that I need to make it work later. So the beauty of word processing, God bless my word processor, is that it keeps the plotting very fluid. The prose becomes like a liquid that you can manipulate at will. In the old days, when I typed, every piece of typing paper was like cast in concrete.

All the humor in my books comes from Kinsey. Some of the books get very funny because she's very impish. In the process of writing I swear she's standing looking over my shoulder going, Do this, do this, nudge nudge wink wink. And she gets tickled. There are times I write things I get so tickled with myself. Sometimes I can't keep them in the book. They are either beyond the bounds of good taste or they are not pertinent to what's happening. She takes over and does something waggishly funny. It's a fun process because she's so helpful to me, whoever she is.

Mostly it is a question of connecting with her inside of me instead of imagining her as a separate creature. It is getting in touch with the piece of my nature that is linked to her. So instead of projecting it outward I need to stay very calm and centered so that I am joined with her. It does sound like channeling, and it's not quite that, but truly it's not that far from what I imagine channeling would be about.

In order to get in touch I have to block out ego. Ego is the piece of me that's going, How am I doing, champ? You know. Is this good? Do you like this? Do you think the critics will like this? Because that has nothing to do with creating. That has to do with the finished work that's out in the world and that's a very separate creature. So I need to work from within instead of an out-of-body experience. And that's a question of not being self-conscious, not being cute, not thinking I'm so hot. Not thinking anything. Not making judgments about myself. Not sitting critiquing myself but being still enough to hear the voice that'll tell me what I'm supposed to do next. Which is maybe the unconscious, maybe the subconscious. Maybe it's right brain. Maybe it's the soul. I'm not real sure.

Sometimes I do this through meditation. Something as simple as self-hypnosis, a process of relaxing and breathing properly, trying to still the yammering. And then I feed in a suggestion that I'll be productive, energetic and imaginative. I also feed in the suggestion that I will solve the problems I'm facing. Which I do either at the machine or elsewhere. There are moments of insight—sometimes you'll be out driving in your car and you'll have a flash of real ingenuity. Once, for instance, and this is not even a mystical experience, I was lifting a sash window and I heard the window weights banging in the wall. And I thought, now wouldn't that be a great murder weapon. You take the frame off the window, you take the window weights and untie them from the ropes, bash somebody on the head, tie them back in, put the window frame back and who will ever know the difference? And in fact, in one of the books, that's how Kinsey figures a murder out. She's lifting a window and she hears that weight bang. That's the way the creative process works.

I work from nine in the morning 'til about 3:30 or 4:30 in the afternoon. I get up at six, run three miles, come back. I have breakfast and shower and clean up, read a little bit of the newspaper to see what's going on in the world and then go up to my desk. I find, as I get older, the work hours are stretching. I used to work maybe two hours a day and I'd fall back exhausted. Now I can stay connected to the work for much longer. Then late in the day I take a walk just to sort of blow off some of the tension.

Until the last couple of books, I was earning a living writing movies for television with my husband. I would work on the books in the morning and do a teleplay in the afternoon. There was even a period of time when I would get up at twenty to five and write. I was translating one of my father's books into screenplay form from five to six, then I would go run, eat breakfast, come back, work on a book in the morning and work on a teleplay in the afternoon. Which I only did for about four months. I just needed to know I could do it. I really feel we don't quite stretch ourselves as much as we could and I wanted to test myself.

I think there's a sort of mystical process of getting information. I swear. It couldn't be luck because it happens too often. I always find exactly the right person to help me. It's like I'll look in the yellow pages and I'll pass up six names and pick one, inevitably somebody who's reading my books, somebody who has just the perfect touch of information.

I have a private investigator who helps me, he's out in Columbus, Ohio, and he'll just spin off stories in asides, giving me other pieces of information. Later I'll go, that's a plot to a novel. So, I keep a running set of files. If I think something belongs to another book I just tuck it in the file 'til I'm ready to deal with it. But it is mystical to me that inevitably I find people who are just perfect for what I need.

For a while I was writing dreams down and I could see the pattern. I think if you tell your unconscious to give you information in your dreams it will oblige you. It's really amazing how the unconscious longs for ways to get in touch with us. And dreams are a perfect way to do it because they often seem so unrelated to our conscious worries.

At one time I was in an unhappy relationship and I could see how my unhappiness would translate into dream objects. But I never analyzed it. I know that I kept a journal of dreams and later, when I went back and read them, it seemed very clear to me what the dreams were saying about the unhappiness. But at the time I didn't have a means by which to interpret them. And from my point of view I'm not sure I believe that an object always means the same thing. I think we all carry our own talismans and our own magical objects with us, so a book of dream symbols would do me no good whatsoever. What's important is learning your own personal vocabulary.

I have a mystical side. It isn't part of my belief system in a curious way. It's not as though I believe certain things are true but, for instance, the house I live in has a ghost. I am absolutely sure of it. And yet I don't believe in ghosts. I just know there's this ghost in my house. And the contradiction means nothing to me. I don't care. I don't have to be logical. When we first moved into this house I would see someone out of the corner of my eye and I was always thinking to myself, Well, who is that? But the minute I turned it would be gone. And there was always a closet door that would be somewhat ajar and the door was very difficult to close. My husband's theory was that it was the cat. But I swear there was no way the cat could have jimmied a door that was this difficult. Yet I would get to the head of the stairs and I would think to myself, I'm not going to look to see if the closet door is open. I absolutely will not look to see if the closet door is open. And inevitably I would have to look and it would be just slightly open. Which is very fearful. But the ghost is not malevolent. It is sometimes playful. I'll be sitting and working and I think, Oh, Steve's home. You know, I hear him walking around and so I'll call out something, Hi Dear, I'm up here working, blah, blah, blah. A few minutes later I think, I don't think Steve *is* home. And I get up and I go and he's not home. So I don't know who it is walking around my house.

A great caravan of real estate people went through when the house was on the market and later I heard this story. This woman got to the head of the stairs and felt a presence but she was afraid if she remarked on it to the other real estate people in the group they would think she was crazy. After the tour was over, and they were emerging from the house, she turned to a friend and said, Did you feel that? And the friend said to her, Oh, the presence at the top of the stairs? And she went, *Oh!* The hair just went up at the back of her neck. But this is an instance where my conscious beliefs have nothing to do with my emotional reaction to the world. And I think it's the same with dreams. It isn't that I necessarily believe that dreams can be translated point for point into any particular statement, but I know that dreams sometimes have a meaning.

I don't think all dreams have meaning. Sometimes I have dreams that I believe are not mine. I have dreams in which the images and the landscape and the interior architecture are so alien that I am convinced it is somebody else's dream material. And those I don't even try to interpret. Often they have no connection to the reality I know. And I will have a sense of what happened but it is impossible to describe. There is no way to say last night I dreamed about X because the X is not of this earth. So I have that. I don't know what that's about.

And I have some dreams that I know are trivial. It's like, not every thought we have is profound and significant. Sometimes we're just shallow and absurd. So I'll think of someone and then I dream of them, or the other way around, and I know the dream doesn't have any strong message. The emotional dreams are the ones I love.

SPALDING GRAY

BEST KNOWN for his solo performance in Jonathan Demme's film version of *Swimming to Cambodia,* writer/actor Spalding Gray has been a fixture in the performance art world of theater for years.

Seated behind a desk on a bare stage, with a notebook and a glass of water, Gray delivers his intensely personal, wildly digressive monologues in a nearly deadpan manner. He has been aptly described as a "WASP Woody Allen."

He is the creator of fourteen monologues including "Sex and Death to the Age Fourteen," "Booze, Cars and College Girls," "A Personal History of the American Theater" and "Gray's Anatomy."

Gray's first novel, *The Impossible Vacation,* became the subject of his thirteenth monologue entitled "Monster in a

Box." The book deals with the autobiographical issues that
permeate Gray's work, including his fears and the reper-
cussions of his mother's suicide, which occurred while he was
vacationing in Mexico in 1967.

Shortly after our interview Gray married his long-time
companion, director Renée Schafransky. He claims he was
finally prompted to propose after discovering how difficult it
was for her to get hospital visiting privileges while he was
recovering from eye surgery. The proposal took place in his
therapist's office.

▬▬▬

I WAKE UP in the morning and usually I'm going *tooom!*
Gears just grinding, thinking about what I want to do, because
I have to make myself up every day. I really have to pull myself
up by my bootstraps and figure out who I am and what I want
to do unless someone has made a schedule for me. That's why
I like working in films. There's this schedule. So a lot of the time
the dreams are floating around but I don't lie there with them.

Bringing this up now, reminds me of the most vivid dream
that I ever had. The most classically Freudian. I thought I had
dealt with my mother in my work—I am writing this book and
it deals with my relationship to her and crawling out from under
that. One of the things that I realized, working on my book, is
that I equate the sea with my mother. Those were the most
intimate and infantalizing, without boundaries, situations that
I ever had—in Jerusalem, Rhode Island, in Secaunet Point,
Rhode Island—summers at the ocean, playing.

Just recently, my girlfriend Renée and I decided to get married. After thirteen years. Mazel Tov. What we decided to do
was get married by the ocean. In January we went out to stay
alone at a friend's to look for a house that would be relatively
close to the sea. We're out there at the ocean and it's very quiet
and easy to sleep without earplugs—I usually plug my ears with

wet toilet paper when I'm in any kind of urban situation—so I had this intense dream that I was lying on top of some ashes, almost like an Indian fakir. They were not hot ashes.

I have to add, as a footnote, my mother committed suicide and she was cremated. I was in Mexico and missed the entire event. When I came back there was nothing but a box, the monster in a box—that's what the monologue "Monster in a Box" is about—next to my father's bed with an urn containing her ashes. Over the years I have fantasized, why didn't I ever go for it and open that box, and open the urn and see the ashes?

So here I am, I'm dreaming. I have this dream, or it's dreaming me, one never knows, and there are these ashes. And my body is dripping down into the ashes and the ashes are coming up into my body. And there's no boundary between the ashes and my body. They're all one.

I woke up and I kept thinking: I was lying on these ashes that were shaped like what? I knew clearly what the shape was and I was trying to recall it. I remember drawing it out in my journal. It looked like one of those sleeping bags. What kind of sleeping bag was it? A *mummy* sleeping bag. And I went, *Oh no!* I'm still not past it. This is the crisis of the wedding coming up, because marriage is a kind of rite of passage into finally committing to another woman besides mom. And not holding out. In a way it's clearing up all of that stuff. It was a very strong dream for me. It just made me realize that no matter how much I talked about it my mother is still deeply in my unconscious, subconscious, whatever that is. It was one of those memorable classic dreams, the ashes shaped like a mummy.

I don't really look at it as a negative dream. The fact that I could remember the dream and see it so clearly made me very high when I wrote it down. It was about awareness. And merging with my mother's ashes. Pretty intense!

I found out that my mother had killed herself when my father picked me up at the Hills Grove Airport. I was coming back from Mexico. They couldn't reach me there. I was not reachable. He picked me up at the airport and I said, "How's Mom?" And he said "She's gone." Like that. "She's gone." And then he started to cry. And I just had this image, like from a fairy tale—died of a broken heart. She died of a broken heart. I just had this vanishing image. Then, when I got home and he showed me all of the evidence, all of the things she'd left behind, and sympathy cards, I immediately got a horrific head cold and went to bed. I was in bed for four or five days. The dreams began not long after that.

Actually, my father remarried about nine months after my mother's death, very fast, to a woman down the road. Her husband drank himself to death, so they had that in common. I would have these recurrent dreams in which my father and stepmother were in a kitchen. They had moved—to get away from the two houses of pain—to this big suburban palace with a swimming pool and all of their kitchen items: the trash masher, the electric can opener. In the dreams they'd be in the kitchen fiddling with their gadgets. I would be there, and my mother was this holographic transparent ghost passing through us. This was a recurrent dream that I had for a long time. I could see her but they couldn't. They would just go on babbling about the toaster, the trash masher, the juicer, the mixer, the this, the that, those crazy things.

I don't think that I really began to pay attention to my dreams until I was in college, when I started keeping a journal. The one childhood dream that comes to mind is a kind of fever dream that was very very vivid and never to be forgotten. It was in summer and I had a high fever. Who knows what it was because I grew up as a Christian Scientist, so who knows. Luckily it passed. Everyone was outside I remember, at a cookout, when I was in bed with a fever. It was summertime. And next thing I knew, I was running down the upstairs hall, outside my bedroom with a herd of American Indians chasing me. I was terrified, and I ran, ran, ran, into my grandmother Gray's bedroom, which was down the far end of the hall. The hall

seemed enormous. I might have been seven years old. I ran into
her closet and shut the door. It was a tiny little closet with lots
of shoes in the bottom of it. I just kind of came to in this sweaty
heap on top of my grandmother's shoes. I had no idea how I
got there and then I remembered the Indians. It was a strange,
intense hallucination. A dream of sorts. Almost like a waking
dream.

For years I kept a dream journal. Every morning I would
write the events that I remembered from the previous day. Then,
using asterisks, I would always record my dreams in the back.
I think they're fascinating to go over. In the past I've had classic
castration dreams, Oedipal dreams, that I was very intent on
recording in college. I was taking a course in Freud and dreams
so I think that stimulated the dreams. It programmed them.

God, I remember one! I was born in Barrington, Rhode
Island. I grew up there. In the dream I was running naked
through the streets of Barrington in broad daylight and feeling
that shame—really a Garden of Eden kind of thing—of losing
one's innocence. I was diving behind hedges and trying to hide
my nudity. I got to my grandmother Horton's yard and ran over
to the rose garden, naked—my Grandmother Horton used to
have a beautiful rose garden—fell down on it and climaxed. I
came into the earth. I woke up and it was a wet dream. I thought
that was pretty intense that you could have a wet dream falling
down in a rose garden.

Another one was: my father, my older brother and I were on
the steps of the back porch in Barrington and we were in the
configuration of Christ and the two thieves. I was Christ, I was
in the middle and the thieves were on either side, the crosses
were on Golgotha. And there was this very evil type man—
archetype of the burglar, heavy beard, unshaven—standing in
the yard and he was challenging us. He was saying "Come
down." And I came down from the steps. He had a straight-edge
razor and he said, "You have a chance to kill me first. You have
the first blow, the first strike," and he handed me the razor.
Then, "If you don't do it, I am going to pulverize your face. I

am going to destroy your face." I went to slice him. And as I
lifted the razor I brought it down and sliced my side. Blood shot
out just like in those classical paintings of Christ. I had that
dream many years ago and it still stays with me. I might have
been seventeen years old when I had it.

Another one was that I had lost my testicles—I might have
been in college then—and was looking all over for them. I went
to a football field in Barrington, Rhode Island (I was never
involved in sports at all), and found them hanging from under
the bleachers. There were my balls hanging from under the
bleachers. It was a very strange dream.

I used to write them down but dreams like those stay with
me. You don't have to write them down. My God, they stay
with you for a lifetime.

I lean toward the school that one must work very carefully
to make your own dream language. I used to look up Freudian
symbols. I had the symbol book, the Jungian book and I'd say,
now what does Jung say about that? Now I try to interpret for
myself. But I haven't taken time to do that, though my dreams
are all recorded. I haven't done an interpretation book. Writing
them down was enough for me.

I'm very interested in lucid dreaming. I have friends that go to
bed at night and decide what they're going to dream. I had a
person in my storytelling workshop at the Omega Institute—she
is deeply into Native American Indian rituals. She lives in
Toronto and she's a sorcerer's apprentice. The sorcerer lives in
the desert outside of L.A. She said that she can't afford to fly to
him anymore so they meet in dreams. He comes to her and they
do these workshops in these waking dreams. All in the same
breath she said, "In fact I'm thinking of breaking away from
him because he's getting rough with me in a way that I don't
like. He grabbed me in the dream last night and left this bruise
on my arm." And then she showed me the hand mark on her
arm. I didn't know whether to draw the line on that one.

* * *

One of the things that people don't realize is that the best way to approach *Swimming to Cambodia* is not just to see Jonathan Demme's film but to read the book. You see, originally it was an epic monologue. It was in two parts. It was three hours long. But Jonathan wanted to cut it to eighty-seven minutes so we combined part one and two and made it much more universal to reach a larger audience. When I published it, there was a very strong dream at the end of the monologue. Every time I would do that dream in performance I would have new insights into it. It had to do with me baby-sitting a straw boy. The boy is playing and gets burned up in the fireplace and I have to go tell his mother about how I'd not been able to be a good baby-sitter, that the child had burned up. Then the child gets reborn in the dream. I scrape up the ashes from the hearth and re-create a live boy out of that. It was almost like a Pinocchio odyssey—going from the straw boy to a real live boy. I end the monologue and the book with that. That was a very powerful experience for me. The straw boy dream was one of those classic dreams about an identity quest.

I'd had the dream when I was working on *Swimming to Cambodia* so I thought it was important to include. Sometimes my editors at Random House would circle my dreams when I was doing *Sex and Death to the Age Fourteen* and say things like, "What does this have to do with anything?" But Theater Communications, they let me publish the manuscript exactly the way I wrote it. They didn't question it. It was good that they didn't because I assume that if you have a dream as powerful as that one in the midst of creating something, it has to do with what you're creating.

Because I would do that dream every night, I would get people coming up to me after the show to tell me their interpretation of it. I would have a dialogue with them and I would get letters, you know, fan letters. People would really harp on that dream.

They would have various interpretations about who the straw boy was and why he was allowed to be burned up.

Ashes are a classic and powerful symbol, aren't they?

* * *

In the second monologue "Booze, Cars and College Girls" I
open with a couple of dreams. One of them was the testicles
hanging from the bleachers dream. I had that dream when I was
in college. I remember that it was connected to me trying to
close myself in. I couldn't stand any outside noise. I wanted to
sleep in a coffin like Sarah Bernhardt. A box or an isolation
tank. I put boards all over my windows on Beacon Street in
Boston. They were beautiful arched windows and the Back Bay
Community Association came and knocked on my door and
said I had to take them down because it looked like the building
was under construction. They didn't like the look of it. I
remember connecting the dream to that. Juxtaposing it.

I would say that a subconscious or unconscious state doesn't
work for me so much in dream life as it does when I'm putting
a monologue together. I'll forget certain things or block on
certain things and realize that I hadn't put them in. As I'm
speaking a monologue I'll be juggling in my mind—where can
I fit this information in? All of a sudden I'll find a natural
opening and *zoomp,* in it goes and there's a new structure. I look
at it or I hear the tape afterwards and I think, that works better
there. That's where the so-called fiction begins to work because
what you're doing is starting to work with the way you
re-remember memory. So in a way it's like a dreamscape.
Because one has to always remember that the experience you're
talking about is the memory of the experience and not the
experience. Then the following monologue is the memory of the
previous performance. You're remembering the way you
remember and so it gets turned into fiction. Memory is a fiction.
That's why I don't fictionalize—I try to stay very close to
reality.

I was talking to Paul Krasner recently, down in Esalen, and
he said, "You know I do a routine where I talk about blowing
coke with the Pope—I've done that so many times now I'm not
sure if I did it or not." I know what he's saying there because
I begin to get a structure through mistakes and reinterpretation.

I'm not working specifically with a conscious mind. I'm not at all a person who works through contrivance and manipulation of reality where you think, What would make a good story? But rather I work very passively with dreams, mistakes, serendipity, coincidence, synchronicity.

Synchronicity plays a big part in my life. I like synchronicity. It gives me the chills. The major synchronicity that I experience is while I'm writing. I'll often have the radio on—background classical music. The news will come on, or some spoken event, and the words will begin to hitch up. I'm in the midst of writing the word when I hear the word on the radio. It would be an uncommon word that would come up on, say, an in-depth report from National Public Radio about the Kurds. But it wouldn't be as strange as *Kurd*. You wouldn't catch me writing *Kurd*. But *death,* that's a pretty common one that might come up a lot, or something like the word *languishing.* Something like *languishing* really gives me the chills when I'm hearing it the same time I'm writing it. That will happen as often as one or two times a week. Which is a lot. I used to keep a record of those but I just don't any more. There are too many of them.

I used to take it as a confirmation that I'm in the right place, doing the right thing. I'm saying, Right, Right, as in *write*- -both uses of the word. It centers me in a way. It's like a mystical confirmation.

I do monologues to try to figure out what's going on. I see life as chaos essentially and then the structure is in trying to put the puzzle together. So right now, next to my desk in New York, I have a cardboard box. And I throw everything that's unanswered, disturbing or relevant to some of the things I'm thinking about, into that box. Then, when I have time, maybe a year later, I'll dump it out and begin to put together the puzzle of a new monologue. I will take a spiral notebook and make an outline of progressive anecdotes, of stories that I think apply to the puzzle. So I begin to have a new take on my life, on where I am historically. What I'm thinking about. How I'm interacting with people. It grows out of a series of anecdotes. Then I begin to see the common theme by speaking it.

What I do is speak it in front of a small audience from the outline. And then I listen to a tape and I go, Oh yeah, like in psychoanalysis. What's the connection? What's the underlying theme? I thought "Monster in a Box," my new monologue, was about all the interruptions that were happening to me while I was trying to write the book *Impossible Vacation*. Because of *Swimming to Cambodia* people were making me all these offers and I was saying yes to all of them. Well, that was one aspect of it. And the more I performed "Monster in a Box" the more I saw that it was also about my mother. That kind of Oedipal monster. And the book that I was trying to write was that other monster in a box. So the more I'd play it, the more I'd see the levels of themes. A monologue really gets mature after maybe performing it a year.

It starts as innocent and the audience likes this because they're in on the innocent process. We're equal. I'm not really sure what it's about. And they're telling me by the way they react. Then it gets more and more polished and then it gets ripe and then it gets reflexive and then when it gets overly reflexive it has to stop. It goes through this arc where it gives me insight and information. And then it becomes entertainment. Or both. When you can get those two things going it's wonderful.

We haven't done this recently, but for many years in our relationship, when Renée and I would wake up together, I'd say, What did you dream? And we'd share our dreams. That's what we do. And I have to say that hers are outstanding. Very complicated. Very Jungian. Very Freudian. Very symbolic. Having a lot to do with her father who also died early, at fifty-two—the same age as my mother—through certain self-destructions. So there's an element of suicide there as well. She's much more able to help me with mine. Renée has more stick-to-itiveness, fortitude and relentlessness at getting to a theme. That's why she makes a very good script writer. But we do share dreams in the morning. If we're on any kind of open time, that's when things get really good in our dreams. When we're on a vacation—in that open period where you try to vacate, all of a sudden the dreams get very active.

What I think is happening often in sleep is that that stuff is in the air. Like radio waves. And they intermingle. I had a very strange experience with that and I'm not an intuitive ESP type of person. I was asleep next to Renée and the telephone rang at, oh God, who knows what time it was. It was in the middle of the night. I was dreaming, and it woke me from the dream. Renée is always good at jumping up for the phone, she's always quicker to get to it. While she was running to the phone I was trying to recollect my dream. The dream was quite a simple one of how I was being called to go to Amsterdam. I happen to know someone that teaches at the mime school over there and he wanted me to teach storytelling at this school. In the dream, he was saying, "You don't have to look for a hotel because I can move in with my girlfriend and you can use my apartment." I was going over the dream, trying to recollect it, while Renée was running for the phone. She said "It's Amsterdam calling," and he was on the other end, apologizing for waking us up. He'd forgotten the time difference and was calling to find out if I could come teach at the mime school. That is strong stuff!

I wonder if it is not so much synchronicity in this case but simply that his message overflowed out of the wires and he was much more telepathic than he realized. All of sudden there were no boundaries and his need to get me to Amsterdam was coming right out of the telephone ahead of time. It got to me telepathically.

I think that that happens a lot to people. It doesn't so much to me. But when those things do happen it opens me up and it makes me much less narrow in my thinking. I'm much more open to people who do lucid dreaming when I talk with them. One student of mine, who was in the workshop—she has some busy, busy nights. Her astral body is moving around the house and she's meeting various entities that her spirit, the guide, is sending her. When she first told me this dream she said, "I left my body from the bed and my astral body was up and I was moving it around the house." Doing, well, I don't know what, maybe she was cleaning the house with her astral body, and the first thing that occurred to me was, "But didn't you ever want to make love to yourself?" You know, coming from a typical narcissist, I said, "Didn't you ever just want to get back into bed and make love to your body with your astral body?" And she said, "It never occurred to me."

Two weeks later I get a call from her, the little devil, and she says, "I did what you suggested. It was great!" I was so jealous.

My mother hasn't visited me in my dreams. It's funny, when I think of it now, that it hasn't happened. I've felt that I've been open to it but I'm also fearful. Renée's father has visited hers. Often. But I think that I'm still resistant. I did a theater piece called "Rumstick Road." It was the most healing piece I ever did about my mother's suicide. It was an exploration of it. I went back and tape-recorded my relatives talking about why they think she committed suicide. It was a very strong, healing piece. A way of dealing with the mourning that I didn't go through, artistically.

When I was writing my novel *Impossible Vacation,* I had a kind of breakdown around my mother's suicide. A collapse, because I had a fantasy that there was a dark feminine side of my mother, the dark spirit, that was trying to take me back to the other side by stealing me away. Soon. At age fifty-two. I guess there's some trepidation coming up because I'm soon going to be as old as she was when she killed herself. I think there's fear and resistance still around that act of suicide and how violent that was.

My mother was the theatrical inspiration in my life. She was always acting out, in a fun way. And then it became the crazy way, the dark way. When she would feed us in the high chair, as little babies, she would have tap shoes on. She was a frustrated performer. She would tap dance while feeding us. I remember her tap shoes. Or she would be doing the opening bars from Beethoven's Fifth. She would always be singing a song: "Pharaoh's daughter went swimming down by the Nile, someone saw her there and stole her underwear and left her with a smile" or "Adam and Eve and Pinch Me went down to the river to swim. Adam and Eve fell in. Who was left? Pinch me, Pinch me, Pinch me." And pinch, pinch, pinch, scream, scream, scream. Yeah, she was there—on—all the time. See, I didn't recognize that is what the therapists diagnosed eventually as manic. But there it was, she was pushing all three of us toward creativity.

All three of us, my two brothers and myself, are writers. And we all write in different forms. My younger brother is music critic for the *Providence Journal;* my older brother, strangely enough, writes about autobiography. And here I am in the middle, doing it. So someone there is a muse and a great inspiration and a great sanctioner of creative spontaneity. I know when I go to my therapist for my checkup, I always am complaining to him about struggling with the paranoia that I go through and how I can make that more positive. And he points out to me, and I do agree with him, he says, You can't have the kind of organized creative mind that you have without having the dark side of it. The shadow of it has to be there. You may be able to create things as light and comic and transcend the darkness but you just can't cut the other off. That's the one I'm always grappling with. It threatens to take me down but I'm usually able to integrate it in the work.

I write every morning. That really is therapeutic for me. Whatever it is I'm writing—if it's a dream I'm writing down or an event, a little story that happened to me on the road that I see as a meaningful anecdote that might fit in somewhere—I'll mark it down.

I find that it's more difficult to listen to people's dreams than it is to listen to people's waking states. I think that the most important thing in using a dream is to work in the same way that you work when you're trying to make a waking state story good. And that is to be very concrete in the details: the colors and the details. That's the first thing. What we would do in a workshop, if we were doing a dream workshop, would be to have a person tell a dream and then have the other students listen and react as critic and audience, saying, Where was it vivid? Where did I start nodding out? Where did I lose my attention? Just that business of clarifying, working with detail and not having "and then"s and "this happened"s. Look for what the "and then" is. What is the image in the "and then" where you're doing a jump? Is there something there that you're not able to put into words yet and that you have to struggle with more? There's no blank in my opinion. There is no nothing. There is no such thing as nothing because as soon as it's observed, it's something. So when I sit down to speak I'm really recounting a kind of memory film. And I'm trying to do it in as much detail as I can. There's no way I will ever go blank unless I have Alzheimer's or something like that. There is always something happening. So I would encourage the dreamer to talk about what wasn't happening. What was the block? What is going on at all times? In order to solve the dream sometimes it's good to free-associate on what the block is. What's there? What is completely there? Be as conscious as possible about it. I've experienced so-called reality as so much like a dream that I only stick to the facts. Because it's so strange, it's so much like a dream when I retell my stories that I sometimes don't know the difference.

I grew up as a Christian Scientist and was influenced by Swedenborgianism and Hinduism. It was all filtered down through the New England Transcendentalists and the ideas of Mary Baker Eddy. And certainly the Indian idea of Maya, life being a dream, so infiltrates my consciousness that when I finish telling a story or writing a story down it's not that much different than a dream to me.

When I was doing my first monologue "Sex and Death to the Age Fourteen," I was working only from memory. I was remembering when I was six, seven and I was only taking the memory that came to me, not trying to bridge the gap. There's a line about this guy shinnying up a tree and showing us his ass after we were watching "Howdy Doody." And I say, "shortly after he shinnied up the tree and showed us his ass they developed the house next door." That was the way that I remembered those events. I never tried to bridge them. And that reads not unlike the way you would have a dream.

I often ask people when I'm doing interviews on stage if they've dreamed recently. I had the opportunity to interview His Holiness the Dalai Lama in Santa Barbara for a new Buddhist magazine called *Tricyle, Buddhism in America,* and that was one of the questions that I asked. And he said, Oh yes, he does dream. He actually said he didn't have any that he remembered the night before but that just two nights ago he had dreamed that his guru had come to him dressed in a business suit. Then, before that, his mother had come to him with his favorite Tibetan dish to serve him. He saw those both as portentous and good dreams.

When I interview the audience, what I try to do is stay very close to the details that I know in my own life. I went a little off with the Dalai Lama and I missed my rule. Maybe I was overexcited. Both the Dalai Lama and I were on tour and we were both ending up in cities at almost the same time. So I started by telling him who I was and what I did and how I'd been touring and I asked him what it was like to tour. We were both staying in Fess Parker's Red Lion Inn in Santa Barbara. Davey Crockett's motel! And I said, "What's the first thing that you do when you get to one of these hotels?" And he said, "Oh, I look around to see if there's anything interesting and then I go sit on my bed and meditate." Well, the place to stop, and the next place to go is "Did you find anything interesting about this hotel?" Right. I missed my mark and I said "What is your meditation like?" Oooh. Twenty minutes later we got onto the next question. Interesting but very complicated and not something I knew about because I'm not a meditator.

I try to go for the detail that lights up in me like a neon light. You can see it there. You can feel it in your gut. You go, Yeah. That's the first thing that you want to ask about. And you go with it and from there on out it's going to be a progression of associations. Because when one ends you go with that next one.

I did an interview recently with someone who asked me if I liked jazz and I realized that I used to listen to jazz all the time and how much it influenced me in my work in terms of digressions, improvisation, the way that I take off. I realized that when a monologue is finished for me it's musical and it has those rhythms. Recently, seeing the film *Swimming to Cambodia* at Penn State, I went, Oh yeah, this is where it works the best—when it moves into its lyrical modes. Working now as a writer I have a terrific problem getting that lyricism into my work. Because in the monologue I'm doing a rewrite every night for a year. I hate rewrites. I write in longhand and I don't have a word processor so I don't do as many rewrites. I haven't got the patience. I realized that my real form is the oral form. One of the things that I do in my writing to try to bring that rhythm into it.

I write in longhand, first of all because I'm allergic to machinery, but also I see it as an extention of my musculature. It's like being a painter. It's the closest thing I can get to my breath. I go over everything I wrote in longhand with a red pen, make corrections and then I get out the tape recorder and I read it. I read it fairly rapidly and begin to find the natural rhythms. I immediately skip over and cut words and interpret and do an interpolation of what's on the page. But I need that page as the spine to come off of, the way in a monologue I need the audience as my edge or my spine to come off of. My wall. My very responsive wall. My human wall. People have asked me, Why don't you just sit down and write orally, speak into a tape recorder? I've tried it. Nothing happens! There is no *other* there to work with. The audience is the other and the written page is the other. It's the dialogue I need.

When Random House wanted me to publish the monologues I thought they meant that they wanted me to write them like a writer and I sat down and tried to write them. I was writing like the person I was reading at the time, Raymond Carver, because I hadn't found my own written voice. Then I thought, I'll just speak into a tape recorder and work on them as transcriptions. And that's what I did. In doing that I learned a technique. How do most students try to find their personal voice? By imitating other writers. And that doesn't really work. So what I had the students do first was to speak their stories, their autobiographic story, into a tape recorder. Then I'd have them transcribe it and begin to work on making the transcription like writing. My theory was, and it works, that they will find their personal voice in that way because it *is* their voice. It is their spoken voice. It comes from the life, the breath, the rhythm. That's so important to me. The lyricism. That's why the monologue form is my bottom line and always will be what I do as long as I have voice and breath. Because it's the most satisfying. I come to lyricism sooner and in a more fulfilling way than I do when I work on the written page.

I'm aware of voices in my head. It started as chatter. This was before I did the monologues. My head was so busy. I wouldn't say they were diverse entities but I did have an interesting thing happen when I was working at the McDowell colony writing my book. I tell about this in "Monster in a Box." I was put in the Bates House. And this freaked me out because it was named after Nurse Bates who nursed McDowell in his final stages of syphillis. So I was equating it with death and was writing about death in my book and I was a little nervous about the whole situation. I had this icon that a Balinese healer had given me to lay my mother to rest. I decided to put it on the mantelpiece to bless the house with that spirit. The Balinese shaman had said that I should talk to this icon, a little drawing that he had done, and bring it flowers. Just talk to it like I would to a friend, a companion. For the longest time I thought this was the silliest thing. And I wasn't doing it. And the more freaked out I got being in the Bates House, the more I would come in and use it as a presence. "Good morning. Hi, how you doing? You know what? I'm going to take you for a walk this afternoon and show you the New Hampshire woods. Now I know it's going to be very different from the Balinese but I tell you—the forsythia! It's early spring and we may even see some daffodils." Right? So I had this relationship going. And I wasn't hearing a lot back. But then I would get so immersed in my book that I would forget. I'd charge out for my obsessive walk to let off steam and I would forget about the icon. And one day I was going across to the door and I heard this voice in my head. "What about the walk?" And I turned and I went over and cradled it in my arms like a child and we went out and explored the New Hampshire woods. And the more I began to work with this icon the more I began to hear this other aspect of my self in the form of a voice. Not Joan of Arc voices with different tones and not Son of Sam ones that couldn't be turned off. But there it was.

The chatter I had was an incessant internal monologue that needed to be aired and gotten out into form. It was almost like talking to myself. And once I began doing the monologues it was an interesting progression of language, of coming into myself. I saw it as a kind of Pinocchio oddysey: coming in as a wooden boy into Gepetto's workshop, which happened to be the Performing Garage. And then breaking away from that and being the person without speech, moving, just the body. Then, speech coming gradually, taking identity. And then doing the first monologue to the Wooster Group. They were my first audience. They would say, "Come in and speak this."

When I was doing the first show, which was the dumb show, the movement show, that's when the chatter was there. I am a dialectician and I think that not having the talk, and just moving, created the talk in its absence. It just came up. It needed to be there. But I had to free it physically first. I'm a very physical person and worked in Tai Chi and yoga and body work for years with the Performance Group and the Wooster Group. So when I sit down at a table now, all I'm doing is centering myself right at the base of my spine to that chair. And I'm moving out of that all the time. I'm coming up. I'm three inches off the chair. My feet are moving, my arms are moving. I'm sweating. It's a physical event for me to tell these stories. They're very animated.

But here I am going on and on with you and it's because you're my witness. I proposed to Renée in front of our therapist. It's audience. Witness. Mom.

ALLAN GURGANUS

Aᴌᴌᴀɴ ɢᴜʀɢᴀɴᴜs is the most morally responsive
and technically brilliant writer of his generation," wrote John
Cheever, describing his friend and former student.

Born in Rocky Mount, North Carolina, into a family he
has described as "shabbily genteel," Allan Gurganus started
out to be a painter. He discovered literature while serving in
the Navy aboard the USS *Yorktown* during the Vietnam War
and pursued his interest in writing at the Iowa Writers'
Workshop.

His 718-page first novel, *The Oldest Living Confederate
Widow Tells All*, spent four months on the *New York Times*
best-seller list and won, among other awards, the Sue Kauf-
man Prize. *White People*, a collection of novellas and short
stories written over a twenty-year period, won the *Los
Angeles Times* Book Prize and the Southern Book Award.

Allan Gurganus is the kind of person whose warmth is contagious. The first time he walked into the "DreamTalk" studio I found myself literally jumping up and down trying to express my enthusiasm about his work. Gurganus, picking up on my excitement, started jumping too. We must've looked pretty strange to the other people at the station!

When, at the close of a second radio interview, I thanked Gurganus for helping make this book a reality, he responded with a sentiment that seems to pervade his life, "We are all angels for each other."

═══

IN MY BOOK *White People*, there's a story called "It Had Wings." The derivation of the story is completely connected to a dream. Some years ago I had a dream in which I was standing at a kitchen sink in a suburban house, like the one I grew up in when I was a little kid, and I saw something fall in the backyard that was the color of a Caucasian. It fell with a kind of smack onto green grass near a picnic table. It seemed to have fallen from about five miles up in the sky, straight down into this little yard. The thing that I remembered when I woke was the sound it made hitting. It was a sound that I registered on the page, when I finally wrote the story, as *thwunk*. I knew that the thing had wings. The phrase "It had wings" was a part of the dream. I saw it sort of emblazoned, like the motto in Latin over the door to a library. I woke up thinking, What an incredibly beautiful set of words! "It had wings." It seemed to me one of the most perfect sentences that I'd ever thought of. And it was sort of presented to me on a tray in the dream.

Years later—there's often a delay in between having a dream and finding a use or place for it—a composer called me up and said, "I'm looking for a story to set to music. Do you know of anything three pages long that I could use?" I couldn't think of anything immediately. But I used this occasion to write the story "It Had Wings." In this story, an old lady, retired from

selling formal wear at Wanamakers for seventy years, is standing at her kitchen sink and sees an angel fall in her backyard.
The first thing you see is the angel falling, and then the old lady
attempting to minister to this wounded angel and helping him
fly away. It was a perfect image in some ways for dreams
because part of the gorgeousness of dreams is that nobody
knows you actually had them except by your own witness and
testimonial. So that if you tell me a gorgeous image, I don't
know if you're just sitting here making it up or if you actually
dreamed it at night. But in some ways it doesn't really matter
because it's all a dream.

What I had to do, and what I always have to do, is find the
character to whom this happened. Character is the center of
fiction for me. To have that event chronicled in the third person
in an abstract way means nothing. It only means something in
so far as it relates to the life and experience and readiness of a
single person who's open enough to the fact of an angel in her
backyard to take her cup and go out and feed the angel a little
milk and ask him questions about heaven. And his answer is,
"We're just another army. Don't expect much. We miss it here.
Notice things more. We're just another army." And I think that
that's true. I think that we're all waiting to be transformed into
something else but in fact the luckiest of us are the people who
realize that this is it. And that to honor our dreams and to honor
our loved ones and to honor our rituals and our lives is precisely
what literature is endlessly trying to teach us. That this is the
moment. And that we are happy and immortal only insofar as
we know and notice that.

Finding a shape for the story was enormously satisfying. I
wrote twenty-two pages and then boiled it down to three and a
half pages. Partly because of the requirements of the composer
but also it was such a joy to have been given this kernel of
something and then to develop it and to find its larger meaning.
It's one of the stories that speaks to me of the subject of dreams
with a special resonance.

*   *   *

I think storytelling is inherently curative. I went recently to an AA meeting with a friend and listened to forty people tell their stories, sometimes in three or four sentences. "Hello, my name is George and I'm an alcoholic. My mother drank. My father drank and then I drank and one day I . . ." Suddenly you're in the middle of a narrative which is inherently curative. In the middle of another person's dream, another person's reality.

There's a strange combination in writing of using images and fragments from actual dreams, but also finding a way to have a governed conscious dream life, which is what writing is. Which is what being an artist is. It's to have access to your own unconscious but also to direct it and to be able to drag in facts and figures that you've found that please you: stories that you overhear as well as stories that you make up. The joy of being a storyteller is precisely that I have two dream lives, at least two: the one that happens the eight hours a night that I close my eyes, and also the one that happens the rest of the time when I open my eyes. That's because I can pull images from that literal dream life and also have this rich kind of alternative sideboard, this kind of sidecar on the motorcycle where you have a measure of control that is all too rare in the world now.

Writing is a kind of free fall that you then go back and edit and shape. I think the best things that I've ever got as a writer come frequently all in a burst. You don't ask too many questions at the outset. You can analyze belatedly and retrospectively but there's a kind of physiological sensation that happens when you are really on the trail of a story. When I'm working well, I wear a moving man's zip-up uniform because I perspire so freely that I sweat my way through the fiction. Finally the body is the ultimate testing ground of what works and what doesn't on the page.

When you think about the English alphabet, twenty-six letters, pictograms, that are asked to bear all the human investigations and all the aspirations and appetites that we have and that have ever existed in human history, it's terribly abstract. It's beyond algebra, so that making that abstraction real, to me, as a very physical person, means to enact it physiologically. One way I do that is to read everything I write out loud many many many times. All the stories in *White People* have been read aloud at least thirty or forty times so that there's a kind of ear music that operates as an editorial principal on the page even when a reader is not moving his or her lips. There's a kind of rhythmic synchronicity which sets up in their biological chemistry which somehow pulls them rhythmically into the fiction and creates a kind of heartbeat on the page. You only get that, I think, by reading the work aloud endlessly.

There are so many things you can do on the basis of these twenty-six letters. You weep, you laugh, you get turned on, you get hungry. It's pretty basic in some ways. By trusting my body and by making that my active collaborator, Hammerstein to my Rodgers, I have a kind of company in the isolation of working.

We all have our own crazy rituals. I pace. I say lines out loud a lot. I live alone and my neighbors think I have a very active and busy apartment. All the voices are me and mine or us and ours. I don't know which. That for me is maybe the greatest fascination. It's how many voices are packed into this single voice? It's how populated each of us really is. Not only with the people that we might've become if circumstances historically and personally had been different—if daddy had not bought the farm in 1936, if I'd been born black instead of white, or if I'd been born in Africa instead of America—but how many other possibilities are encoded in us narratively?

In my first book, *The Oldest Living Confederate Widow Tells All,* I imagined myself into the body of a slave named Castalia who was abducted from Africa when she was three years old, along with her royal family tribe. There was something that happened when I was writing that chapter, about coming out of the river Niger into the ocean and crossing to the slave auction at Charleston, that was almost like a memory. It was not just a kind of narrative invention that I was cooking up detail by detail, knowing that I got this detail from anthropology and this detail from something I'd overheard. It was almost like a preexisting map. And I knew when I imagined the ship turning a bend in the river what was going to be there next. It was just a question of mapping it. So, I think when you're really cooking, when you're really sweating so freely that you have to wash your moving man's uniform every other day, you know that you're in touch with a kind of waking dream life that frequently is the one that hooks up with the most people, the most readers.

It's mistaken to say that you go into a kind of dream state and come out with a 719-page novel. It's a combination of knowing when to be trusting and when to be suspicious. It's a question of knowing when to let the pages flow and then having the good sense to come back and say, "This is better than that. This has to go." It takes a strange combination of being enormously intellectual and willful and smart and also being as trusting as a baby. There are lots of very smart people and there are lots of very trusting people. But it's very hard to get both of them together in one body. That's why there are so few great artists and so few great books. You either get a sweet trusting book or you get a smart cold book.

It's an odd combination of being ruthless, in the sense that you can't be sentimentally attached to an image just because you have had it. You have to be pure in the service of your characters. And it's precisely that seeming selflessness, that giving up of your own ego and your own willfulness, and your own self-congratulatory "Look at me, aren't I brilliant?" that purifies and let's you become clear and at one with the character that you're seeking to save.

I think that the first impulse in writing is to flood it out, let as much run freely as you possibly can. Then to take a walk or go to the bank or go to the store and come back in a day or six months later. To read it with a cold eye and say "This is good. This is not. That sentence works. This is magical. This is crummy." You have to maintain your critical sensibility and not just assume, because it was an extraordinary dream for you, that it will be a dream for other people. Because people need maps to your dreams.

My dreams often tend to be fairly literal. It's almost like a ticker tape comes across the bottom that says "Order flowers for your mother's birthday tomorrow." "Invest in salt mines." I have pretty hardheaded dreams in some ways. They can be very lavish in terms of stage values and special effects but they tend to be about people in situations, on expeditions or errands. It's very hard to typify a good night's dreaming. I tend to remember a lot of images in the morning. I tend to have at least three or four moments from my dreams and, as everybody understands, you can train yourself to do that. I've found it very valuable and entertaining. I tend not to talk about it a lot to other people because I feel that, until you've found out what a dream means and translated it into action, it tends not to be as magical for other people as it is for you. But I always assume that the dreams mean something and part of my joy is decoding the dream. "What does this mean? Oh, I see, I overheard that in the bus and I made that connection to my anxiety about this." It's not that I think I'm infallible at reading my dreams. Part of the beauty of dreams is that they're eternally mysterious. And that's part of their meaning and power for us. They seem to have a kind of wisdom that we don't have in our waking lives. But they have narrative beginnings, middles and ends the way my stories do.

I believe in Whitman's vision that we're all composed of a thousand voices and that those of us who have chosen to use our imaginations on a daily basis instead of suppressing our imaginations, which is what the culture frequently demands, are very lucky because we are always in company. We are always surrounded by voices that are like and unlike our own and that are our own. And part of the joy of having written for twenty-odd years is that as I'm now sitting here, I seem to be alone but in fact I'm trailing about sixty people. They're people that I've created but also people that I've actually, to be more precise linguistically, *discovered* because they preexisted me. They've always been around and waiting to be heard.

When I'm really doing it right, I know not only what's in my characters' wallets, which is what the creative writing classes tell their students you should know, but I could tell you what the great-grandmother's wallet was like and generationally, classwise, historically, where the matrix that made this particular person possible came from. Genetically and in terms of nationality and in terms of aspirations. It's like Stanislavsky's admonition to actors to always know everything about your character so that even when you just scratch your back on stage you're scratching your back in a context.

It takes work. Not necessarily on paper. I don't have dossiers for everybody but one example would be that when I started *Oldest Living Confederate Widow* I recognized, on the basis of the first thirty pages, that I was writing in the voice of an ungrammatical woman. She said "ain't" a lot. She was very colloquial in her speech and yet I was confused because I thought she was from an upper-middle or upper-class small-town family. That interests me very much, to have a character who can go anywhere but chooses a particular perspective. I was confused about why she was saying "ain't," so I typed "Why I say ain't" at the top of the page. And that became a chapter which was my explanation to myself. It turns out that Lucy Marston had a working-class farm father and an upper-class socialite debutante mother and opted to speak in the voice of her father because she found her mother pretentious and overweaning. So you wind up explaining things to yourself.

I wanted to create the ideal companion, the best company in the world. Lucy, who had a fifth-grade education and lived to be ninety-nine, is a born survivor, a great storyteller and a person who saves her loved ones by imitating and remembering them. So that creating her meant creating her community. All novels are about communities in time and how time changes communities and what parts of communities are not changed and altered by mortality. They're all about accountability. How much I owe you and how much you owe me and how far I can go in helping you. And where that jumping off point is where, much as I care about you and much as I love you, you're on your own. And I'm on my own. Those kinds of basic transactions that are tribal are really at the center of fiction and at the center of our lives.

I've tried to conceive in Lucy of a single voice that was capable of delivering a choral work, a titanic kind of humanity and majesty. So that a single voice could register all the concussions of history and yet come back with a kind of Pan's pipe song, a kind of ebullient folk music, that pulls her through and gets us through.

What you need to be to create a character is terribly hardheaded and sensible. You say, I will now create a ninety-nine-year-old woman. Where is she? She's in a charity rest home. She doesn't have any money left. She gave it all away. Who does she see in the course of a day? She sees the people who help her. Who are they? There's a nurse and, because it's a low-paying job, probably a black nurse. And how do we make the black nurse particular? Well, he's gay and he's swishy and he wears a T-shirt that says "Disco Ain't Dead Yet" and he makes quilts for people, and he does massages for old people and he does their hair and he does whatever they will pay him to do to get pleasure in their last days. So that by virtue of a process of elimination and by paying enormous attention to how most people live, you wind up concocting a very particular person out of that situation. And they take on a life of their own. Then your obligation is, having set this set of circumstances in motion, to then take dictation from those precepts, those points of the compass. And to trust your own creations to lead you and to tell you what they are like and what they consider funny and how they would, in fact, connect to her.

One of the joys of Lucy, and living with her for seven years (she's the longest monogamous relationship of my life), is that she overattributes. She's a person who, unlike most of us, gives more credit than she probably should. She thinks Jerome, who has a high school degree and is, to the naked eye, a very swishy and temperamental queenly gentleman, is the most talented person she's ever met. He can do quilts, he can lip synch Olivier's soliloquies off records he borrows from the public library. He is utterly adorable and important to her. She lets us see his larger capacities and his possibilities, which have been cut off by his circumstances, by the facts of his race and his life and his time. But through Lucy's eyes we suddenly see him as an heroic figure. And at the same time we understand that he's just this swishy orderly. The joy of living in her eyes for those years was precisely that I found myself mythologizing everybody who came in contact with her. Not just the grand figures but people like Zondra the candystriper, so that by the time you finish a book there is a new additional wing in your own interior mansion. You become a bigger and more comprehensive soul by having followed this identity to its logical conclusion as a storyteller.

My characters have made guest appearances in dreams. Little cameos. The strange thing is that other people, who've read the novel, have written me about visitations in their dreams by characters from the book who wind up doing surprising things. That's one of the incredible things about having published a first novel that sold a million and a half copies. It would seem that a writer is dreaming for other people but this strange transaction happens, which is a classic sort of Jungian archetypal situation, in which the initial dreamer is relieved in a kind of relay and then his readers begin dreaming for him. So that if you really tell a story—and for me that's the holy unit—that becomes the history of your readers, then they begin telling you stories that grew out of your own stories.

Somebody told me that at the Convention of Manager-Directors of Old Age Homes in America the keynote speaker opened by reading my description of Larry, the manager of the old age home where Lucy lives. He's a sweet, fat sort of mama's boy who knows everybody on a first-name basis, knows everybody's stories and tries to make this impoverished cinder block building a home. This was read as a description of the ultimate manager of such a place and as a kind of testament to what these people should be doing for the old people who are dependent on them.

It's an astonishing thing to have created a person alone in your room which then becomes an exemplar for his whole occupation. It's an enormous privilege. And the paradox is, that instead of making you feel puffed up with pride and ego, it's hugely humbling. It sounds like something you say in interviews but it's actually completely and utterly true that you feel that your relation to your readers is a sort of priestly relation. And you realize that there's a reason that, in the original Catholic Church, priests were not allowed to have sex with any one person. Because if you deny yourself a certain kind of genital contact with a single individual you then give away that spirit, that translated libidinal energy, to the little old humpback lady whom you would never consider touching. And to children and to old people and to everybody. And it's that transaction, of reaching into your own dream life, your own smartness, your own aliveness, your own knowledge of the world and handing it over to other people—the extraordinary way in which they then give it back to you quadrupled—that becomes an incredible metaphor, not just for art, but for life. Because all the real metaphors apply to both dimensions. If you are one of those people who gives everything away, what you get back is so enormous, so rewarding and so strengthening that it gives you the kind of courage and energy that you need to go back and find more stories. And to turn them back over to other people.

I had a dream when I was about eight years old that was one of those dreams that's so real you're sure that it's happening. You can't quite believe that you've imagined it because all the details are in place. They say God is in the details and that's certainly true in this case. I was in my knotty pine bedroom in my maple bed with the bed quilts pulled up over me—the history of the locomotive across my bed quilt—and I heard a sound in a black walnut tree right outside my window. That was strange. It was a kind of shuddering, tinsely, rustling sound. I leaned out of my bed and looked and I saw the tail of an enormous beautiful bird. We're talking about a bird that was probably forty feet long from head to toe. It had a kind of peacock tail and the feathers were as big across as palm bows. It was the most ravishing thing I'd ever seen. It was all the colors. All those rich blues and greens and purples and reds that you see in a peacock, but it was a huge, seemingly mythological bird that had somehow come to rest in our tree outside my room. We lived in a ranch house. It was a long, long house and my room was on the far end. And I had this terrible dilemma. I wanted more than anything else for other people to see the bird. I wanted so much to have an audience because I wanted to be confirmed that it was not a dream. That it was reality. Of course there's an ego connection here. I wanted credit for having found it. I wanted to be the tour guide so I had to make a decision about whether to stay in bed and enjoy it and see it a long long time or whether to run and make a noise and risk having it not be there when I brought the others from the far end of the house. I made the decision in the dream when I was a kid to just sit there and watch it. That, in some ways, I was all the witness that I needed and that I didn't need to enlist other living bodies and witnesses in order to have it real. That seeing it for myself which, of course, meant dreaming it and inventing it for myself, was all the reality I needed. And so I got an extra fifteen minutes with this extraordinary creature who was preening itself. Probably on the way to Miami Beach. I don't know. But it was a great seminal dream for me.

I guess the message was that the audience was in me. That I was the jury and that rather than jeopardize the experience by enlisting a kind of outward affirmation of the experience, my responsibility as an artist and a dreamer and the keeper of the tree as a kid was to notice as thoroughly as I could. To drink it all in because I knew that I would never see this magical creature again and that the very act of trying to prove it meant that I lost it. Saving it was being alone with it in the moment and drinking it in forever.

JAMES W. HALL

JAMES HALL was born in Kentucky in 1947. It was while teaching a course in the art of the best-seller at Florida International University that Hall decided to test his theories and try writing a thriller. Hall had published four volumes of poetry and numerous short stories but the mainstream audience had eluded him until *Under Cover of Daylight* was published in 1987. *Tropical Freeze* and *Bones of Coral* followed shortly thereafter, both suspense novels set in the Florida Keys.

Bringing a poet's skill with language to the art of the mystery novel, James Hall has created some of literature's most memorable bad guys. He continues to bridge the worlds of popular fiction and academic literature through his courses at Florida International University, where he is a professor.

Hall's poetry and short stories have been published in

The North American Review, The Georgia Review, American Scholar and his own collection entitled *Paper Products.* Other titles include *The Lady from the Dark Green Hills, Ham Operator, The Mating Reflex* and *False Statements.* He lives in Miami with his wife, Evelyn.

WHEN I WAS a college student I came across a book by Howard Nemeroff called *The Journal of a Fictive Life* in which Nemeroff was keeping an account of his dreams and doing a sort of self-psychoanalysis. Each morning, after he recorded his dreams, he would write down a lot of thoughts about them. The book had a strong influence on me. I like Nemeroff's poetry very much and decided, in the spirit of trying to be just like all these great writers I was falling in love with left and right, that I would try to do my own journal of a fictive life. I would write down my dreams every morning, spending thirty minutes or so going over what I could recall from the night before. And, as everybody seems to know, the more you pay attention to your dreams the more you seem to dream or the more you recall what you've dreamed. That happened to me as well until thirty minutes in the morning stretched out to two and three hours. I was spending all morning in my college dorm room writing down, analyzing, figuring out and mulling over my dreams. Seeing the connection between last week's dream and this week's dream. It just became so exhausting to do, to even face going to bed at night, that I thought, oh my God, here I have to go to sleep again and work all night dreaming and remembering my dreams. Eventually I just threw up my hands and said, "I can't do this any more!" I had done it for months, and I just stopped cold because it had become something larger than I really wanted. I didn't see any way to scale it back

But it was a very very profitable thing. For one thing, it got me writing and examining myself and my life in a way that was much more like what I think writers and other artists do—

which is to examine the meaning and weight of images—rather than trying to examine psychology or the recollection of incidents or your relationships with people, which is what you do a lot of times in psychoanalytical investigations. Because dreams are primarily visual, you spend a lot of time doing what poets do anyway, which is use images: describing them first, then trying to weigh them and understand what they mean and how they might be connected to the other images they are surrounded by in the dream itself.

There was an image that, though I didn't realize it at the time, changed who I was in certain fundamental ways. I dreamed one particular night about a dark carriage. A dark carriage that came very, very fast out of these mountains, down through a little village and went back up into the adjacent hills. It was a scary, scary dream and in the carriage was, I suppose, a deathlike figure. There's a famous Emily Dickinson poem, "Because I could not stop for Death" something "He kindly stopped for me." I can't remember exactly how the poem goes but it's about a carriage. Perhaps I got the original dream image from that, but it stayed with me for a long time after I had the dream.

It seemed like I'd had almost a visitation. Something that had come out of the hills in my own imagination and scared the village part of me, the daily life part of me, and then disappeared back into the hills again. I wrote a poem about it. It was called "The Lady from the Dark Green Hills," which became the title of my first book of poetry. In my poem the lady wasn't in a carriage, she was in a Jaguar XK150, a big, long, black Jaguar. She drove out of the hills and scared the people of this village. And they created myths and stories about her. The poem was about two pages long. This was my first published poem. It was published in *Antioch Review* when I was nineteen years old. *Antioch Review* was, and probably still is, a major university literary magazine.

Someone read that poem, "Lady from the Dark Green

Hills," and wrote me a letter. The woman who did this was a poetry editor at Harper and Row and she said, "I read your poem and I loved it. Do you have a manuscript?" I'd written maybe twenty poems and all of them were terrible except this particular one. I sort of lucked out because the dream image was so powerful it just went from one part of my mind to the paper. But I thought, oh, this happens to every writer: you publish a poem and then editors from New York start to call and then your life changes and then you become a writer. I ran over to one of my professors and showed him this letter and he just could not believe it. This sort of thing just doesn't happen to writers. It's very, very rare. Especially for a nineteen-year-old kid. And I was so innocent, blasé and stupid, really, that I thought, oh, no problem, I don't have enough poems for a book? I'll spend a couple of weeks and write them. I thought I could actually pump out a book of poetry, 'cause they're awfully thin and there's a lot of blank space. I thought, yeah, sure. So I did it. I sent them all to her and she wrote a very polite note back that said "I still like this poem very much but this other stuff is just crap." Which was true. In a way it was a very bad thing to have happened to me because it gave me false hope, a kind of hubris, a pride in something I really had not earned the right to feel yet. I paid my dues retroactively. It was five or six years before I had another poem published in a magazine of that stature and really earned the right to get some of the things I got so easily that first time. So I blame dreams!

I haven't had many dreams about my fiction although sometimes, when I'm writing very intensely, when the writing is going very hot, I have dreams of words. I mean, I'm lying there and listening to words go by my head. Sometimes I worry this is sort of leftover energy from a lecture I've given because I've taught too much that night before I went to bed. I continue to talk in my head. When these dreams start to come I usually try to wake myself up because they're so boring. They're very tiring. I talk and talk and talk in my dream and hear myself in my own words endlessly rattling on and I kind of pinch myself and make myself wake up, if that's possible. I don't know exactly how it happens but I try to erase that dream. It's a tedious one.

One of the things that I've discovered through reading a lot of best-sellers, studying a lot of popular fiction for courses that I've given at the university, is that there are certain recurrent, mythic qualities in books that we could consider, from an elitist academic viewpoint, to be pulp or low-life, mass-market fiction. But obviously they have a certain kind of power or else three million people wouldn't buy and be excited about them. One of the things I found out was that there were these recurrent patterns. One, for instance, that I feel has a kind of mythic quality, is what I came to call, in a particular class on best-sellers, "the golden place." This is where the novel begins to picture a time and place, usually both of those, where the grass was greener, the flowers smelled better, the birds chirped more purely and everything was simply better. Usually associated with childhood and long ago. It's a form of nostalgia, I suppose, but when you see it in a fictional form it has a tremendous power to call us to our best, ideal selves. We feel in ourselves that such golden places are possible to return to, to reacquire, to rediscover and I think that one of the hungers we bring to the reading experience is to go to other people's golden places and live there, temporarily. A place that is coherent, that makes sense, where values are still valuable and ideals are possible to achieve.

I don't see that the dream state that we have at night is that much different in some ways from the dream state that writers learn to put themselves into as they're writing. I know that sounds like kind of a romantic notion but it's very true for me and I've heard other writers say similar things; that when you are creating at the highest pitch, or the lowest pitch, whatever it may be, the most extreme conditions of creation, you're not there. You're witnessing it, perhaps, or you witness it when you wake up at the end of a writing period. I can be at the word processor for hours and hours and not even know what I've written, not know it in a real rational way. And then find out later. Of course, there's always got to be some sort of interaction between the right brain and the left brain as you're doing this, because it is a rational activity. You are sitting upright and your fingers are moving across the keys so it takes a certain amount of rational intelligence to simply do the operation. Nevertheless, it's a kind of self-hypnosis that you learn to put yourself into when you write well. It doesn't always happen, I can't always get back there. To me it's the golden place that I can return to on a regular basis.

Many years ago I brought a hypnotist to one of my freshmen composition classes. This was how desperate I was to kill time and do anything else but teach grammar. This hypnotist hypnotized the group, and the posthypnotic suggestion he gave to us all was, When I come to you, you will not be able to say your name. And, as he was going around the room and asking people if they could say their name, I kept saying to myself James Hall, James Hall, no problem, I wasn't hypnotized, oh shucks, darn, I was hoping I could be hypnotized. When he got to me he said, "What's your name?" I couldn't say my name. You don't know exactly whether it's because you want to be part of the group that was hypnotized that you willfully refuse to say your name or whether you really literally cannot say your name. I knew my name. I knew it in my head. I simply didn't say it.

He told us that if we wanted to put ourselves in a hypnotic state again, all we had to do was knock on a piece of wood or a table three times and relax and we would fall into that hypnotic state again. I did that for a while afterwards and I could re-create some of the kind of comfort and quiet of that state. But it sort of disappeared because I didn't use it all the time.

What I think now is that I have developed a kind of self-hypnosis. Most writers do, whether they want to put it in these terms or not. It sounds kind of hocus-pocus when you talk about it this way but maybe the rituals of sharpening your pencil or getting your coffee or everything just right around your work space are part of it. Mine is sort of warming up my fingers on the keys, just writing automatically. I go back to something I've written previously and start tinkering with that to warm up to the writing. The actual movement of my fingers across the board and hearing the characters start to talk is what eventually gets me back to the world.

When I hear the characters speak in ways that seem true and real and authentic, then the rest of it all falls into place around them. What they see, what they do, how they act with each other, that all flows out of how they sound as characters, what their speech sounds like.

This is all happening on the page. I'm not vocalizing in the room. You wouldn't sit next to me and say, yes, listen to Hall, he's muttering to himself again. But what I am doing is subvocalizing them: saying these things in my inner ear and hearing the cadences of people's speech, how they talk, how they respond to other people who talk. And when those cadences start to sound real and possess me, convince me, seduce me into believing that these people are really there and talking, then I just let go and they do the work. It's a fascinating operation.

I'm currently working on a new novel so I'm getting the characters; they aren't quite talking right yet. And, I don't know, when they don't talk yet, they aren't interesting. They simply don't say anything that has any juice in it, any excitement, any electricity. They are saying things that normal people say in normal ways. There's nothing special about them. I haven't fallen in love with them. I haven't fallen under their spell yet. And part of that is because I haven't gotten myself energized enough about them, who they are, especially, what they want, what their inner motivations are. I don't know them well enough to know how they sound.

I see characters in fiction, as being more like actors on a stage. The audience is listening raptly to whatever they say and my job is as the director of a play. It's to say to them, Dougie, you're not being interesting, people are dozing off in the first row. Perk it up here. Get a little more excitement in what you say. I sort of counsel him to do that and when he starts talking right then I don't have to do any more of the directing.

I think of Dougie in *Bones of Coral* as sort of Rain Man with a 357 magnum. He's like Dustin Hoffman only his skill is not math, unfortunately, it's killing people. And being violent towards people. I'm not sure where those characters come from. They must come from some zone in my consciousness that we all have. That place where our nightmares bubble up. These images that are in us all. They're not exterior to us, they're in us. They're our own deepest fears, worries, anxieties. I think my bad guys come from those places in myself just as Poe's bad guys and crazy people did. They come from the id perhaps—the unrestrained creative, disobedient, bad boy part of consciousness that we all have. In writing the books that I write, one of my jobs is to make bridges to that dark zone and let the gremlins walk over the bridges into the light of the reasonable world. Give them a chance to speak their minds, to say their piece, to do what it is that the scary, bad, unrestrained parts of me want to say.

Why do I do that? Well, I guess in a psychological sense, it's purgative. You get it out of yourself. I do it because it's fun. Because seeing these characters, seeing someone like Dougie for instance—who is able to act in ways that are so much more free, so much more unrestrained, so much more creative, extreme—is a pleasure for me. To tear off my own bonds and restrictions that the world puts on us, on me, and temporarily, in my fantasy life, to enact things that I could never permit myself to enact normally—there's a pleasure in this—a kind of sinful pleasure I suppose, but it's a deep pleasure and part of the whole creative impulse. I believe, for me, the creative impulse is to let those sides of yourself that normally you repress and restrain have their day in the sun.

My students are a very interesting mix of people. They're not all college-age students. I have a retired psychiatrist in one of my classes. When I was first working on *Bones of Coral*, I read a passage about Dougie doing something. And when I was finished there was this dead silence in the room. And the psychiatrist, I think speaking for several in the class, said, "You ought to consider increasing your visits to two times a week." Assuming I was going one time a week already. There is a certain taint that I feel as these Dougies and the bad guys in the other books emerge from me. It's sort of like that alien breaking out of the guy's chest in the movie, *Alien*. This horrible grotesque thing that's been hiding in you, that's buried in you.

There's a famous moment in film history that I'm sometimes reminded of in my own life. In *Double Indemnity*, Fred MacMurray played a very bad guy that helped kill his lover's husband. Fred MacMurray had always been a good guy in previous movies and, after that movie came out, Bette Davis supposedly said to Fred MacMurray, I can never look at you the same way again because you were so good as that bad guy. Friends of mine have said virtually the same thing to me. That they can never look at me with the same kind of innocence and so on as they could before because of Dougie and Irv and Vinnie and Ozzie and some of the other characters I've created. But the fact is we've all got those people lurking in us. The aberrant version of ourselves. Given the right kind of pressures and the right kind of strains on our life, we can act very irresponsibly, very violently, in very ugly ways in brief moments. We just tend to restrain ourselves better than the characters I create in my books.

When I started my publicity tour for *Bones of Coral*, I had a dream in which I woke up and I was in a morgue. I was lying on a morgue table and my doctor was there from Miami where I live. I said, What is this place? And he said, It's a morgue. I looked over and on the slab next to me, was a woman with part of her leg gone. And blood. She was clearly dead. Part of her arm was gone. She sat up while we were looking at her and I asked the doctor, "How could that possibly be? How could she be sitting up? She's dead." And he said, "Didn't you know that for fifteen minutes after you die you're still alive? And you can still witness everything." That's when I woke up. And I started thinking about that. My God, it was such a scary proposition. Are these minutes that we're in right now those fifteen minutes? And we just don't realize it's happened yet and we're living beyond that moment where we're actually on the slab? It was a dream, I think, about feeling a loss of connection with the stream of time that I am normally in, where you simply wake up in the morning and you know what your day is going to be and you go through one minute hooked to the next minute. On a book tour your day is totally irregular. Time is really screwed up. You're flying around the country, you're jet-lagged, you know you're doing all this stuff and in a way that's a kind of death. This is my nickel-plated interpretation. And it bears on the thing that I'm writing now too, which is another suspense novel in which the dead live on. Not literally. They're not vampires or anything like that, but people who seem to be dead come back to pull the strings of the living. They come back to haunt us in very explicit, direct ways. I think both of those things were at work in that dream

I don't usually write down my dreams any more, but when I do think about them, like I've been forced to with this dream lately, I find that there's a lot of potentially interesting material that can be extracted. It helps crystallize other things that I've been thinking about but only in a marginally conscious way.

When I was keeping my journal of a fictive life I noticed this thing happen I call decay. As you're telling the dream it seems to be disappearing. When you articulate it, give it words, the images seem to evaporate almost as fast as the words are coming. And when I saw this was happening on a regular basis with my dreams, what I started to do was to lie. I began to fabricate the dream in the journal, to pretend this was the dream I had when in fact I could no longer clearly recall the dream. But my feeling at the time—and I still feel this—was that there is a time when you wake up in the morning where you're still in the aura of the dream state. There's still kind of dream dust hanging around you and almost anything you do or say during that time is infected by the dream or caused or shadowed by the dream in some way.

For many years I believed that the only time that I could write was in the morning when I had a lot of energy, when I was still a little foggy and had a little bit of a dream hangover. That's a romantic idea that I've abandoned. I write at all times of the day, whenever I have a chance I write and I have equally interesting discoveries later in the day as I do earlier in the day.

There was a dream that I had several times when I was a kid that I wrote a poem about. It was a kind of burial dream, a premature burial. In fact the poem is called "Premature Burial." It was a very scary, claustrophobic kind of a dream. I was scratching my way up out of sleep, or the dirt. And when I reached the surface—where I'm out of breath and struggling, fighting towards the light of day and towards nondreaming— my mother was there, waiting for me in the dream as I woke up.

That's one of the only dreams I really remember from being a kid. But over the long term, this is the way I've spent a lot of my adult life, going down into dark or mysterious or uncharted places in my memories and my consciousness. Then, having to wake up again to life, to claw my way back into ordered, reasonable, rational, everyday, responsible life. That world down there is irresponsible. It's scary. There's no time. It's all dark. I guess the most literal way I can put this is that when I disappear into the word processor in the morning—I may stay there for hours, depending on how long I have to work that day—I'm burying myself. In a way it's a very selfish act. I'm dying to the world, to people who care about me and whom I should care about, to my responsibilities, my duties, my job and all that. I disappear into this sort of tomb. And stay there for a while and live that dark other existence.

And then I have to fight my way back on a regular basis. Day after day after day. To get back into taking the rest of the world seriously. Because the rest of the world doesn't seem as serious when you first come out of this state, when you claw your way back to the surface of the earth and there's your mother waiting. There's responsibility, there's promises to keep and miles to go before I sleep. There's all that world of duties and requirements, so that sometimes the wonderful world that you've been in seems so much better, so much more desirable, that it's hard for you to give yourself fully to that other world. And this can create all kinds of very real problems. You're not paying enough attention to your marriage. You're not paying enough attention to your students. Or job. The details of your finances. You can get sloppy in all kinds of ways if you become too addicted to the dream world, to the creative world that writers, on a very regular daily basis, and artists of all kinds put themselves into. They go down there and stay there, willfully, for as long as they can before the alarm clock rings and the world says, Okay, get back to work.

The truth is that I screwed it up before. I gave myself over too much to that other world to the exclusion of my marriage. I lost a marriage as a result of that. And I was less than responsible in a lot of other ways: to my friends, to my parents, to other people, because I was indulging myself in myself. I was in this sort of tomb of self-absorption and nowadays I just see that the two worlds are important, that I want to be healthy. I want to be happy. There's no reason you can't. There's this romantic picture of writers, sometimes, that you either are going to be a great writer or have a great life. And you have to choose one or the other. I don't think that's true for me. I don't believe that that has to be an either-or choice. But you have to consciously decide that. You can't let your ordinary life drift and just sink into the creative world all the time.

It's a great relief to me to know that I can actually be

creative and be happy at the same time. For a long time I didn't think that was possible. I thought the creations came out of darkness and sadness and pain. And they still do, you know. There's a lot of unresolved pain in all of us all the time. Flannery O'Connor used to say that anyone who's had a childhood has enough to write about for the rest of their lives. You could just go into a sensory-deprivation tank at the age of seventeen and have plenty of material for the rest of your life. And I think that's true for me. It's true for most writers. We continually go back to those first discoveries, those first pains, which were very very excruciating and which we still haven't quite understood.

My first novel, which I wrote when I was a graduate student, was called *Being Dreamed To*. It was about a guy who thought that the reality he was experiencing was actually being given to him on a planet in his head, not unlike that terrible Arnold Schwarzenegger movie in which one is confused totally about what is the exterior reality and what is the interior reality. That's another way of picturing the struggle I've been talking about with the creative process, when those two realities tend to intermingle all the time. It's important, in order to be healthy psychologically, to know that the world out there is just as good and at least as important as the world in here, the interior world.

CHARLES JOHNSON

B ORN IN Evanston, Illinois, in 1948, Charles Johnson
began his career as a cartoonist for the *Chicago Tribune* in
1969. In 1970, he created a fifty-two-part series on cartooning
for PBS called *Charlie's Pad*. By the time he came to study at
Southern Illinois University with writer John Gardner,
Johnson had already written six "apprentice" novels. With
Gardner's encouragement he completed *Faith and the Good
Thing,* which was published in 1974. This contemporary folk
tale told of the young Faith Cross's journey North, searching
for "the good thing" she'd been promised by her dying
mother.

Johnson's second novel, *The Oxherding Tale,* about the
coming of age of a young mulatto slave, was published in
1982. *The Sorcerer's Apprentice,* a collection of short fiction,
was nominated for a P.E.N. Faulkner Award in 1986. *Middle*

Passage, recounting the adventures of a young black sailor aboard a slave ship, won the National Book Award in 1991.

Johnson described his work, in an interview for *Contemporary Authors,* as an attempt to "interface Eastern and Western philosophical traditions, in the hope that some new perception of experience, especially 'black experience,' would emerge."

Charles Johnson lives in Seattle with his wife, Joan, and two children. He is the Pollack Professor of English at the University of Washington.

———

I W O R K E D six years on *Middle Passage.* I had a draft done after a year and it didn't work. So I went back and rewrote it for five years. And somewhere, I think it was around year four, I knew that chapter three needed something. At that point the main character is on this ship. They've reached Africa and the slaves are going to be put in the hold. That's all fairly straightforward and linear. But I knew something more, in terms of the story and the plot, was needed to up the ante in chapter three, to introduce a new element. I couldn't figure out to save my life what that was. I have this tendency to write until I'm just exhausted and then go and take a nap or something. So I did that. I stopped writing. I had no answer and I went and I lay down. As soon as my head hit the pillow I started to drift off into that marginal place that you enter between wakefulness and dreams. I wasn't out and yet I wasn't fully awake—it's that moment when your mind is just opening up—and I saw this image. Of sailors. They were Yankee sailors hauling something out of the jungle. It was in a crate.

I woke up and I said, What's in this crate? Is it human? Is it animal? Is it vegetable? Mineral? Then it hit me. It's a god. Now what does that mean? I had no idea. How could they have a god? Basically it was this little puzzle. I looked back and said, Okay, it's a puzzle for me. I don't know how yet but that's the way I'll do it in chapter three. The other sailors won't know what it is yet either that the captain has captured. Later they'll find out and by then I'll know more. Literally it was a kind of cryptic, encoded dream image. I thought about it and I said, Well, where does that come from? The thing that leaps immediately to mind, and reviewers thought of this too, is King Kong. I mean seriously. I've seen it dozens of times, but not recently. And so I said, Well, okay, if that was a germ or a seed I don't mind, but this goes way beyond. It's not an animal, it isn't a big prehistoric ape, it is, literally, an immaterial deity.

In earlier drafts the god actually talks. And he has all these things to say about the universe and ra ra ra. It was so hard to do. It didn't work to have the god talk. As soon as he spoke, it was going to be a disappointment. So in this version he doesn't speak. He communicates in images, unfolding images. Because that way diction, word choice, don't anchor him to a particular region.

I spent a month and a half on that simple passage where the god appears to Rutherford. Just doing it wrong 'til I finally decided that he would be quiet. The god would not speak but it would have a means of basically opening itself up for Rutherford's enlightenment and illumination. It must have been two or three thousand pages into the mix before I got the 250 pages for the finished manuscript. It must've been year four and a half when the god became a subplot or element in the story. I knew the book needed something. But it wasn't until I sort of halfway went to sleep that something popped up in my mind.

Years ago, when I first started writing, I used to write down my dreams. I'm sure a lot of writers do that. You keep a pad by your bed and, soon as you wake up, you write it down. I even wrote a story once after a dream, but it was so surrealistic I couldn't understand it. I mean, I wrote it, right? And that's what I dreamt, but I couldn't publish it. It was for my own benefit. I really don't write down the dreams that often any more. But they're there. The unconscious works for me.

I remember sometimes I would get ready to go to sleep and I would hear dialogue. I'd literally hear a line and then I'd hear a response. And at that point if it really sounded good to me I would get up and write it down. It's just like the mind is churning away and thinking. I might be just lying there thinking about something I'd just written, someone saying something, and then I would hear a better reply than I'd written before so I would jot it down.

There's a section in *Middle Passage* where Captain Falcon is talking to Rutherford. Rutherford says something about Falcon's paranoia and Falcon says, "Do you think I'm overly cautious?" and Rutherford says, "Yes I do think you're overly cautious," and Falcon says, "I guess you like people, don't you?" and Rutherford says, "Yes, I do. Don't you?" And Falcon says, "Not really." And he goes into this thing about "I guess I've never trusted other people. I only really think I'm real. No one's real but me in terms of my experience." That whole little speech of his came to me when I was almost falling asleep. And I got up and I wrote it down verbatim. I heard one sentence after the other. It was exactly right for his character, I think, because he is a very solipsistic person.

When I write it's a very visual experience for me. I'm seeing things as they happen. I'm sometimes not seeing ahead of the character. For example, in *Middle Passage:* When Rutherford first enters Captain Falcon's cabin, Falcon is facing away and Rutherford only sees him from the back. I knew Rutherford was going to speak to him and then I knew Falcon was going to spin around in the chair. And when he spun around, when I wrote that sentence, I saw that Falcon was a dwarf. And I said, Well, let's go with that. Let's see what happens with that. And suddenly that gave me ways to characterize the scene visually. Suddenly his physical size gave another dimension to what would have been a fairly typical dialogue between a new sailor and a captain. But then later, and this was not planned, it occurred to me that, given the nature of what he's doing as a slave trader, he's spiritually very small. So the lack of size is a sort of correlate to his smallness of soul. Really, when you're writing you don't always know what an image means. Later you figure out how it hooks up with other images in the book. That's what happened with his size. In Falcon's case, he's so big and so much larger than life in his adventures, that the contrast in size suddenly was very interesting. He could've been six feet four, but that would've been too predictable. Even if he was of average size, it would've been too predictable. For him to be a short man, hardly bigger than the cabin boy, but nevertheless a scrapper with a real strong bantam fighting spirit, that's more interesting.

The characters in *Middle Passage* are all very different physically and I hope in other aspects of their character too. Psychologically, biographically, they're all very different. That was a challenge because I wanted to make everybody more individuated than in my previous books. I wanted to stay with their individual characters and let them determine the action. Not impose my sense of plot but let them all come together and find out what they wanted to do, to each other and with each other, during the course of the voyage.

In the earlier draft the ending is very different. Rutherford survives, but it's Tommy the captain boy who survives with him and not Squibb. The plot changed in different versions so that different characters, given their nature, survived, and others didn't.

I think what happens, really, is that when you're writing, part of the process is mysterious. You can plot out things and it's all conscious, you can do that and make decisions about what characters you want to have. And then you stop and you just trust instinct and you don't know where a certain thing will come from. Maybe from somewhere deep in the back of your memory. I mean, when I'm writing, a phrase I haven't said or heard spoken since elementary school will pop into my mind when a character is talking. And I'll be stunned. I'll say, Wow, now that is interesting. How did that get dredged up?

There's something Squibb says when he is first talking to Rutherford on the ship. He says, "The reason I look so bad is because I've been living." That is a line I heard when I was nine or ten from one of my mother's friends. She was this wonderful old lady, not old, she was maybe thirty or something and I was eight, but she seemed old to me. She said that to me, "The reason I look so bad is 'cause I've been living." I never forgot that. And then there's a line, Ngayama says to Rutherford about one of his people's myths or practices. He says, "My people have a saying, wish in one hand and piss in the other and see which hand fills up first." That was one of my grandmother's sayings. The first time I heard her say that I said, Oh, that sounds terrible. Because I was probably saying, Oh, I wish I had this or I wish I had that, and she looked at me and she said that. What a terrible thing to say to somebody, right? But then I never forgot it. But you know, it didn't kick into my memory in a vivid way until I started writing. And then files open up suddenly because of the pressure of the creative process. That's what's so exciting to me. Because when you're working you're not censoring things. You're just hoping all the gates will be open and you'll get something out of your past that will be useful. Apparently we never forget anything. Everything we've ever seen, literally, every image, every sound, is somewhere in there on a cell. And all it has to be is activated.

If I'm writing, and if it's really happening right, sometimes the words'll pop up. I know I've heard them somewhere before. I have some friends who are very vivid with language. One of my friends in L.A. has been saying lately, "Oh, man, this project just went south on me." It just went south! What does that mean? So I have to jot this down. Somewhere I will use that. All that stuff you hope will come up again. Things you've heard. And it will be right for the character that you're creating.

Sometimes I meditate before or after writing. That's a good way to sort of clear everything immediate out of my mind. And things just kind of pop up at times. But I don't rely on that. I think the creative process itself is so like meditation. It's all about concentration over a short period of time. Some people write for two hours a day. I write until I just stop. And that can be twelve straight hours, working on something. So by that time, it's so focused, everything that's in memory is coming out. I'm asking myself questions about the characters and getting answers from logical and illogical places.

You know the kind of questions I ask when writing something? I basically ask the same questions a playwright asks. Like, in that scene with Falcon I described, I'm saying to myself, What does a character see when he walks in a room? What props are there? What is the lighting like? When somebody crosses the room, how do they cross the room? How do they walk?

I don't know if this is a connection but long before I was a writer I used to be a cartoonist. I think visually more than I do otherwise so that when I look at a scene I really want to know every gesture and particularly the idiosyncratic gestures, the character's visual persona. I can see the quality of light in a room, whether it's late afternoon or early morning, because it really does create a different mood for the drama to take place. I look at as much specificity as I possibly can. One of our graduate students once said something in class that a theater director had said to him. He said "Specificity is generosity." The more detail that you give to the reader, the more you help their imagination. Specificity becomes the vehicle for their imagination. So I really try to carve out the scene all of those different ways.

And sometimes one of those images resonates on more than one level. Even the ship itself, the *Republic*. From research I found what those ships were like and how the water would tear them apart, and how the sailors had to rebuild the ship. That's why they had carpenters on board. Everybody had to be able to help in chores other than the one that they had signed on for. And it suddenly hit me, this is a process. As it crosses the waves this is a process. And on top of that, since I'd named it the

Republic, that meant, okay, that the governmental institution that we live under is also similar, being rebuilt and torn apart from day to day. So the specifics of the ship became, then, this other metaphor of politics. That's what I'm always looking for when I'm writing. I'm looking for different levels of meaning. But it all has to be anchored concretely in the world that the characters are in: the weather of their world, the props of their world, the physical nature of their bodies among other bodies in their world. That to me is interesting.

The name *Republic* was there from the very first paragraph. That's all I had in the beginning, I started writing the first paragraph then the second. The ship was called the *Republic* because I'd never heard of a ship called the *Republic* before. I didn't know until later that I would use that *Republic* to represent the ship of state. But, you know, you get an idea and say, Okay let's see what happens later. And then you do find something else to add to that or it does open up in a new way. Part of it is mysterious. As you go along, the job for the writer is to clear up the mystery.

I had a good teacher, a cartoon teacher, named Lawrence Larier, who was cartoon editor for *Parade* magazine and a detective novelist in the forties. He had a couple of best-sellers: terrible books with titles like *Stone Cold Blond*. He told me something once that was really interesting. He said when he wrote a novel, a mystery novel, he would just put in all these things that were interesting in the world of the character in the first chapter. And in every chapter after that his job was to unkey the mystery of all the elements. Because he didn't know what they were. So as he discovered what these things meant, the reader would discover them. And I think it's almost the same thing for me. A character gets introduced and I say, That's an interesting person, but how does he fit in all of this? And later, four chapters later, you see him do something that does make his inclusion comprehensible. But again, first it's unconscious and then you make it conscious. And if it doesn't work you have to go back and take it out. Which often happens. If it's a blind alley. Some things just don't really have a place during the course of the working out of the book.

Now Squibb, for example, is a bigamist. He has several wives. And in the earlier version of *Middle Passage* he has a long speech about how hard it was to maintain three marriages at once: running all over the country checking in over here for a week, getting an excuse to go over there for another month. I had a long passage about that. But it didn't fit. So that got weeded out and all we know is that he says he's a bigamist. And he has his little speech about always wanting to find, in other women, the first woman he ever loved. And that's it.

Usually when I'm writing I explore as much as I can and then I look at it and say, Well, does that really make sense in the overall design of the book? If it does, it stays, and if it doesn't, you just have some writing that maybe you can publish later in a separate short story or something.

I've had dreams that I thought were prescient at times. Even when I was a kid I had a couple of dreams here and there that turned out to be true. I once had a dream about my family, when I was twelve, that was really weird. At that time, as kids, we didn't think about dying. And suddenly it hit me that people died, somebody in the house could die. That made me very sad. And then I had this dream that made it okay. Suddenly there were these other people in my life. I don't know who they were but there was a woman who I was married to. There was a kid, a son, or something like that. That's all. It was a dream of looking forward.

I really think Freud is right about some things. We take the questions of our daily conscious life into our dream life and the dream has its own language for trying to answer the question for us. According to Freud, in one night it will answer the same question over and over again through several different dreams. It's so odd because dreams are often narrative in form. You know, this happens and that happens and this happens. And it's just a little bit of work to unkey them. For me it's a lot of work actually. You really have to say to yourself, Why was that symbol chosen? What does this represent? I mean you can be in your dream in several different guises, not just as the protaganist but as one of the minor characters. To me it's fascinating.

I think dreams are one way that we use to answer questions from our daily conscious life. And they're unpredictable. I mean you don't know what kind of answer you'll get. I think that's why Freud was so fascinated in *The Interpretation of Dreams* with unkeying that language. Some of it's literary language. It's like we draw from movies we see, books we read, something that might even be a casual conversation. The dream uses all of that in a very unpredictable way. Freud's whole thing was to try to understand the logic of that. And it seems like for almost every patient it was different.

When I have a dream, it's with me when I first wake up but by the time I finally stumble around, wash up in the morning, go get a cup of coffee, it's starting to fade. Because I'm becoming really conscious, waking up. And then it's gone. So usually I'll try to jot it down just instantly and look at it later after I wake up and see if the scribble made sense.

If I'm really dreaming and something wakes me up briefly, I can put my head back on the pillow and resume the dream. It's like it's still so vivid in my mind, I can go back. I can do that actually two or three times a night if I want. I can actually almost will the dream. Not quite, but almost. If I fully wake up then it'll be gone. But if I'm still sort of halfway groggy I can go back to it.

Writing is a lot like dreaming. You're creating a dream for the reader. John Gardner used to call a work of fiction a vivid and continuous dream. Vivid because a work of fiction should have all of that vividness that a dream has in its details. And it should be continuous in the sense that nothing interrupts the reader in the same way that nothing wakes you up because you're so immersed in the book. I do think that when I'm reading something I really enjoy, I forget about what's going on in the room. I forget about what's going on outside the house and I'm just in this alternate universe. That's what you try to create with a work of fiction for the reader, that same dreamlike quality. For the writer to do that it takes incredible concentration during the periods of writing. And the reader is infected by that. You become absorbed, as you're reading, in the characters: what they're going to say next, what's happening, little sounds that go on around them. I mentioned before I was very visual in my imagination so I have to work at other kinds of imagery. Imagery for taste, smell, sound. I really have to work to get that in there because I think that makes for a fully sensuous experience.

You really have to be so immersed in the unfolding story before your eyes that you forget about everything else. For me, writing a novel is a very difficult thing to do because I know this is a marriage of a year or two years and that it's going to be totally absorbing. I mean I teach, I work, but my mind is really on the unfolding world of the fiction. My family is now used to my going off into this dream state. They'll say, Oh, Dad is a little distracted right now. Because everything I see in the world is interesting to me only if it relates to the unfolding world of the book during that period of time. After the book is over I can be totally interested in it. I can go from this to that to this. But with a book, if I'm reading something, if I'm looking at something, if I'm learning about something, it's got to be related to the novel or the story at that moment. That's the kind of head I have to get into just to write a story.

When you're doing early drafts on something, I think what you're really doing is knocking at that door saying, Let me in, let me in, 'til finally you get to something and the door opens. And then it's just like you aren't writing it any more. It's like you're following truth—everything that took so long to set up, all the implications and premises and following them

through—at that point it isn't a struggle. You aren't outside the
room, you're inside the room. I think it takes a while.
Sometimes you can start out right, crack, first draft and it goes.
You sit there for twelve hours and you've got the whole thing
just unfolding before your eyes. Other times you've got to figure
out the language of the narrative and the diction and the tone.
You've got to figure all that stuff out and it's more methodical
and then it's draft after draft 'til finally it all gels and doesn't
seem mannered, doesn't seem decided but seems organic. Then
other times you get this gift and it's all there and you just
ride it out.

In *Oxherding Tale,* the book before *Middle Passage,* I was
knocking on that door quite a lot. There are similarities between
the two books. A lot of the things I figured out in *Oxherding
Tale* became strategies I used in *Middle Passage.*

Middle Passage was always fun to do even when I went
down blind alleys. I didn't have to worry about tone. I knew
Rutherford's voice. I knew the comic-tragic tone was there. I
knew it was about the sea. All I had to do was just unpack what
was already implicit in the material, in the premises. There's an
old phrase that when you write something what you do is you
give your characters nature and you let that nature perform. So
in the beginning it's all decision. I want this person to be like
that. I think he should have this trait or should speak this way
or should respond this way. You make all those decisions and
after that you don't have to make that many more decisions.
They're acting in accordance with all of these premises that
you've set up. I think the hard part is developing and making
those initial decisions. This is their world, these are the laws of
their world, this is what's possible, this is what's not possible.
And after that the drama can happen within that context
without your having to force it. You get into that frame of mind
by defining a world and then just letting the people and things
in that world perform.

I worked six years on *Middle Passage* and one of the
differences between the earlier drafts and the later draft is that

I changed emotionally over six years. Different things happen in your life. And when I came back to the earlier material I didn't feel the urgency of what Rutherford and these characters were going through. I had to address them or they had to speak to me in terms of what I was feeling most at that moment, emotionally, for it to have any kind of animation or life. I always have to do that with a story. It's almost autobiographical in the sense that, this is not literally happening to me in the story, in my life, it's not literally transposed, but rather my emotional concerns are sufficient that these characters in this story can become the vehicle for whatever I'm feeling right now. All my feelings go in there.

I guess the questions I really was emotionally dealing with in *Middle Passage* were questions of personal identity, racial identity. The meaning of home in particular. Of being displaced and figuring out just where home is. And who is at home that you want to get back to.

That was not what it was when I started in '83. I had different concerns, I forget what they were, but I grew out of them during the course of writing the first draft. I'd go back and look at it and it'd feel cold. Almost like with your dreams, issues are being worked out through the characters in dreams. Same thing in a novel or short story. For it to work for me, for me to come back to it with suspense and interest, I have to believe these characters are working out something important to me, that I need to know about my own life. And by the time I get to the end of the novel I really feel I can move beyond those emotions. I don't have to go back to them again.

I look at my first book, *Faith and the Good Thing*, and there are questions that I was working through as a twenty-five year old. They're not questions for me anymore. It's like reading somebody else's life. Because it's sixteen, seventeen years ago. I couldn't write it now. There's no way I could. I couldn't be twenty-five or twenty-six again.

What you have to figure out, before you write, is what is happening with you right now that you can objectify in a story, that will be entertainment, that other people will be able to identify and sympathize with and feel at the same time. That's the hard part. How do you start that process? I think it's finding the emotional door that you have to go through. You have to find a way, an angle in on the characters, so that your emotional dope, your limits, concerns, needs and hopes at that moment can be expressed through the vehicle of the made-up story. And then you have to shape the story as entertainment so other people can feel that same emotion.

STEPHEN KING

STEPHEN KING has the ability to tap into our deepest
unnamed fears and, through his fiction, give them confront-
able, conquerable shape. By creating likeable, multifaceted
characters with whom readers can identify, Stephen King
allows us to metaphorically face our anxieties about death,
sex, abandonment, dismemberment, pain, betrayal, ostracism,
disease and failure.

Stephen King was born in Portland, Maine, in 1947. In
1970, shortly after graduating college, King sold his first
short story to a mass market men's magazine. For the next
several years he worked as a laborer while continuing to
write short fiction.

King was teaching high school, living in a cramped
trailer, when his wife, Tabitha, rescued a discarded manuscript from the wastebasket. *Carrie*, King's first published

novel, became an instant best-seller in 1974. More than just the story of a girl with supernatural powers, *Carrie* is a powerful portrayal of the pain and cruelty of adolescence.

In 1975 King published his second novel, *'Salem's Lot,* a tale of vampires set in contemporary Maine. This was followed by *The Shining* in 1976, *The Stand* in 1977, and at least one book every year thereafter.

Writing under his own name and that of Richard Bachman, King has produced more than twenty novels and has sold more than 100 million books worldwide. These include *Christine, Cujo, The Dead Zone, It, Pet Semetary, Needful Things* and *Gerald's Game.*

Different Seasons, a collection of short fiction published in 1982, demonstrates King's talent as a great storyteller outside the horror genre. Books such as *The Shining, Misery, The Tommyknockers* and *The Dark Half* offer insight into the creative process as King's author-protagonists confront such problems as writer's block, renegade fictional characters and ardent fans who refuse to let their artists-heroes change or grow.

Stephen King lives in Bangor, Maine, with his wife and three children. When not writing, he sings and plays guitar and is a member of the band, Rock Bottom Remainders.

———

ONE OF THE THINGS that I've been able to use dreams for in my stories is to show things in a symbolic way that I wouldn't want to come right out and say directly. I've always used dreams the way you'd use mirrors to look at something you couldn't see head-on—the way that you use a mirror to look at your hair in the back. To me that's what dreams are supposed to do. I think that dreams are a way that people's minds illustrate the nature of their problems. Or maybe even illustrate the answers to their problems in symbolic language.

When we look back on our dreams, a lot of times they

decompose as soon as the light hits them. So, you can have a dream, and you can remember very vividly what it's about, but ten or fifteen minutes later, unless it's an extraordinarily vivid dream or an extraordinarily good dream, it's gone. It's like the mind is this hard rubber and you really have to hit it hard to leave an impression that won't eventually just erase.

One of the things that we're all familiar with in dreams is the sense that familiar or prosaic objects are being put in very bizarre circumstances or situations. And since that's what I write about, the use of dreams is an obvious way to create that feeling of weirdness in the real world. I guess probably the most striking example of using a dream in my fiction was connected to the writing of 'Salem's Lot.

Now, I can think of only maybe five or six really horrible nightmares in the course of my life—which isn't bad when you think that that life stretches over forty-four years—but I can remember having an extremely bad dream when I was probably nine or ten years old.

It was a dream where I came up a hill and there was a gallows on top of this hill with birds all flying around it. There was a hangman there. He had died, not by having his neck broken, but by strangulation. I could tell because his face was all puffy and purple. And as I came close to him he opened his eyes, reached his hands out and grabbed me.

I woke up in my bed, sitting bolt upright, screaming. I was hot and cold at the same time and covered with goosebumps. And not only was I unable to go back to sleep for hours after that, but I was really afraid to turn out the light for weeks. I can still see it as clearly now as when it happened.

Years later I began to work on 'Salem's Lot. Now, I knew that the story was going to be about a vampire that came from abroad to the United States and I wanted to put him in a spooky old house. I got about that far in my thinking and, by whatever way it is that your mind connects things, as I was looking around for a spooky house, a guy who works in the creative department of my brain said, Well what about that nightmare you had when you were eight or nine years old? Will that work? And I remembered the nightmare and I thought, Yes, it's perfect.

I turned the dead man into a guy named Hubie Marston who owned a bad house and pretty much repeated the story of the dream in terms of the way he died.

In the story, Hubie Marston hangs himself. He's some sort of black artist of the Aleister Crowley kind—some sort of a dark magician—and I kind of combined him with a stock character in American tabloidism—the wealthy guy who lives and dies in squalor.

For me, once the actual act of creation starts, writing is like this high-speed version of the flip books you have when you're a kid, where you mix and match. The cover of the book will say, "You Can Make Thousands of Faces!" You can put maybe six or seven different eyes with different noses. Except that there aren't just thousands of faces, there are literally billions of different events, personalities and things that you can flip together. And it happens at a very rapid rate. Dreams are just one of those flip strips that you can flip in there. But they also work in terms of advancing the story.

Sometimes when I write I can use dreams to have a sort of precognitive effect on the story. Precognitive dreams are a staple of our supernatural folklore. You know, the person who dreamed that flight 17 was going to crash and changed his reservation and sure enough, flight 17 crashed. But it's like those urban fairy tales: you always hear somebody say, "I have a friend that this happened to." I've never actually heard anyone say, "This happened to *me*."

The closest that I can come to a precognitive experience is that I can be in a situation where a really strong feeling of déjà vu washes over me. I'm sure that I've been there before. A lot of times I make the association that, at some point, I had a dream about this place and this series of actions, and forgot it with my conscious mind when I awoke.

* * *

Every now and then dreams can come in handy. When I was working on *It*—which was this really long book—a dream made a difference.

I had a lot of time and a lot of my sense of craft invested in the idea of being able to finish this huge, long book. Now, when I'm working on something, I see books, completed books. And in some fashion that thing is already there. I'm not really making it so much as I am digging it up, the way that you would an artifact, out of the sand. The trick is to get as much of that object as you possibly can, to get the whole thing out, so it's usable, without breaking it. You always break it somewhat—I mean you never get a complete thing—but if you're really careful and if you're really lucky, you can get most of it.

When I'm working I never know what the end is going to be or how things are going to come out. I've got an idea what direction I want the story to go in, or hope it will go in, but mostly I feel like the tail on a kite. I don't feel like the kite itself, or like the wind that blows on the kite—I'm just the tail of it. And if I know when I sit down what's happening or what's going to happen, that day and the next day and the day after, I'm happy. But with *It* I got to a point where I couldn't see ahead any more. And every day I got closer to the place where this young girl, who was one of my people—I don't think of them as good people or bad people, just my people—was going to be and they were going to find her.

I didn't know what was going to happen to her. And that made me extremely nervous. Because that's the way books don't get done. All at once you just get to a point where there is no more. It's like pulling a little string out of a hole and all at once it's broken and you don't get whatever prize there was on the end of it.

So I had seven, eight hundred pages and I just couldn't stand it. I remember going to bed one night saying, I've got to have an idea. I've got to have an idea! I fell asleep and dreamed that I was in a junk yard, which was where this part of the story was set.

Apparently, I was the girl. There was no girl in the dream. There was just me. And there were all these discarded refrigerators in this dump. I opened one of them and there were these things inside, hanging from the various rusty shelves. They looked like macaroni shells and they were all just sort of trembling in a breeze. Then one of them opened up these wings, flew out and landed on the back of my hand. There was a sensation of warmth, almost like when you get a subcutaneous shot of Novocain or something, and this thing started to turn from white to red. I realized it had anesthetized my hand and it was sucking my blood out. Then they all started to fly out of this refrigerator and to land on me. They were these leeches that looked like macaroni shells. And they were swelling up.

I woke up and I was very frightened. But I was also very happy. Because then I knew what was going to happen. I just took the dream as it was and put it in the book. Dropped it in. I didn't change anything.

In the story "The Body," there's an incident where several boys find themselves covered with leeches. That was something that actually happened to me. There's a lot of stuff in "The Body" that's just simply history that's been tarted up a little bit. These friends and I all went into this pond about a mile and a half from the house where I grew up and when we came out we were just covered with those babies. It was awful. I don't remember that I had nightmares about the incident then but of course I had this leech dream years later.

I really think what happened with this dream was that I went to sleep and the subconscious went right on working and finally sent up this dream the way that you would send somebody an interoffice message in a pneumatic tube.

In the Freudian sense I don't think there is any subconscious, any unconscious where things are going on. I think that consciousness is like an ocean. Whether you're an inch below the surface or whether you're down a mile and a half deep, it's all water. All H_2O.

I think that our minds are the same nutrient bath all the way down to the bottom and different things live at different levels. Some of them are a little bit harder to see because we don't get down that deep. But whatever's going on in our daily lives, our daily thoughts, the things that the surface of our minds are concerned with eddy down—trickle down—and then they have some sort of an influence down there. And the messages that we get a lot of times are nothing more than symbolic reworkings of the things that we're concerned with. I don't think they're very prophetic or anything like that. I think a lot of times dreams are nothing more than a kind of mental or spiritual flatulence. They're a way of relieving pressure.

One way of looking at this water metaphor might be to talk about jumbo shrimp, everybody's favorite oxymoron. They're the big shrimp that nobody ate in restaurants until 1955 or 1960 because, until then, nobody thought of going shrimping after dark. They were there all the time, living their prosaic shrimp lives, but nobody caught them. So when they finally caught them it was, "Hello! Look at this. This is something entirely new." And if the shrimp could talk they'd say, "Shit, we're not new. We've been around for a couple of thousand years. You were just too dumb to look for us."

A slightly different way of looking at this is that there are certain fish that we get used to looking at. There are carp, goldfish, catfish, shad, cod—they're fish that are more or less surface fish. They go down to a depth of maybe fifty, sixty or a hundred feet. People catch them, and we get used to seeing them. Not only do we see them in aquariums or as pictures in books, we see them on our plates. We cook them. We see them in the supermarket in the fish case. Whereas if you go down in a bathysphere, if you go down real deep, you see all these bright fluorescent, weird, strange things with membranous umbrellas and weird skirts that flare out from their bodies. Those are creatures that we don't see very often because they explode if we bring them up close to the surface. They are to surface fish what dreams are to our surface thoughts. Deep fish are like dreams of surface fish. They change shape, they change form.

There are dreams and there are deep dreams. There are dreams where you're able to tap sources that are a lot deeper. I'm sure that if you wanted to extend this metaphor you could say that within the human psyche, within human thought, there really are Mindanao trenches, places that are very very deep, where there are probably some extremely strange things floating around. And what the conscious mind brings up may be the equivalent of an exploded fish. It may just be a mess. It may be something that's gorgeous in its own habitat but when it gets up to the sun it just dries out. And then it's very gray and dull.

I remember about six months ago having this really vivid dream.

I was in some sort of an apartment building, a cheesy little apartment building. The front door was open and I could see all these black people going back and forth. They were talking and having a wonderful time. Somebody was playing music somewhere. And then the door shut.

In the dream I went back and got into bed. I think I must have shut the door myself. My brother was in bed with me, behind me, and he started to strangle me. My brother had gone crazy. It was awful!

I remember saying, with the last of my breath, "I think there's somebody out there." And he got up from the bed and went out. As soon as he was out I went up and closed the door and locked it. And then I went back to bed. That is, I started to lie down in this dream.

Then I began to worry that I hadn't really locked the door. This is the sort of thing that I'm always afraid of in real life. Did I turn off the burners on the stove? Did I leave a light on when I left the house? So, I got up to check the door and sure enough it was unlocked. I realized that he was still in there with me. Somewhere.

I screamed in the dream, "He's still in the house." I screamed so loud I woke myself up. Except I wasn't screaming when I woke up. I was just sort of muttering it over and over again, He's in the house, he's in the house. I was terrified.

Now, I keep a glass of ice water beside the bed where I sleep and the ice cubes hadn't melted yet, so it had happened almost immediately after I fell asleep. That's usually when I have the dreams that I remember most vividly.

Part of my function as a writer is to dream awake. And that usually happens. If I sit down to write in the morning, in the beginning of that writing session and the ending of that session, I'm aware that I'm writing. I'm aware of my surroundings. It's like shallow sleep on both ends, when you go to bed and when you wake up. But in the middle, the world is gone and I'm able to see better.

Creative imaging and dreaming are just so similar that they've got to be related.

In a story like "The Body" or *It,* which is set around the late fifties or the early sixties, I'm literally able to regress so that I can remember things that I'd forgotten. Time goes by and events pile up on the surface of your mind like snow, and it covers all these other previous layers. But if you're able to put yourself into that sort of semidreaming state—whether you're dreaming or whether you're writing creatively the brainwaves are apparently interchangeable—you're able to get a lot of that stuff back. That might be deep dreaming.

I'm aware, particularly in recent years, how precious that state is, I mean the ability to go in there when one is awake. I'm also aware, as an adult, of the vividness of my sleeping dreams when I have them. But I don't have any way of stacking up the number of dreams that I have as opposed to anybody else. My sense is I probably dream a little bit less at night because I'm taking off some of the pressure in the daytime. But I don't have any inherent proof of that.

I can remember finding that state for the first time and being delighted. It's a little bit like finding a secret door in a room but not knowing exactly how you got in. I can't remember exactly how I first found that state except that I would sit down to write every day and I would pretty much do that whether the work went well or the work went badly. And after doing that for a while it was a little bit like having a posthypnotic suggestion.

I know that there are certain things that I do if I sit down to write: I have a glass of water or I have a cup of tea. There's a certain time I sit down around eight o'clock—or 8:15 or 8:30—somewhere within that half hour every morning. I have my vitamin pill; I have my music; I have my same seat; and the papers are all arranged in the same places. It's a series of things. The cumulative purpose of doing those things the same way every day seems to be a way of saying to the mind: you're going to be dreaming soon.

It's not really any different than a bedtime routine. Do you go to bed a different way every night? Is there a certain side that you sleep on? I mean I brush my teeth. I wash my hands. Why would anybody wash their hands before they go to bed? I don't know. And the pillows: the pillows are supposed to be pointed a certain way. The open side of the pillowcase is supposed to be pointed *in* toward the other side of the bed. I don't know why.

And the sleeping position is the same: turn to the right, turn to the left. I think it's a way of your mind saying to your body, or your body saying to your mind—maybe they're communicating with each other saying—we're gonna go to sleep now. And probably dreaming follows the same pattern if you don't interrupt it with things like drug use, alcohol or whatever.

The dreams that I remember most clearly are almost always early dreams. And they're not always bad dreams. I don't want to give you that impression. I can remember one very clearly. It was a flying dream. I was over the turnpike and I was flying along wearing a pair of pajama bottoms. I didn't have any shirt on. I'm just buzzing along under overpasses—*kazipp*—and I'm reminding myself in the dream to stay high enough so that I don't get disemboweled by car antennas sticking up from the cars. That's a fairly mechanistic detail but when I woke up from this dream my feeling was not fear or loathing but just real exhilaration, pleasure and happiness.

It wasn't an out of control flying dream. I can remember as a kid, having a lot of falling dreams but this is the only flying dream that I can remember in detail.

I don't have a lot of repetitive dreams but I do have an anxiety dream: I'm working very hard in a little hot room—it seems to be the room where I lived as a teenager—and I'm aware that there's a madwoman in the attic. There's a little tiny door under the eave that goes to the attic and I have to finish my work. I have to get that work done or she'll come out and get me. At some point in the dream that door always bursts open and this hideous woman—with all this white hair stuck up around her head like a gone-to-seed dandelion—jumps out with a scalpel.

And I wake up.

I still have that dream when I'm backed up on my work and trying to fill all these ridiculous commitments I've made for myself.

ELMORE LEONARD

ELMORE LEONARD had been writing for three decades when the general public finally discovered him. He began his career writing westerns for the pulp magazines. Eighty-four editors rejected his first novel before it was finally published as a paperback original. Intent on commercial rather than literary success, Leonard switched to writing crime novels after the market dried up for westerns. In 1982, after twenty-three novels, the thriller *Stick* became a best-seller.

Born in New Orleans in 1925, Elmore Leonard started out as an advertising copywriter. He made his living for many years writing educational and industrial films in the Detroit area, where he still resides with his wife, Joan.

It is the colorful dialogue and eminently likeable villains that distinguish Leonard's action-packed thrillers. Grover Sales, writing in the *Los Angeles Times Book Review*, praised

Leonard for his "uncanny use of plot, pace and his inexhaustible flair for the nervous rhythms of contemporary urban speech."

Leonard's novels, many of which were made into films, include *The Big Bounce*, *Mr. Majestyk*, *Fifty-Two Pickup*, *Glitz*, *Freaky Deaky*, *Killshot* and *Maximum Bob*.

======

I DREAM a lot. I'll get up to go to the bathroom at four in the morning and I'll have a dream in my mind but by the time I come back it's gone. I'll bet I dream every night and then lose it.

For years I remember dreaming that I fell down a very steep, narrow flight of stairs. I would hold back, try to hold back, as I was about to hit. I don't think I ever hit, but holding back took a strenuous effort. It seemed to take something out of me. But it was never a hit.

This was in the sixties and seventies before my writing became well known.

In the eighties, I remember dreaming several times of climbing a rickety ladder. Not a real ladder but a ladder that had been formed out of driftwood or scrap lumber. None of the rungs matched and some were very loose. I tried to climb that a few times. I fell a lot but I kept on climbing. I hung on. And then I'd get up into an area where there would be some vines and bushes. That was later. Now I wasn't falling anymore, I was climbing up. I thought, Boy, finally!

I always assume that my dreams are so obvious. I wanted to prevent failure. That's what these dreams were about. But I don't know. I was never holding back. I was never writing down. I was doing the best I could. Always. I continue that. I try to do better all the time.

The other recurring dream I used to have was all of a sudden being naked in public. It might be in a church, or on a street corner. There'd be bright sunlight, people around. No one was really looking at me. And then I'd realize where I was. And that I just had to go walk from wherever I was over to some doorway. Or, for example, in the church I'd be in the front pew. I simply had to walk across the aisle and get out. That's all. Just do it. Try not to pay any attention to anyone who was staring at me. Just get it done.

In another recurring dream I would find myself back at the ad agency where I had worked from 1949 to 1961. In this dream it was always my first day back and I was standing in the hall with someone who had hired me. Several other people were there, too. They were showing me my office when a guy I had worked with before walked by real fast. He was a link with the past. I would see him and I'd say "Chuck!" or "Charlie!" And he'd say "Catch you later. See ya later." He was off to a meeting. He'd always run by. In one of the dreams I remember that the office that they were giving me was huge, but the walls were lined with shelves filled with canned goods. And in the middle of the office was a wooden school desk with a pen—the type where the top raises up and you keep your books inside—and I would think, "Oh my God. I'm going to be in here forever! I've failed and I'm back."

It wasn't until the eighties that I finally felt—this is what I do—I write novels. I'm always going to write novels. And I'm successful enough at it that I'm not going to have to go back to ad writing.

I sold my first story in August, forty years ago. A novel that appeared in the December issue of *Argus* magazine. I got $1,000 for it. And between the time that I wrote it, sold it, and it came out, I had written several more stories. When the story appeared an agent, Marguerite Harper, contacted me. She represented me until '66, when she died. She sold everything that I wrote. Most of it went to pulp magazines, but she was aiming everything at the *Saturday Evening Post,* where I had no business being. I didn't write their kind of stories at all. Mine were all westerns. I didn't have enough blue sky or comic relief in my westerns, but she was selling them. I remember one time, probably in very early 1952, I said, Why don't you critique my work and then we'll get fewer rejections. I'll fix the story before you send it out. She said, "You learn how to write and I'll sell it." I was very anxious to learn how to write and very anxious to do it full time. Especially after that first sale, a thousand bucks!

The next four or five sold immediately to the pulps but for a hundred bucks—short stories, two cents a word. I wasn't making that much money, only about $250 a month.

It would've been possible to hammer out one a week at a hundred dollars a week—which would've been more than I was making—but I was warned by her and by an editor at *Popular Publications,* Don't do it. You'll become a hack. You'll have to turn these out to make a living. The quality will suffer and you will not have really learned how to write. You will not have reached your potential. I think what they meant was you will not have developed a style, a natural style. So I stayed on until '61. Finally I quit because my profit sharing in the company came due. It was my first opportunity to quit with some money. Not much, eleven, twelve thousand bucks. At that same time we bought another house, and that money went into the down payment. So I did a lot of freelance writing, advertising writing, industrial movies, things like that for the next five years until *Hombre* sold to Fox. That gave me enough to write a book and I wrote the *Big Bounce.* It was rejected by everybody until I rewrote it and the film rights sold. It was a terrible movie but it got me going again.

Success seems like kind of a fluke to me. It's not based on merit, since not everyone has the same opportunities. For me, it was just something that happened. I was in the right place at the right time. In 1985 I became an overnight success after thirty years. Everybody liked that idea and played with it. I didn't think that I would ever have a best-seller. I never thought that my writing was either good enough or bad enough to make the list. I didn't write the right kind of book. Of course now there are more and more crime books getting on the list.

Humor came in as I discovered my style—the most natural

way for me to write. I had been studying and imitating Hemingway when I realized that your style really comes out of your attitude, how you see things. And I didn't share Hemingway's attitude at all. I didn't take myself or life as seriously as he did.

When you begin to read Hemingway he makes it look so easy. There's a lot of white space often on his pages. You see the lines of dialogue, the page running vertical rather than horizontal. You see all that white space and you say, Whoa, that looks easy. I should be able to do that. I know how people talk. And then you realize that it isn't nearly as easy as it looks. Because there's a lot in between the lines that he didn't say. Like in his short story "Hills Like White Elephants": you know everything about these two people and he hasn't told you anything. She's going to go get an abortion or she isn't, you don't know. So you study and see ways to do that. See ways to describe people. You don't describe in detail all the features but just perhaps something that stands out.

And then I found other writers to be inspired by—not crime writers as it turns out. I was never inspired by Chandler, Hammett or those guys who are responsible for most of the people writing in the field today—that first-person style with all the similes and metaphors.

I was inspired by a writer by the name of Richard Bissell who in the fifties wrote *Seven and a Half Cents,* which was turned into the musical *The Pyjama Game.* He was a pilot on the Mississippi River. When I was researching *Killshot* I reread a lot of Richard Bissell's work and then it really hit me how much he had influenced me.

Early in the morning things will come to me. I'll wake up with ideas, specific plot ideas, scenes. Sometimes, as I wake up in that half sleep, I'll have ideas that I think are great and then, as I come fully awake, I realize they just don't work at all. Or I'll wake up with scene ideas that don't necessarily fit. Not ideas that I feel are worth writing down. I'll only write something down if I see it as the answer to something that I've been having a problem with. And that does happen.

I don't believe in writer's block. I don't know what that is. There are just certain little areas that I know I'm going to get through. It's just a matter of finding a way.

I try not to think at all at night. From six P.M. on I try not to think about my work. I don't want to. I want to let my unconscious or subconscious work on it. And then in the morning I wake up and look and think, Okay, where am I? What's going on? Do I have any ideas? And usually I do. Very very often what was a puzzle, what was a problem at six o'clock, having worked all day, gets solved over night.

From four o'clock on, if it has been a difficult day, I'm probably getting kind of tired. If it was a great day, if I just swung through and did six, seven, eight pages, then I'm not tired. I have to fight with something a little bit more before I'll throw it aside and say it's not going to work. It always happens in expository scenes. This is when I, as the author, would normally describe where the person comes from, how she grew up and so on. But that's not my style. That's not the way I write a book. I write a book in scenes, always from somebody's point of view. So when I get into the exposition I have to think of a way to dramatize it. I have to think of a way where someone in the book, if not the person herself, could tell where she came from and why and so on. That is the hard part.

There was one scene in *Get Shorty* that took me days, and I don't know why. There's a scene where the older producer, Harry, and Karen are in bed. She hears something downstairs. Finally, after about eight pages, Harry admits he hears it too and goes down to find out who turned on the television set. It's his scene. You follow him down the stairs and he walks into the den. The lights go on and there's a guy sitting behind the desk waiting for him. I do this scene for another ten pages, and then go to Karen upstairs, who's now outside the bedroom. She's got a Lakers T-shirt on and she's standing by the railing looking down into the front hall, listening. Every once in a while she hears Harry's voice. She tries to interpret what a line means out of context and decides that Harry is not talking to one of her friends who might be pulling a joke. But it's not a burglar or someone to be afraid of, not the way Harry's talking to this person. So then this is where I want to say something about Karen. I've got Karen all alone standing here by the top of the stairs. Now this is the place to fill in some of her background. And what do you say? Well, Karen was born such and such a place and she came out to Hollywood to be a movie star, da da da da. No. How do you get into her background? What is she to Harry? Things like that. I worked on it and worked on it and it just sounded trite—until I used something that he said in bed to her. She says, "Do you hear that, Harry?" at whatever the sound is downstairs, and he says, "Maybe it's only the wind." Now she recalls him saying that once before. It was a line that she had objected to from one of her movies. She had worked for him as the female lead in his horror movies—because she was a great screamer. In the movie there's this noise—the monster is tearing the shingles off the roof with his bare hands to get to them—and she says to the hero, with her eyes raised, "Maybe it's only the wind." She had been in this same house, down in the study reading the script, when she'd said to Harry, "You've got to be kidding. Come on, I'm not going to say that." And this is what she thinks about at the top of the stairs. She thinks about why the line works. She'd said, "Everybody's going to laugh," and he'd said, "Right. That's good. Nervous laughter. Let 'em get a little of that out of their system." It's all bullshit but it's what he tells her and it does begin then to explain their relationship—how she first auditioned for him and so on. See?

I went back and rewrote that scene again and again over a period of a month. I kept going back and I'd get so tired of it! Retyping that one page to get to the point where I had to do something different. Actually, I'll only retype something to make it readable; otherwise I'm writing in the margins and between the lines. My daughter, who does my typing, can read my writing and so it doesn't have to be perfect. I write in longhand and then I put it on my typewriter. I bought the typewriter, an Olympia manual, secondhand in about 1975 for $120. I like the sound of it. And I like the type, and as long as I can get ribbons I'll keep using it. I think I can get through with this next book without ever having touched a word processor. I don't like the sound of the word *processor*. It's like hitting wood or plastic. It doesn't have that ring.

Anyway, I think I finally made the scene work. Those are the kinds of things that I wake up thinking about in the morning. Sometimes, more often than not, I have the solution to it. I wake up knowing how to work it out.

LEONARD MICHAELS

LEONARD MICHAELS was born on the Lower East Side of Manhattan in 1933 to Polish Jewish immigrants. Until he was nearly six years old, Michaels spoke only Yiddish. He sold his first story at the age of twenty-nine.

Michaels's two collections of short stories, *Going Places* and *I Would Have Saved Them If I Could,* deal mainly with male-female relationships. His first novel, *The Men's Club,* published in 1981, anticipated the men's movement of the 1990s. *Shuffle,* an autobiographical novel, appeared in 1990. In 1992, Michaels published *Sylvia,* a novella based on the story of his first marriage, which re-creates the violent spirit and revolutionary atmosphere of New York City in the early sixties.

Michaels is the recipient of numerous prizes including a Guggenheim Fellowship and an award from the National

Foundation for the Arts. His short stories have appeared in the O. *Henry Prize Stories* and *Best American Stories*. His essays have appeared in *Best American Essays*.

A resident of Kensington, California, Leonard Michaels teaches at the University of California, Berkeley. He is the father of three children.

THIS IS a dream I had in early adolescence. I have long imagined that it was a prophetic dream and it said something about my career as a writer.

What I see in the dream is this stone stairway leading down into a dungeon. Big steps covered with moss. Everything all around is dank and dingy, ugly and scary. Sprawled on these steps is this figure that I think is me. His head is twisted to the side and his tongue is nailed to one of the steps.

I think it suggests that, well—the tongue has to do with speech. You can imagine that it has to do with writing too. And, in so far as I'm in a dungeon, it seems to suggest that my writing will always come out of some dark place. People have said that all writing of any real interest comes out of the subconscious, but since my tongue is nailed to one of the steps, it suggests that maybe I was trying to get out of this dungeon, but was forbidden to do so. I have been obliged to draw my writing career from this dreadful place.

There is perhaps something about sacrifice implicit in that dream. And enormous suffering. I've always seen it mainly as imprisonment, being trapped and being committed against my will to a certain kind of writing, a certain sort of expression. But who knows? Look, this dream may really have had to do with something else. This is merely my sense of it as prophetic, telling me, as an adolescent, what my fate would be.

My best book is my last book, called *Shuffle,* which has dream material in it of a very particular kind. The book is also full of sexual business and the tongue is by no means neglected. In the book I talk about waking up beside a woman who tells me her dreams the moment she wakes up every morning. Sometimes I'm still asleep and I hear her voice beginning as she recounts the dreams she had that night. Sometimes it's a little irritating because I'm not quite awake yet and she's going on and on about her dream. On the other hand, sometimes it's extremely fascinating, her dream is wonderful and I urge her to keep going, don't stop, see the whole dream. In order for her to do this she must keep her voice very neutral. She can't be rhetorical when reporting a dream. She has to not let her voice—her personal sound so to speak; her needs; her desire to create certain effects—she can't let any of that enter into the report of the dream. All of that starts to interfere with her memory of the dream.

I make this point because this is very much like what happens in writing. In some way a writer has to strike a certain voice, a certain note, a certain tone and sustain it. The writer really should not, if the writer's going to be any good, try to lunge off the page and grab the reader by the neck and make the reader think or understand or feel something. All of that should be implicit in the story he or she is telling. In the case of this woman and her dreams, she instinctively told her dreams the way a good writer writes: Letting the dream happen. Not getting between the listener and the dream.

This is going to sound a little mystical but I had a woman friend who, in response to problems that appeared in my life, problems that had only to do with me, would dream solutions or illuminations of the problem. That is to say she would formulate the problem in her own dreams without my telling her what the problems were.

I was writing something—I had been working on it very hard—and it had to do with popular Latin music, salsa. I hadn't discussed it with her or anybody except the magazine editor I was writing the piece for. In the midst of this essay, when it was really tough and it had really become problematic, we had dinner and she said, "I had this dream and it was full of musical notes." She started describing the notes and it was the stuff I was writing about! Now where did she get that? She'd never had a dream like that in her life. She doesn't even know music.

I suppose it's quite possible that dreams are expressive of the deepest levels of intimacy between people. At least that has seemed to be the case in my life. When I say between people I mean not only between a man and a woman but even between you and yourself. You, at one point in your life. and you, at a much later point in your life, when you're really a considerably different person. There you are in an earlier incarnation dreaming your future, your fate.

It's been my experience, during certain periods of my life, to feel a kind of fear just before I went to sleep because of what I might dream. There were certain things I simply didn't want to know about and I was afraid they'd come up in my dreams. I would literally stay up late, not so that I could work or read or anything, but only so as not to sleep. The dreams were very intense and were coming night after night. I was afraid of them.

There are certain things one really doesn't want to know. You want to walk away from certain things. And you often find you can't. Your dreams tear at you, demand attention. Let's say you have a really good friend, or a lover—someone crucial to you—and you feel as if, in one way or another that you can't even specify, you're being betrayed. And you don't want to know it. You don't want to think it. You can't live with this idea. Your dreams may then become terrifically turbulent and show it to you. They may even tell the truth, which is the worst thing of all. Along comes your dream and there it is. Your dear friend is in the dream and he or she is doing exactly what you fear most.

It's really weird when it happens. You discover how profoundly you're connected to other people. There are all these subterranean forces, deep dark forces, that flow about—holding you to this person, or separating you from that person, binding one human being with another—and our understanding of this kind of force is often very, very limited. I think it's mainly because we just really don't want to know. We're much too civilized to want to know that we feel and think certain things.

I went through one particularly bad period where I was afraid to go to sleep because I was afraid to dream. It went on for months. I was trying not to sleep because the minute I fell asleep I'd be attacked again by my nightmares. I don't remember any of them, but I do remember they were awful. It's not as if they were terribly violent nightmares. They were nightmares about things that were so horribly disturbing that it was worse than seeing monsters or being chased by dangerous creatures. It was just finding myself in some state, some condition, some hideously uncomfortable place: a dreadful apartment where every inch of the room, the air, would be full of fear and distress and I'd have to get out. The floor would be slightly tilted and the ceiling low. I'd have to get out not even knowing why. I'd go down this endless flight of stairs. I'd be on strange streets and suddenly see people I knew and they would be vacant and unavailable to me. That kind of a nightmare. Low-keyed horror stories.

The truth is that the whole period in my life was so awful that I did other things aside from not sleeping to avoid confronting what was happening inside me and what was happening between me and other people. I spent hours sitting in my office at school, hours and hours sitting there, not wanting to deal with the world.

Time passed and the dreams stopped. I think that had to do with meeting new people, having new friends. Somehow or other this stirred within me some sort of healing process. It was good psychological nutrition so to speak. The new people, the new voices, the new feelings. I guess new people somehow suggest to you that your world is really not as narrow as maybe you believed it was. You're not so limited by your psychological environment as maybe you thought you were and so on.

* * *

The vast majority of us find that when we sit down at the typewriter all sorts of inhibitions begin to make impossible the statement of even something that means a very great deal to us. We have a strong feeling about this and that and we run to the typewriter and then what? Either the writing is bad or we tell some kind of lie. We betray the feeling in fifty different ways. We never get it right and the writing kind of stinks. I'll give you a quick example of what I'm talking about.

Something happens to you, something very interesting or very exciting and you run into a friend and you tell the friend what it is that happened. Very very often you will tell the friend what it is that happened in a way that's masterful, that even a great short story writer couldn't've managed. Then you go home and you want to sit down at your typewriter and write all of that. And it's awful! You'll spend weeks trying to do what you did in three minutes on the street corner. And you can't do it. You may even spend your life trying and you won't be able to do it. But, just talk to a friend: everything is easy and loose. You've got this kind of freedom and you know exactly who your audience is. It's through your friend somehow that you have access to these feelings that are otherwise not very available.

This is going to sound absurd but I think what makes the difference is rhythm. It's maybe the most important thing. You really can't be a writer without it. There might be rare exceptions, but every novel, every short story, anything that's any good has rhythm. And if it isn't moving in you, if you're not hearing it, if it isn't controlling your sentences, your feelings, your thoughts, it's unlikely that you're really writing. It's the most basic music. It has to be in your heart, in your brain, and then you get to talk.

Rhythm is something that develops between two people. They have a way, they have a vocabulary, they have the beat.

Between each of my books there's usually a long period, six years or so. But between *Shuffle* and *The Men's Club* there were

nine years, the longest layoff. I always write. I'm always
publishing something here and there but I don't do a book a
year. There are a lot of writers who do that, as if that's the
definition of a writer. They've got a kind of obligation to keep
at it and in quite a few cases it pays off. In money and in
reputation and so on and so forth. You become a significant
presence on the literary scene. It's never been that way for me.
I don't know exactly why. I think it's because I'm more of a
fanatical reviser than I am a writer. I can never leave anything
alone for too long. I always go back and I want to do the story
over. This is not right or that's not right. Believe me, if that's
your disposition, you're not going to get to do a book a year.
You have to pick up speed and I've never been able to. I've tried.
In fact, at this very minute I have the first sixty, seventy pages
of two novels that I went into with this new spirit, trying to see
how fast I could write. I saw that I could probably do two or
three books a year and so I've satisfied my curiosity. Whether I'll
finish the books is another matter. Probably not.

It's interesting to me that you can dream on demand. If you're
in a therapy session and your psychotherapist asks you to
dream, you will produce dreams. Another remarkable thing is
how difficult it is to recover a dream. Even as I'm trying to tell
somebody what I dreamed, it vaporizes. I can't get my hands on
it. Things start vaguing out more and more.

   I don't think I can remember a single time in my life when
a *man* told me a dream. I'm sure it must've happened at some
point, but I can't remember ever hearing a dream from a man.
On the other hand, I've heard dreams from women again and
again and again. I have women friends who seem to dream in
a very regular way, like the way they eat. They like to tell what
it is they dreamed and very often it's quite fascinating.

   Men probably dream as much as women do but there's
something that inhibits them from reporting dreams. Maybe it's
just cultural. *Just* cultural! As if that were not too important.
Maybe there's something in whatever it is that constitutes men

psychologically in American society that denies the validity or the value or the experience of dreaming. Maybe it's the kind of experience that is not good for a man to have in a highly competitive society. Who needs that sort of sensation? The sensation of being seized by powers and forces and ideas and thoughts and feelings inside yourself. That is what happens after all. The dream is entirely yours but it's taking place without your will. You're not deliberately dreaming. It's just going on. And it belongs strictly to you. Maybe this kind of experience indicates too much passivity for a man. That's my guess. Whereas women are familiar with the experience and quite at home with it for the same reason that they're generally more at home with their own feelings. You know, men have the same number of feelings, I'm sure, maybe even more in many cases, but they may not feel as comfortable with the idea of a rich and perhaps turbulent psychological existence.

Borges has said that all writing is a guided dream. Now that's an interesting definition, don't you think? I mean the idea that the lyricism, the force, the mysterious energies are happening on their own, a little beyond your control. In writing, something has to feel as if it's happening but you're guiding it. You're not imposing your will on the material, you're allowing its freedom and dream nature to continue to exist, to continue to be felt and respected. That's the distinctive feature of real writing.

BHARATI MUKHERJEE

BHARATI MUKHERJEE was born in Calcutta, India, in 1940 to a family of Brahmins. Educated in Europe and India, she went on to earn her doctorate at the University of Iowa and began writing fiction in 1972.

While living in Canada, Mukherjee became conscious of herself as a "brown woman in a white society" and wrote her first novel, *The Tiger's Daughter*. With her second novel, *Wife*, she continued to explore the emotional challenges faced by women trying to bridge disparate cultures. Her first collection of short stories, *Darkness*, was published in 1985.

After winning the 1988 National Book Critics Circle Award for *The Middleman and Other Stories*, Mukherjee expanded her story "Jasmine" into a novel bearing the same name.

Mukherjee is married to writer Clark Blaise, whom she

met at the Iowa Writers' Workshop in 1961. With her husband she cowrote *Days and Nights in Calcutta* recounting their experiences in India. She and Blaise maintain a commuter relationship while she teaches at the University of California, Berkeley, and he chairs a department at the University of Iowa. They have two sons.

A year before our interview, I was introduced to Mukherjee by a mutual friend. When we met again she suddenly remembered our first encounter and remarked that the words "dream facilitator" on my card were the inspiration for a story she had just completed.

═══════

I'M THE KIND of writer who in the very first draft really doesn't know what adventures the character will get into. In the stories I've ended up liking, and in the novel *Jasmine,* the endings have definitely come to me in dreams. The very first time it happened was in my second novel, *Wife.* The ending took me by surprise. *Wife* is about a young woman who comes as an immigrant wife to New York and has a great deal of difficulty adjusting to the new world. I thought that like a pliant, good, obedient Indian wife she would probably either give in to her depressions or commit suicide, which is a traditional and honorable way out for women like her. But instead, in my dream, she decided to kill her husband. The first thing I said to my husband as he woke up was "I got it! The guy's going to die!" Therefore I wrote the novel in which the wife, in a misguided but very self-assertive act that was very important to me personally, actually does murder her husband while he's having his breakfast. And, so, the poor husband bleeds into his Wheaties.

As I'm getting towards the end of a story, the ending that, during my waking hours, I think will happen is sometimes subverted or obliterated by the dream. It happens just as I'm getting ready to write that scene.

In many of the stories in *The Middleman,* the endings are

not the way I had planned them. There's a story called "Buried Lives" in which I thought the man, an illegal alien, was going to drown as he tries to make a dash, by boat, into Nova Scotia. But the character refused to get on the boat. He found himself a girlfriend in Germany who was willing to marry him and he said "Sorry Mukherjee, I want a happy life for myself" and just didn't get on the boat.

I thought again Jasmine was going to take a socially acceptable way out of a crisis but instead she did something very bold and unpredictable and at the same time headed for California. This was long before there were any plans for me to come to UC Berkeley. Deep down I must've been planning it.

I have come to trust very much the unconscious within the creative process and the efficacy, the value of dreams. Art really is quite often anticipated by or resolved by dreams. My husband, Clark Blaise, is a wonderful writer and he trusts them even more than me. He actually sees the characters in very thick and solid ways.

I've also been visited by a ghost. I was writing an autobiographical book called *Days and Nights in Calcutta,* which I coauthored with my husband. I must have been under tremendous pressure. Perhaps Western psychiatrists will say it was simply pressure and I imagined a ghost, but I felt the man breathe on me. I knew who this ghost was. It was an uncle. Not someone that I thought of very much or had spent much time with when he was alive. He had juvenile diabetes and eventually many complications. But in the dream he breathed on me as if he was trying to warn me about something.

I was so frightened that I had to call my parents. I couldn't be in a room alone for the rest of the night because the ghost was so real to me. My mother's reaction was, "Of course there are ghosts, but there are good ghosts and there are bad ghosts. The man whose ghost you saw was a good person so he's not going to harm you in any way."

Several years later my younger son developed juvenile

diabetes. Now there was no reason why any logical person should connect the two events. I do.

I believe in ghosts and I believe in an invisible world that is very solid, very real. The world we cannot see is probably more substantial than the one we can see.

The very first novel that I wrote includes a universe in which there are gods, there are angels, there are ghosts, there are bad spirits, as well as human beings. Everything is in perspective. In some ways I suppose it comes from my childhood Hindu background. I've carried that childhood reality into my adult life. For a very long time, in fact until fairly recently, I was terribly afraid of the dark. The solidity of spirits made me afraid of the dark. I knew they were there. But I told myself that I had to survive in the new world and that ghosts probably had a harder time in America. Overcoming my fear was an act of will. I still know they're there, but most of them are good spirits. They look after me.

As a child in India I lived in dreams. We bought wholesale astrological predictions but did not intellectualize dreams. The word *Freudian* was something foreign and funny that applied to people out there in the West and not to us. So I never tried to mess with my dreams. But I have been burdened with superstitions all my life. I still will not leave the house if someone sneezes just as I'm getting ready to leave. When we're ready to leave the house we say "I'm coming" rather than "I'm going" because if you say "I'm going" it will be a permanent exit. You'll never come back. I still don't cut my nails on certain days of the week.

I also am terrified of snakes. I don't think it's the usual Western phobia having to do with sexuality. Snake equals phallus is not true in my case. When I was about two, I pulled a snake by its tail. It was in its viper's nest, embedded in a hole in the floor of my grandfather's garden estate. As a result, when there's a crisis, what I dream of is an immense, enormous—I know this sounds horrendously sexual and perverted—snake.

I'm terrified. As a result, snake sequences, snake hallucinations, snake nightmares or snake phobias turn up in many of my fictions.

As a child, I remember a couple of servants saying that if you dream of birth then a death is about to happen to a friend or family member. And if you dream of death then something good, a birth, will take place. The opposite takes place. Same with food. You must never eat in a dream, then you will starve in real life.

I don't remember my dreams that much. I just know that I've had a wonderful feeling or that I've been terrified. Maybe it's part of my old childhood fear of overintellectualizing the unconscious life. I let a dream work underground. If you talk too much about it I feel you'll lose the capacity to use your dream.

I dream in color. My dreams are very visual and very emotional so there's a big gut reaction to whatever has happened in the dream. My dream self has either been tortured or is ecstatic. There is no middle ground. These are not sensible, logical, ordinary dreams. Sometimes a dream will give me a glow for the next two or three days.

I'm the kind of writer who doesn't take notes. I tell myself, trust the unconscious. If something is important enough in my unconscious life I will remember. It will come to me when I need it. So I don't keep a notebook of good lines, good thoughts or dreams.

I have too many stories in my head rather than too few. Until very recently I had to grab whatever time I could because I worked at one full-time job, three part-time jobs and so on. When I was ready to sit down at my word processor my head was so full of stories, the sentences were just pounding against my skull. And even now I realize that there really isn't a single second in my life when I'm not thinking story. There are just thousands of people inside my head and if they're ghosts they sure shriek real loud, all waiting to tell me their stories. I just transcribe. At my best I'm a transcriber of those eerie voices.

I hear them. Voices. Mine are really quite literally voice stories. I become the person I'm writing about. Thats why it's easy for me to write from the point of view of a male Vietnam vet, because I enter the character so fully.

As a Hindu I've been taught that this life is a dream. So the intersection between what I've anticipated in art and my actual life is like dream and fulfillment, like dream and premonition.

For Hindus, the goal is to drop out of life, right? What human beings think of as reality is really an illusion, a Maya. A dream. Or a nightmare. You reach salvation when you can extinguish that illusion and become one with the cosmic soul. So if the cosmic soul sends out little hints through dreams or through the unconscious then art is my satellite dish for hearing the signals, and quite often my life imitates art.

I used to dream of cutting wings off birds and sewing them together so I could make a pair of large wings and fly. In a story called "Angela" in my first collection of stories, *Darkness,* this image appears.

I can't remember lifting off, I only remember the process of trying to make those wings. I realized even as a child, brutally, that I had to get those wings from the birds in order to make the giant pair for myself. I shudder to think what Freudian analysts would make of that. But I realize now that all my fiction, and certainly my own life, has been an attempt to leap out of the limitations that gender, caste, class, imposed on a young woman from a very orthodox family in a very, very traditional society.

If I had been poor instead of privileged as a child, you can imagine how much more restrictive my life would've been. What I have needed to escape is the tremendous confinement that even well-off women from educated families in the Calcutta of my generation faced. I could have had a very comfortable life if I had stayed in Calcutta. I'm sure I could have had a contented life and I'm sure I would have been a very competent witty novelist of manners. But that's not what I wanted for myself. I wanted chaos. And I got it.

I don't believe that one should hang on to an old culture, an old life just out of fear, paranoia or cultural arrogance. The characters I'm most sympathetic towards are those who are willing to take risks, even if it means getting hurt sometimes.

It's not a smooth process, the remaking of oneself.

I think dreams serve a very important function. And that is to keep the individual and the culture sane. I really do think that dreams are wholesome and that if we could read them, without overintellectualizing them, that the dreams would put us in touch with solid and sane selves. I believe in reinforcing the unconscious. The best stories that I write are about characters who hear the wake-up call from the unconscious. Who, until the moment when the story begins, have deadened themselves to their dream selves or the unconscious. And suddenly, on that day on which the story begins, something happens, suddenly ordinary and routine life, the conscious bunker level of consciousness, is shattered and they must delve deep down into the unconscious.

We're all trying to figure out a middle ground between acceptance of the crises that occur to us and a desire to think that individual effort can help us change some things. I have solved this in my own life by saying, let me treat every moment with reverence because I don't know what the mission of any of my moments in life is. That's why I'm not embarrassed to admit that I believe wholeheartedly in dreams.

GLORIA NAYLOR

GLORIA NAYLOR was born in New York in 1950.
Recognizing that the presence and perspectives of black
women were underrepresented in American literature, she
began writing fiction.

Her first novel, *The Women of Brewster Place*, was designed to reflect the diversity of black female experience. It
told the powerful and often painful stories of eight women—
residents of an urban housing project—who differed from
one another in age, socioeconomic status, political and sexual
orientation. This book, which was later turned into a TV
miniseries produced by Oprah Winfrey, won the National
Book Award in 1983.

An upper-middle-class black suburb became the location
for Naylor's second novel. Her third took place in a black-
owned island in the south and her fourth book in and
around an urban cafe.

With each book Naylor set out to explore a different aspect of human existence. *Brewster Place* was her emotional book. *Linden Hills,* her more cerebral. *Mama Day* explored the spiritual realms, and *Bailey's Cafe* dealt with the sexual. Having completed this quartet in 1992, Naylor finally felt she could call herself a writer. She views the ten years spent on these first four novels as a period of apprenticeship.

Gloria Naylor is a resident of New York City.

═══

I 'V E   H A D , what my mother's called all of my life, a vivid imagination. I am very much a daydreamer. When I was younger—I don't do it any more—I used to literally dream serials. I'd have daydreams where one dream would leave off and then the next night I would pick it up and take it someplace else. The dreams would be in segments, like a soap opera. I was always the star. It was always me, five years later, or older, in some situation I thought pleasing.

This started in my teens and moved into my twenties. They'd last sometimes a week, sometimes a month, it would depend on how interested I was in that particular fantasy. These daydreams would deal with either career aspirations or romantic aspirations. I'd ultimately finish one off and start a new fantasy.

I'm still a very elaborate daydreamer. When I'm stuck in the writing of a book I will lay down and play it out in my mind to get myself past that bump some way. I will replay the words—because at that point they're practically memorized—and try to make a mind picture out of what I want to happen. Then I'll get up and go back to the word processor and attempt to look for the words for that mind picture.

For example, in *Linden Hills* I was taking two boys from Upper Hell to Lower Hell and I was stuck about how to do that. Tupelo Drive was supposed to be the Tower of Dis where the demons were—you know *Linden Hills* is just a reworking of

Dante's *Inferno*—and they were at the gate and they were to enter then into Lower Hell. What Dante had done at that point—when, with the poet Virgil, he had reached the Tower of Dis and demons were blocking their entrance into Lower Hell— was have Beatrice send the Archangel Michael to scatter the demons. I wasn't following *The Inferno* concept by concept, but at the beginning, middle and end of *Linden Hills* I just totally reworked his images. So I was at that point and I said, Okay now, I have these boys here but they don't know anyone in the really posh part of the neighborhood. How am I going to get them there? That's when I lay down and inverted the idea of having a policeman come and stop them. Which is very plausible. You simply cannot walk in some neighborhoods in this country because you're suspect. So the police were the demons I used to stop the boys. And then I had Ruth—who was my Dante Willy's symbol of divine love—send her husband, Norman, on an errand and he gets them into Lower Hell. That's an example of daydreaming a solution.

I remember that specifically because I had just won the National Book Award for *The Women of Brewster Place*. All of that hoopla had happened, and was over, and I was sitting back down with the *Linden Hills* manuscript. I was frustrated, going, Oh my goodness, How am I going to do this? Don't these boys understand that I'm a writer? They didn't understand that. They only knew that they were stuck up there in Linden Hills and I hadn't pushed them down into the other section. I remember that because it was a humbling experience. Which said to me it never gets easier, I don't care what.

If you don't keep things like acclaim in perspective they can literally stop you. I've known it to stop people from writing. It's what Hemingway said, "If you believe 'em when they tell you you're good, you'll have to believe 'em when they tell you you're not."

I've always kept everything in perspective because I have other goals for myself with my writing. I have things I want, challenges I want to meet with my work, and only I can determine if, indeed, I'm up to doing that. The reason that this last novel, *Bailey's Cafe,* is so important to me is that it finishes a quartet that I had dreamed about when I started *The Women of Brewster Place.* Because with *Brewster Place* I had dreamed—and this is a waking dream if you will—of having a quartet of interconnected novels that would serve as the foundation for a career I wanted to build in writing. Now if I had gotten waylaid by reactions to laying down that foundation, either good or bad, positive or negative, I wouldn't've fulfilled what I'd wanted to do. Now I feel that I am indeed a writer. I believe that I now have the basis for a career that I'm going to build. It's always been a matter of my shutting out the din of other people and what they think of my work and understanding what my own goals are.

So much of what I do is unconscious. I choose not to dissect why certain images appear when I'm writing. I just let them lead and take me where they will. I tend to feel, Okay, this is here. Is it working? Is it right? And then I proceed to craft the language around it the best I know how.

Now, after the fact, when I'm speaking about a piece of work or when I'm trying to answer a question coherently, I will attempt to make connections. But I often feel that my connections are just as good as someone else's in that regard. Because, when the process is going on, it lives at the level where dreams are born. And I don't tamper with that too much.

For the most part, I have, before I start a book, a very broad outline of where I want to go. Very broad. I always have my first sentence and I have my last sentence. I write from the first sentence, not knowing why the last sentence says what it says. But it comes and that's when I know I'm ready to start the work. Not maybe that exact week, even that exact month, but I know that it's there to be found. Because my work, for me, is sort of a peeling away of layers. It's discovering what already exists.

But it's a matter of my doing whatever work I have to do to get there.

The images start first. I will be struck by these images that haunt me and say, Okay, that means that's a story that's waiting to be told. After that it'll be the first line. And then it will be the last line.

With *Mama Day* for example: for years I saw this young man and young woman walking by water. I knew that they were falling in love—or that they had fallen in love—and I knew they were troubled. I did not know what that meant. I knew the place was New York. At first I thought maybe it was the Brooklyn Promenade overlooking the Statue of Liberty in Brooklyn Heights. I went over there. That wasn't right. I knew *Mama Day* was going to be a water book so I wanted to live by the water. And then one day I was walking along Riverside Drive, looking for an apartment, and I passed a little cafe. I said, Oh my God, this is it! I realized that this is where my characters George and Cocoa had been walking when he told her the story of his mother.

That's what I mean when I say the images come. I feel that my characters were waiting. They weren't even born yet. I *did* know their names, that much I knew. But none of their relationship had happened. I didn't know what he did for a living, I didn't know how she was connected to Mama Day. It works like that, you know.

With *Brewster Place* the initial image was the rocking of the women. Mattie rocking Ciel. The first thing I ever wrote that became part of that section was the business of having an earth mother take this woman, who was in pain, in her arms and, through the rocking of her, bring her back to life. I wrote that and put it away for about a year not knowing what it meant and then ultimately I wrote a front story for it. The other scenes all came after that. Because I was curious about that woman who had done the rocking. And then she had a friend named Etta Mae. It built like that.

* * *

With *Mama Day* I remember the initial image specifically. It was a woman carrying a dead baby through the woods. I love *k* sounds—I don't like the word *kiss* because it sounds harsh but—I love the word *keening*. I never used that word in the book, because it turned out that it was a silent scene, but I saw this woman carrying a dead baby. And she was keening. Obviously her soul was keening to Mama Day. The only line I had was the old lady's when she said, "Go home, Bernice. Go home and bury your child." It brought me near tears. I didn't know why. I can recall specifically when that image appeared. I was living in Washington, D.C., finishing up *Linden Hills* when that image came to me. I can see myself sitting on the sofa. I had this rented furniture—I was there on a fellowship at George Washington University—and I was sitting on this couch. It had its back to a window. It was a big studio apartment and I was by myself. I was probably listening to music or maybe smoking a cigarette when the image came.

The same thing happened with *Bailey's Cafe*. I'd be listening to Duke Ellington's "Mood Indigo" and I would hear the sound of footsteps like scraping on a wharf. I knew that this man and woman, they were dancing. And for some reason the sound of their footsteps dragging on that wooden pier brought me to tears. I did not know why. I did not know their names. Ultimately I discovered that was Sadie and the Iceman. And I discovered why that sound.

You know which images are important because they hit you so powerfully. They're almost like psychic revelations or something. But you don't always know what they mean. I feel that I'm a sort of filter for these things. When *Mama Day* began to unfold, and I realized all the trauma this woman had gone through to have this child, I did not want the child to die. But there was no way for it not to happen. Because it had been one of those early images. Little Caesar's death was really a hard one for me but it was unthinkable not to have it happen.

* * *

For me at least a great deal of what I do is mystical. That's why I feel very blessed that, to date, I have been able to do justice to these images and stories that have been entrusted to me. I hope that in the future I continue to do so. I know what it takes. It takes a great deal of research, sometimes a great deal of effort and sacrifice. And yet you're still not promised that the spark of life will hit and that those characters and creations will touch people. I just keep praying that they do. I will do my part. And part of my part is the hard work of it all. And the searching.

Bailey's Cafe was a tough book for me. It dealt with sticky issues for me personally. All of these women have been victimized one way or the other because of their sexuality— or by the whole issue of female sexuality in the Western world—and the constraints on it. It was tough writing those stories. But they had come to me so I said, Hey Gloria, do whatever you must to tell these stories.

The pain of trying to find the words for things that I already know are going to be traumatic or sad is tough. When I finally got Willa out of the basement in Linden Hills I said, Oh, God! I was so tired of being cold and depressed. You know, it was hard being down there with her. A lot of black humor got me through Linden Hills. Midway through that novel, in what I call my basement scenes, I said, "The thesaurus has run out of synonyms for pain. What else can I use to say this damn woman is hurting?" I almost lost it with that book, I'll tell you.

My nephew's been with me since last year and I've written this last book with him here. I've basically lived alone most of my life. Having another person around tells you things about yourself you don't know. He will sometimes come out of his room and say, "Who are you talking to?" or "What are you laughing about?" and it'll dawn on me that I have been laughing aloud about something in the book.

I cried a few times writing Mama Day. I had to go back and do some rewriting because I was too kind to George, knowing he was going to die. I said, No, you cannot feel sorry for this man at this point. He doesn't know he's going to die. He's being a bastard. Go ahead and let him be nasty in this fight. You're affected by these things because they come from a place inside yourself, yet unreachable by you. So you're an audience too. You're the first audience to your work. And the most important audience.

Bailey's Cafe took four years—beginning with early images, on through the gestation period, and the frustration, and my thinking it would never get done and the writer's block. With every book there's been writer's block. *Bailey's Cafe* takes place in 1948 and '49 so it took a lot of research. The physical writing of it took a year but I'd done all the other prep work before.

I don't know how I break through my writer's block. I'm just so thankful I have each time. Each book it happened a different way. Sometimes it was because I was just on the wrong track. I remember *Mama Day:* I was down in Guadalajara, in this rented kind of apartment thing. The first two novels had been written third person, past tense, and I knew that I had mastered that, so I was sort of determined to tell this story that way. And that was not the way it was going to be told. I had to find that out. I remember suffering writer's block there for quite a few weeks. I know that in most cities, if there's an American consulate or an embassy, there's always a library. So I found out there was a consulate in Guadalajara and I said, let me go to the library there—just to kill time, you know, to read books. Rummaging through the shelves I picked up Faulkner's *As I Lay Dying*. I'd always been intrigued by writers who had these six-week wonders. Like *Their Eyes Were Watching God*—Zora Neale Hurston completely wrote that in six weeks. Faulkner allegedly wrote *As I Lay Dying* in six weeks when he worked as a night watchman. I want one of those six-week wonders! Anyway, I picked it up. I thought, Okay, I'll read this, I'd been meaning to. And that's when it hit me—what I was doing that was wrong. *As I Lay Dying* is structured in leapfrogging points of view. They're taking this woman's casket to Jackson, Mississippi—the casket is in the back of a wagon dragged by this mule—and each family member has some recollection of her that pushes the narrative along in the same way that mule is pulling that casket on to Jackson. It hit me that I would have to tell this story in shifting points of view, which is what I was waiting to know all along, you see. I didn't know anything about writing in the first person and I was terrified. But that was neither here nor there. That was what had to happen.

Sometimes you're just on the wrong track. Sometimes it's not ready yet. You know there's still more there for you to discover.

E. L. Doctorow had said once, years and years and years ago—I think before I even began writing "professionally"—that for him, writing a novel is like driving across country totally at night. Your headlights will only show you about two hundred feet in front of you but by going those two hundred feet you can make it to three thousand miles. I never forgot that. And indeed he was right. It is a journey into the unknown where often you're only conscious of, and what's only visible for you, is that step right in front of you. But you take it and you hope. And when you look up you've reached San Francisco. So what can I tell you? That's probably why we're always so insecure that the last sentence we wrote will be the last sentence ever. You're not promised anything. It's not as if it's wood and nails and glue and you're building a box. It's intangible.

Some people say they can actually direct their dreams. They can choose what they're going to dream. I cannot do that and I see my work the same way. I cannot choose that a situation or a character will come to life. I just hope that they do and I think, if I do my work and I open myself up enough and just let the situation talk, regardless of what I think about it one way or the other, it normally happens.

When I'm in the midst of a work, like in the thick of it, I have sometimes dreamt about the characters. It would be almost impossible for me not to have dreamt of those people because that's all I was thinking about day in, day out.

I've dreamt about Mama Day. The physical writing of *Mama Day* took seven months, so it was real intense. I was working twelve hours a day because I had been blocked for a long, long time. So when it began to flow it just gushed out of me. To the point where probably it wasn't real healthy. It would've been impossible for me not to have had dreams about the book.

Do I think that my dreams are telling me something? Yeah. I do, because I know what they are. They're just the subconscious cleaning house. But I connect that to my life—I don't connect it to my work per se. The dreams in my work come from my being a sort of habitual daydreamer.

You know what is interesting in my dreams? The same places will crop up. I dream of my grandmother's old apartment building, which is no longer standing. And there is an elaborate set of train tracks I dream about. It might look like Penn Station where you have the subway at one level and the commuter trains at the other level. I have often returned in sleeping dreams to those locales. Whenever I'm returning to the train station it's because there's something troubling going on with me as far as not knowing what particular direction I want to take with something.

I'll either be on the train in some weird situation knowing I should get off at a certain stop or I'm late for the train. Sometimes the train turns into this elevator. I've had the train-turn-into-the-elevator dream many times. The elevator becomes like a roller coaster. I'm terrified of roller coasters. And although it's an elevator, I know it's a train, and I'm saying, Oh I know what's going to happen, we're going to get to the top and then there's going to be this roller coaster ride. Or it'll be my not catching the train in time. Or I'm on there with unpleasant passengers. Various scenarios, same place.

My grandmother's old apartment building used to be a recurrent setting in my dreams when I was a child. I don't recall, the last ten or fifteen years, dreaming of that place again. Maybe it's been replaced by the return to the train station.

I, once in my life, had the exact same dream twice. That was the night before I got married and on my wedding night. My shrink told me it was just anxiety—marital anxiety or something.

I haven't done it recently but I do keep journals. I will keep them to help me sometimes when I'm stuck in a piece of work. I will write out what it is I want to say and why I'm not saying it. Or why I think I'm not saying it. I don't know why I haven't done this as much in the past few years but I'm not going to question all that for the same reason I didn't question why the serial daydreams phased out. I have countless journals but recently I've only used them when I'm stuck with the work. I've come to terms with a lot of demons that way.

All of my life the journals I've kept, or diaries—they were diaries when I was twelve, thirteen years old—were basically for me to give voice to things I couldn't say with my mouth. I never spoke much when I was younger. I was very shy. So the diary my mother gave me helped me do that. I have often said that I consider my work an extension of this: trying to give form to the inarticulate inside of myself. Always.

If certain dreams plague us they're probably things that plague us in our waking life, so writing—by going to that same level where dreams live, wherever that might be—helps to clean that out. It's one of the reasons I try not to censor the images that will often come up in my work. Some of them have troubled me. I've never physically had children but it's troubled me why babies always die in my work. I don't know why that happens. It didn't happen in the last book. Maybe I have resolved whatever I needed to resolve. I don't know. I don't dream about babies dying. In fact, in the last novel, a baby gets born.

JOHN NICHOLS

BORN IN BERKELEY, California, in 1940, John Nichols began writing at the age of fourteen. He sold his first novel, *The Sterile Cuckoo*, at twenty-two. His second novel, *The Wizard of Loneliness*, appeared in 1966 and was described by James F. Cotter as a "flawless and controlled work of art."

In the late sixties Nichols got actively involved in the movement to stop the Vietnam War and his writing became more political. He moved to Santa Fe, where he wrote long articles about the land and water problems of northern New Mexico for the *New Mexico Review*.

This research produced the germ of a novel, and in 1974 Nichols published *The Milagro Beanfield War*, a human tale of class struggle and cultural genocide. Although the book was largely ignored by critics it became an underground cult classic. *The Magic Journey*, published in 1978, and *The*

Nirvana Blues, in 1981, became known, along with *Milagro,* as the New Mexico Trilogy.

Besides his novels, which include *A Ghost in the Music, American Blood* and *An Elegy for September,* Nichols has written five works of nonfiction, among them the photo-essays, *If Mountains Die: A New Mexico Memoir, The Last Beautiful Days of Autumn* and *On the Mesa.*

John Nichols began writing screenplays in the early 1980s. He collaborated with director Constantin Costa-Gavras on the script for *Missing,* worked with Robert Redford on the movie version of *The Milagro Beanfield War* and developed film projects for directors Louis Malle and Karel Reisz.

He lives in Taos, New Mexico, where he is actively involved in protecting the natural environment.

───────

I'VE USED dreams in different pieces of writing, almost word for word, but the one dream that wound up being a major part of a piece of work was a dream about putting body parts together. It is recurrent in *American Blood.* The hero of that novel, the narrator, is a Vietnam veteran who has a recurring dream that he's wandering through a field of people, victims of war, who have been blown apart. He keeps trying to put the limbs together—you know, the head back on the proper body, the limbs back on the proper body—and he never gets it right. He can't do it. He keeps creating these grotesques until the final scene in the book when he makes some kind of peace with the whole horror that he went through and comes to some kind of resolution. In the dream, he actually manages to put people together again. They get up and walk away, whole. That came out of a dream that I had once. It wasn't making people whole or anything. It was a fractured kind of dream. I remember wandering through some kind of field with a lot of damaged bodies lying around and feeling utterly desperate, trying to get them together. The dream never really went anywhere and they weren't Vietnamese people, they were strangers. But that was a powerful image to me and I wound up using it with a fair amount of dramatic effect.

I embellished the dream. I changed the context, changed the personality that was involved in it. I related it to the Vietnam War, made a lot of the people Vietnamese, made other people friends of the narrator. In the book, the narrator has a girlfriend whose daughter is brutally murdered, almost by accident, the way women often are. She's one of the characters that he winds up putting together. She gives him a hug and wanders off at the end of the scene. I gave personalities to a lot of the bodies. I have characters in the book who are maimed or crippled who, in a sense, are made whole in the end of the novel. All of that came out of the dream which was just a fragment that I remembered as powerful and very disturbing.

There's a dream I had once which I put into *An Elegy for September*—a very erotic dream of being inside a kind of bubble or a placenta, floating through what was apparently outer space with a woman I did not know. It seems like most of the erotic dreams that I've had in my life are with people that I don't know. Just total strangers. That's kind of curious to me. This was a total stranger. I was just floating in this kind of bubble, wanting very desperately to make love, but not being able to because any kind of sharp or passionate movement might rend a tear in the placenta-bubble and let in a vacuum. It was a tremendously erotic dream because I had to withhold. The woman that I was with really wanted to make love. She kept pushing and pushing. I was terrified to actually generate that kind of passion or action for fear of tearing the bubble.

That dream may actually be related to my health. Because when my heart got really bad, it became much more difficult to have orgasms. Simply because I was terrified. Sometimes orgasms would trigger really bad fibrillations so it was hard to push things over the edge that way. Because adrenaline can trigger fibrillation when you've got a bad heart, it can psychologically effect whether or not you want to push to a climax. But what a great way to commit suicide!

Most of the heart medicine that I'm supposed to take has a tendency to make you impotent. It's not difficult to get an erection, but it's almost impossible to have an orgasm. It's like having Novocain in your body. I really don't like taking the medicines because it's uncomfortable to live your life feeling kind of Novocained. It does something to your energy. It controls your heart and makes you feel better but it also calms down that sort of nervous, sensual erotic energy.

I used to have lots of erotic dreams and I loved them. It's been a while since I've had those kinds of dreams. I used to love to have wet dreams because they were so sexy. They ended in great orgasms. I used to even be able to almost *conduct* them to orgasm, you know? When I was young I'd be really embarrassed by wet dreams so I'd kind of wake up and try and stop them. Then I ceased being embarrassed and found that it was fun to let them run their course. I'm not a person who can wake up from a dream and then go back to sleep because I really want to see how it turns out or finish it. But there were years when it seemed like I could do some kind of psychological click inside my body without waking up that would allow an erotic dream to reach its conclusion.

I have lots of anxiety dreams, some that are easy to interpret. God, I remember when I first got married—I was twenty-four— having all kinds of anxiety dreams. And when I was getting divorced this last time, having lots of dreams about my ex-wife, Juanita—like being in houses full of people, searching for her. I'd catch a glimpse in another room of her, disappearing, hand in hand with another man. Then I'd ask people and they wouldn't know where they'd gone, that kind of thing.

When we got divorced I gave Juanita my house, the house that I'd lived in for twenty years. Since then I have had maybe a dozen dreams relating to that house and the loss of it. Dreams she's not in very much. Dreams about irrigating the two little fields at the house where the water gets out of hand and starts flooding everything. Running around frantically, trying to build dikes to stop the water from flooding and to control it.

The other day I dreamt that I was walking down this typical American Mapleville–type street with Juanita. I had a real yearning for that kind of peacefulness. She was talking about friendship and being friendly. I was keeping deliberately aloof, not falling into it, not biting, you know? And yet yearning to do it, to be friends.

Probably the most recurrent situation that I've dreamt about, that's consistent over years and years and years, is one of defecating: taking a shit. It's always in real embarrassing situations. Like I really have to go to the bathroom and I'm in a public place and I cannot hold it in. So I wind up going into a doorway on a crowded street and just squatting and taking a shit and being utterly humiliated. That's a kind of recurrent dream that's very disconcerting. I've got no idea what that means. I'm sure that must be something common.

Obviously many of the anxiety dreams I've had, particularly about women that I've been involved with, have been triggered by the nature of the relationship: by arguments, by breaking up, by getting together, by jealousy, by defensiveness, by insecurity. But that dream about defecating, my guess would be that it's something that probably has occurred in all kinds of situations going on in my life.

I can't think of dreams that really relate to the process of writing books. I have had a couple of dreams which people I've worked with are in. I remember one dream concerning Robert Redford, having a really warm relationship with him. He was in trouble. It was a very gentle dream, very unlike the making of a movie.

I don't remember ever having an antagonistic dream about Costa-Gavras or Robert Redford or people that I've worked with. I have a faint memory of being kind of deferential toward them, but them usually being fairly friendly. The dreams seem to be much more forgiving and compassionate than life.

Film actors, every now and then, will come into my dreams. And people that you would not suspect at all. But also, several times, I've had erotic dreams with people I know. Women who, in real life, don't turn me on at all. Not even remotely. It's very, very weird to dream about them in that way.

I've had lots of anxiety dreams about my kids. I had a terrifying dream last year about Luke, my son, where he was going to rob some old people and beat them up. This would be very unlike Luke. I remember going to a window of this house and shooting my own son to stop him as he was going to attack these people. And then holding him while he bled to death. Apologizing. It was a very disturbing kind of dream.

I remember I had one dream when I was living in Barcelona, Spain. It is sort of my only experience with ESP. It was 1962 or '63 and I had a horrible nightmare about my brother Tim being in very serious trouble. I forget exactly what the dream was but it was one of those nightmares you try and get out of because something so horrible is happening.

I just couldn't get awake. Finally I managed to sort of rip my eyes open. My hands were clenched up in the air in front of my face from tension. And while I was staring at my hands they evaporated because they were really down at my sides all along. Clenched. I was awake, looking at my hands and then they evaporated. It was like seeing an image on a TV screen after it has been turned off.

A few days later I got a letter that my brother Tim was in the hospital with serious heart fibrillations that had locked into something.

Many of my dreams are very violent. There are an awful lot of fights. People chase me, people shoot at me. There's all kinds of hostility and confrontation and struggle—real batterings and that kind of stuff. But those are never nightmares like these things I'm recalling. They're kind of brutal but not in that really terrifying way.

Sometimes I'm the victim and sometimes I'm chased. Sometimes I'm very brutal back, including really mangling people, just beating the shit out of them. Usually the people are pretty threatening. They've threatened me first, so it seems to go both ways.

My dreams are kind of narrative, but they move around so much and they change shape so much that they seem really psychedelic. Usually all I can capture when I think about them are bits and pieces. It's rare that I can really remember a long continuity of dreams. When I was writing them down I found that I got better and better at it. It's almost like you train yourself to pay more attention to the dreams. You train yourself to retain them. I don't know to what extent you actually influence the act of dreaming by being self-conscious about conserving them. I wondered about that, because the experimenter always effects the experiment, but it's almost like getting in training. When I was really paying attention, trying to write down dreams and making that conscious effort I would retain a lot more.

I started recording my dreams when I left my marriage and got divorced. I was living alone in a really tiny apartment and it was one of those stages in life where you say I've got to get my shit together. I've got to do things that I've promised to do all the time. I also wasn't sleeping with anybody so I didn't have the disruption of waking them up if I woke up and started scribbling or turned on the light.

For a long time it was almost like I thought I didn't dream because I never paid attention. Or I just woke up so swiftly that I didn't remember anything. I was getting so little sleep that I never got down deep enough or I never had the time to drowse. I find dreaming is usually a lighter sleeping mode than a real deep sleeping mode. I love taking naps in the afternoon because

you kind of drowse. Then I find dreams will just come up and
go crazy. It's like looking at a kaleidoscope of impressions. I like
that kind of thing a lot.

I have a feeling that if I had kept writing my dreams down
they would have become more and more influential. So many of
them are convoluted and strange and weird: like one I had about
my daughter Tanya turning into a little embryo the size of a
potato that turned into something like a cricket that I dropped
in the mud. They're just sagas that don't seem to make any sense
outside of being sort of dadaistic or surreal. They're dreams like
Salvador Dali paintings. And when you write them down in cold
blood they seem pretty disturbing or grotesque. I mean, they're
not disturbing to me. It doesn't seem to me, particularly as a
writer, that there should be any area of investigation or
indulgence that isn't at least interesting no matter how brutal or
weird or crazy it is. But I think that scares people.

I remember, when I first got married when I was twenty-
four, handing my wife, Ruby, books to read. One of the books
I wrote was about the last week in the life of a homeless
alcoholic in New York City—this was in 1964 or '65—who
went around with a cart collecting cardboard. Ruby was just
appalled. She couldn't read any of my books because my mind
seemed out of control to her. My whole life in writing is a
struggle to free myself from all the censorship that I've been
trained into from birth. That's what the struggle to learn to be
a writer is about.

I've always loved the grotesque. Some of my favorite
painters are Jan Van Eyck and Brueghel and Heironymus Bosch.
Peter Blume, he's a kind of German fantasist. I just love
that stuff.

American Blood is like one bad nightmare. It was very
difficult to write, to find the courage to just do it, to be able to
write that freely about the whole thing.

I'd been working on related stuff going back into the sixties.
I've written seventy, seventy-five, eighty books. Only published
fourteen of them so far. Many of the books that I've written,

they've been out there, but they just were no good. Because it's real hard to control things. I wrote a book in 1967 about a guy who wins the Medal of Honor, comes back to the United States, is appalled by the exploitation within the country and winds up murdering his family at a cocktail party. Then he rips off his Medal of Honor and throws it in the ocean. The book was just about the horrors of both his life post-stress syndrome and the cruelty and brutality of the culture that he was theoretically fighting to save. But the book was so angry, so nihilistic and so undisciplined that it wasn't even worth giving it to a publisher. I've always tried to deal with lots of different themes including those kinds of themes. I guess *American Blood* was a way I finally managed to do it successfully.

Getting into dreams, writing down dreams, paying attention to them and to their structure might be a way of training to produce another kind of literature that has a different control, a literature that is freer and that deals with all the gargoyles and pterodactyls in some kind of coherent way. I don't know.

Dreams may seem chaotic, but one can always create structure. Life really doesn't have all that much structure. I mean books are really putting an awful lot of artificial structure on what often can be pretty structureless. Dreams are just another part of that experience. It's as easy to pull a structure out of a dream as it is to pull a structure out of daily life. I mean I could write a short story about yesterday, but I would exclude ninety-five percent of what happened because that's all boring. Yet there would be four or five incidents that I could put together into some little pastiche or painting that made sense. You can certainly do that with dreams. But you'd have to study them. If you've studied dreams you may understand the patterns that they have. I've always put dreams into books, always used them to explain aspects of structure or emotion, by carefully selecting and shaping the dreams that get used. I don't think I've ever put dreams into books that make no sense on the surface. Many dreams don't. So maybe that's a real lie when I put dreams in.

The great striving in the history of humanity is for order and structure. In science and physics it's to discover a unified field theory that makes sense of everything. And yet the more scientists seem to study the more they're coming up with the idea that it's really much more chaotic. That it doesn't make sense. That there's something we really don't understand and that chaos is more powerful than that kind of unity. An artist is always involved in essentially finding a kind of unity or a structure that you can draw people into, that makes sense, that gives a wholeness to experience. Many artists try and push it beyond, into how you represent that chaos. I'm not real good at that. But it would be fun to pursue dreams for a couple of years. Type them all up and then see where all the connecting things are. I don't know if you would wind up training yourself to actually dream in a pattern that you wouldn't have dreamt in otherwise. That I don't know.

JACK PRELUTSKY

JACK PRELUTSKY may be labeled a children's poet but his phenomenal success must be in part attributable to the laughter his verses evoke in book-buying parents. Prelutsky captures the difficulties of being a child in our modern world—from the horrors of cafeteria food to the frustration of arbitrary bed times. Elephants, chickens, witches and ghouls are among the sundry creatures featured in Prelutsky's pun-filled poetry.

Born in Brooklyn, New York, in 1940, Prelutsky experimented with a variety of artistic forms before discovering his talent as a poet. Over the course of twenty years Prelutsky has published more than three dozen books of poetry including *Something Big Has Been Here, The New Kid on the Block, Ride a Purple Pelican, Tyrannosaurus Was a Beast, The Queen of Eene, The Headless Horseman Rides Tonight* and *The Baby Uggs Are Hatching.*

He is the editor of several classic anthologies including *The Random House Book of Poetry for Children* as well as *Read Aloud Rhymes for the Very Young* and *Poems of a Nonny Mouse.*

In 1991 Prelutsky published his first book designed specifically for adults, *There'll Be a Slight Delay, and Other Poems for Grown-ups.* He currently lives on Mercer Island in Washington State with his wife, Carolyn, and an ever-expanding collection of frogs.

———

*Today I shall powder my elephant's ears
and paint his posterior red,
I'll trim all his toe nails with suitable shears
and place a toupee on his head.*

*Tonight I shall tie a balloon to his tail
and wrap him in feathers and furs,
then fasten his necktie and velveteen veil
and put on his boots and his spurs.*

*There'll be a warm smile on my elephant's face
as we're welcomed to Pachyderm Hall,
to dance until daybreak with elegant grace
at the elephants' masquerade ball.*

That poem came from a dream. It's odd because the elephant came first from a mouse. A little friend, who was then six years old, said, "I had an idea about dancing with a mouse." I said, "That's very interesting" and I went to sleep that night and dreamt about dancing with elephants. There were thousands of elephants and it was a masquerade ball. Now an elephants' masquerade ball is very exciting. After all, you need a big hall. And toilet facilities are important.

I don't know about the psychological significance of it but I've probably written about eight or ten poems about elephants

over the years. I like to take simple ideas sometimes, things that
we've heard all our lives and rework them into new forms. I
remember when I was a kid I heard jokes—How do you know
when there's an elephant in the refrigerator? The answer I
remember is, You can't close the door. How do you know when
you have an elephant in the house? You can smell the peanuts
on his breath. Et cetera. I said, Wouldn't it be fun to put a bunch
of these ideas together into a poem? And, since I do enjoy
writing about elephants, I wound up with "An Elephant Is Hard
to Hide."

I get a lot of inspiration from my dreams. Actually just
about all of the poems in my two nightmare books, *The
Headless Horseman Rides Tonight* and *Nightmares: Poems to
Trouble Your Sleep* came from dreams. The only exception
might be the first poem that I wrote, which was the poem called
"The Bogeyman." That one came from direct experience. My
mother used to threaten me with the bogeyman when I was a
kid. She'd say, "Wash your hands or the bogeyman's going to
get you." Or "Eat your spinach or the bogeyman's going to get
you." And that sort of led to the book.

After I wrote the bogeyman poem, I realized I was on to
something. I wrote all the poems in the two *Nightmares* books
between about midnight and six in the morning. I would wake
up in a cold sweat and I'd be dreaming about a witch or a
werewolf or a goblin or something like that. It was a
particularly unpleasant time.

I had dreamt about the witch but was missing some parts of
the poem. I was having dinner with my girlfriend in Boston and in
the middle of dinner I got up from the table and picked up a paper
napkin and just scribbled the poem. I said "Thank you so much
because you've just inspired a wonderful poem." I showed it to
her and she slapped me and said, "Get out." I never saw her again.
I tried to explain to her that the witch I was writing about was
really the opposite of what she was. But she didn't buy that.
Needless to say, I learned a little about romance that evening.

* * *

Some of my dreams are very pleasant actually. I've had one for the past couple of months I'm trying to hold on to. It's my magic chair. I dream about it about twice a week. It's sort of my magic carpet but it's a big yellow chair, overstuffed and it has a gear shift with five on the floor. No reverse, so you can only go forward. It serves not only as an automobile, it's also an airplane. I fly around the world and see all sorts of things from the comfort of my magic yellow chair. I might do a book about it someday.

When I was living in Albuquerque, I was looking out the window of my studio one day and I fell asleep. I usually keep the radio on while I'm working—usually to classical music, because I need quiet background—so I listen to something like Mozart or Brahms. I was thinking of the plants and the flowers that were growing there and I dreamt that they had all changed to musical instruments. The trees, instead of being trees were oboes and cellos and bassoons. Maybe it was a combination of looking at the garden and listening to the music, but when I woke up after a little nap, I immediately wrote a poem called "I Am Growing a Glorious Garden."

After watching an episode of "The A Team" on television I had a nightmare about Mr. T. He was covered with vegetables. Of course the poem that resulted has nothing to do with Mr. T now. I just kind of fantasized what kind of creature would want to spend its life submerged in vegetables.

Sometimes when I finish writing a poem, I look at it and say, What can I do with this, can I write the opposite? I've done this a couple times. For example, in *Something Big Has Been Here,* I have a poem about my mother's cooking, called "My Mother Made a Meatloaf," about a meatloaf that we never ate because it was uncuttable. We tried everything, blow torches, hippopotamus, nothing worked. And as soon as I finished that I wrote a poem called "The Turkey Shot Out of the Oven," just the opposite, about a food that explodes just before you get to eat it.

Sometimes to get in the mood for work I do a bunch of *New York Times* crossword puzzles. I play a lot of word games and just sort of futz around for a while. Sometimes I'll be doing a puzzle and there will be a little fragment or word that will hit me in a new way. It might be something that I've seen a thousand times before. It'll just hit me and I'll play with that for a while. This happens in life, too.

I was in my local market and I was buying chicken for supper. I was going to do the cooking that night so, being naturally lazy, I decided to get boneless breast of chicken. I'd bought it many times, but that day something occurred to me that had never occurred to me before. I asked myself, what about the rest of the chicken. Was that boneless too?

Well as soon as I thought of that I started asking questions about chickens. I mean can a boneless chicken walk? Can it fly? What do the other chickens think about it? Where does it make it's home? Does it have friends? Can it walk erect? I played with those ideas when I got home. I went to bed and I actually dreamed about this. As a matter of fact from this dream two poems have happened. One is "Last Night I Dreamed of Chickens" and the other is "Ballad of a Boneless Chicken."

When I was writing that poem, I went to bed asking myself the question, How can I end this poem about a boneless chicken? I fell asleep and in the middle of the night I woke up and I said, Yeah! because I knew how I was going to end the poem. I had a dream about a chicken laying an egg. Well, what kind of an egg does a boneless chicken lay? The answer is revealed in the last verse.

> *I'm a basic boneless chicken,*
> *Yes, I have no bones inside,*
> *I'm without a trace of ribcage,*
> *Yet I hold myself with pride.*

Other hens appear offended
by my total lack of bones,
they discuss me impolitely
in derogatory tones. . . .

Since a chicken finds it tricky
To parade on boneless legs,
I stick closely to the hen house,
Laying little scrambled eggs.

I deal a lot with nonsense. Nonsense is a kind of organized chaos. It's setting up a system which does not exist. But you treat it seriously and you stay within the boundaries, like an artist should stay within the frame of the paintings. If the artist starts spilling over onto the wall and onto the floor it tends to mean less. But if you set limits . . .

In the case of the boneless chicken, what I did was ask all the questions you're supposed to ask. All those who, what, where, when, how, why questions, as if you're asking about something serious.

If you start with a ridiculous premise—which is, by the way, what most dreams are—and if you ask just those ordinary straightforward questions about a ridiculous idea, you don't have to stretch anymore. Because all the answers are going to be ridiculous or weird. That's a technique I use with much of my writing.

I think limits are important. Robert Frost, when asked why he didn't write nonrhyming verse said, he'd just as soon play tennis without a net. I happen to like a lot of nonrhyming verse, but I think it helps to have a framework. For example, I'm writing some sonnets for adults. Well, I'm restricted to fourteen lines. So even if I thought I needed sixteen to say something, I'm not allowed to have it. I have to be more creative because I have to fit that extra two lines of ideas in somewhere. And it's a challenge. I find limits very challenging.

Several years ago I was working on a book about dinosaurs.

I wrote about dinosaurs eating and dinosaurs walking around and dinosaurs either eating plants or other dinosaurs, and I'd run out of things to say. But my publisher said we needed one more poem to finish the book. And just that week a new dinosaur was discovered four or five miles from my house in New Mexico. I knew then that I had it. It was then the largest dinosaur ever discovered. It was the first land creature that was longer, if not heavier, than the blue whale. It was called Seismosaurus, which means "Earthshaker." Well I didn't know much about it. All I knew was that it was very big. So I went with that. I live and die by the thesaurus so I opened it up and was delighted because there, in the exact order, were the words that I needed. I didn't even have to turn two words around. There were all the words for "big," which described what I wanted, and it was wonderful because the second word rhymed with the fourth word. And the sixth word rhymed with what I wanted to say at the end of the poem. It was magic. And it's called "Seismosaurus Was Enormous."

> Seismosaurus was enormous,
> Seismosaurus was tremendous,
> Seismosaurus was prodigious,
> Seismosaurus was stupendous.
>
> Seismosaurus was titanic,
> Seimosaurus was colossal,
> Seimosaurus now is nothing
> But a monumental fossil.

And that's it.

One of the secrets of art, whether it's painting or music or anything else, is knowing that it's just as important what you leave out, as what you put in. I could've gone on with that Seismosaurus poem—and Seismosaurus was strong and Seismosaurus ate broccoli or whatever. It wouldn't've added anything to the poem. It's what you don't put in. I find that sometimes I'll have lines and I'll say, wait, this isn't saying anything new, this isn't adding anything. If I've written a four-verse poem there's a good chance it started out as five verses. I didn't need the extra one and combined some of the ideas.

But nothing is thrown out. Nothing. Everything is saved. Usually when I finish a book I have more ideas left over than when I started. A lot of the passages in *Something Big Has Been Here* came from leftover ideas. They were things that just didn't work. They were not ready. Or they were just off-shoots, maybe just a word that I didn't use, and that led to a brand-new poem.

In *The New Kid on the Block* there's a poem called "Forty Performing Bananas" about some bananas who get up on stage and sing and dance. There are some banana puns in there like "our features are rather a-peeling" and "people drive here in bunches to see us," "our splits earn us worldly renown," and I wanted to outdo myself. When I was a kid I had discovered that, if you squeezed a hot dog just right, it would shoot across the room. I stored that idea. And then one day I was in a novelty store and I bought a little Styrofoam glider in the shape of a hot dog. I put those ideas together and said, This could be a poem. So I wrote down all the hot dog puns I could think of. "Mustered in formation" was easy and "ketch up with each other," but there were still some key ideas that were eluding me. I wrote down all those words but I could not think of a way of using sauerkraut in the poem. And then I had a dream about the flying hot dogs and I knew exactly what I had to do. When I sing the poem I pretend to be the lead hot dog whose name happens to be Major Weiner. Some of the puns are hidden, by the way. They're not all obvious.

> *We're fearless flying hot dogs,*
> *The famous unflappable five,*
> *We're mustered in formation*
> *To climb, to dip, to dive,*

We spread our wings with relish,
Then reach for altitude,
We're aerobatic weiners,
The fastest flying food . . .

The throngs applaud our antics,
They cheer us long and loud,
There's never a chili reception,
There's never a sour crowd,

And if we may speak frankly,
We are a thrilling sight,
We're fearless flying hot dogs,
The delicate essence of flight.

I was so happy when I woke up and wrote *delicate essence!*
That's Kosher delicate essence by the way. These are all-beef
hot dogs.

I'd been puzzled by this poem for months and months. I'd
started it, I would try it in the shower, I'd put it away, I'd sit at
my desk, I'd do it on trains and planes and automobiles and it
wouldn't work. I always have a notebook and paper by my bed
and I woke up one Sunday morning with a big grin on my face.
The poem was complete in my head—I'd dreamt the whole
thing, and I just said *yeaaaah.*

My biggest suggestion to writers is: keep a notebook or a
piece of paper and a pencil by the bed. I mean I wake up almost
every night and write something down. It's the rare night that
I don't. Sometimes you dream that you've found a cure for
cancer or something and you think it's brilliant and, of course,
you wake up and it's crap, garbage. There's nothing there. But
about a third of the time there's a very good idea there. It may
be something as silly as sour crowd and delicate essence but you
never know.

In the sixties I was one of those counterculture types. I still have
a lot of the same values I had back then even though I have

reached the half-century mark—people are more important to me than money and property and that sort of thing. I wanted to be an artist but not everything works out the way you want it to. I was about twenty-three years old and I was searching for myself. I had tried all sorts of arts, along with all sorts of day labor, I was also doing things like acting, and singing, and photographing and making pots and terrariums. I used to draw imaginary animals. I remember one creature I invented had four legs, but the two on one side were shorter than the two on the other. It lived under a mountain and could only walk in one direction, so it was perfectly suited to its environment. There was another tiny bird that lived atop a hundred-foot-tall tree. The problem was that the bird couldn't fly. Fortunately it was also perfectly suited to its environment because it had a hundred-and-one-foot-long beak and it fed off the ground. It just waited and things crawled in. It worked very nicely.

I drew a bunch of these creatures, and after about six months, I had about two dozen. They were very painstaking. They took me about a week apiece and they were all two dimensional. I still can't draw perspective.

One evening I sat down, looked at them, and said, Oh well, they need poems to go with them. I do not know where that idea came from to this day. I had never written poetry. I'd never even written. I'd flunked English One twice in college and English Two once. Or the other way around. I'd showed no promise as a writer. I certainly had never written any poetry. But I sat down that evening and in two hours I'd written two dozen little poems to go along with the drawings that took me six months to do.

A friend who had published a few children's books saw what I had done and made me take the whole business in to his editor and she said, You're very talented—we want to publish you.

I said, Really, you like my drawings? She said, You're kidding. You're absolutely the worst artist we've ever seen. You have no talent in that direction. But you have a natural gift here for verse. And it went on from there. She encouraged me. I started writing about real animals and one thing lead to another. Now I've got about forty books.

I guess I have a facility with words. It's certainly a lot easier than it used to be. But still, even the ones that sound easy take a lot of work. Once in a while they do just come out. I sit down and I write and it's done. But even those have a word or two that changes. Some of those poems take ten, thirty, fifty rewrites before they're right. I can work for weeks and weeks on a single poem. The whole trick is to make it seem easy, as though, hey, I could have done that, anybody could have done that. I've even had one of my illustrators say that to me, "God, I work so hard on these drawings and you just sort of put these poems out there. Gee, I could do that." And I said, "Well, good." And he hasn't. But that's okay because I can't do the drawings.

Many poems don't really end up the way they start. I believe in serendipity. Just as I thought I was going to be an artist and I turned out to be a writer. I discovered my talent only because I was looking for something else. Well, it's the same thing with kids. You tell them to do something and they do something else. Sometimes the thing they do is better than the thing you ask them to do and you better pay attention to that. I have a poem, it's kind of autobiographical. It's a bittersweet poem about paying attention to children.

> *The day they sent Sam to the grocery store*
> *To purchase a carton of eggs,*
> *He brought back a pear with a pearl in its core,*
> *And a leopard with lavender legs.*
>
> *He returned with an elephant small as a mouse,*
> *A baseball that bounces a mile,*
> *A little tame dragon that heats up the house,*
> *And a lantern that lights when they smile.*
>
> *Sam brought them a snow ball that never feels cold,*
> *A gossamer carpet that flies,*

A salmon of silver, a grackle of gold,
And ermine with emerald eyes.

They never send Sam to the store any more,
No matter how often he begs,
For he brought back a dodo that danced on the floor,
But he didn't bring home any eggs.

REYNOLDS PRICE

OVER THE LAST thirty years, Reynolds Price has
written more than twenty-one books including novels, plays,
essays, poetry, biblical translations and memoirs. His best
known works are set in the small towns of the rural South
during the 1940s and '50s.

Reynolds Price was born in Macon, North Carolina, in
1933 and began writing at the age of twenty-one. His first
novel, *A Long and Happy Life,* won the William Faulkner
Foundation Award for Notable First Novel in 1962. This was
followed by *A Generous Man* in 1966, *Love and Work* in
1968, *The Surface of Earth* in 1975, *The Source of Light* in
1981 and *Mustian: Two Novels and a Story* in 1983.

In 1984, Price had just completed the first third of a new
novel when a pencil-thin tumor was discovered growing in
his upper spine. Subsequent surgery and radiation treatments

left him paralyzed from the waist down. Unable to write, Price took to drawing pictures much as he had in his childhood. When he finally found the energy to write again, he completed his unfinished novel, *Kate Vaiden,* which earned him the National Book Critics Circle Award in 1986.

Despite being confined to a wheelchair, Price has become even more prolific since the cancer, producing *The Laws of Ice* in 1986, *Good Hearts* in 1988, *The Tongues of Angels* and *The Use of Fire* in 1990, and *Blue Calhoun* in 1992.

Each year Price teaches one semester at his alma mater, Duke University, offering a class in writing and a class in the poetry of Milton. He lives in North Carolina.

———

I GUESS I've been someone who's taken dreams seriously virtually all of my conscious life. I remember being conscious of dreams, in childhood, as scary. I suppose I was in high school and early college when I first learned about Freud and the fact that dreams were taken seriously as clues to the psychic life and to psychic health. And once I really started writing full time, dreams began very quickly to feed quite directly into my work.

Sometimes, when I'm working intensely on a book, especially if I'm working on a particular character that I'm fascinated by, I'll find myself dreaming dreams which seem to me to be very appropriate to that kind of person. These dreams seem to be more appropriate to the character I'm writing about than to me. I really feel as though, not only am I creating that person's life in the daytime while I'm writing the book but I almost seem to be dreaming that character's dreams. I have literally transcribed some of those dreams and attributed them to the character. I did that in a novel of mine called *Love and Work,* and I remember doing a lot of that in *The Surface of Earth.* I felt these dreams were some kind of deep unconscious response to my work on the book itself and therefore were appropriate to the characters.

Obviously I was the person who was dreaming, and the dreams were relevant to me as well, but since I was imagining a particular character and was involved with that character's mind for a period of months or sometimes years, then often the dreams came to seem more relevant to them.

In *Love and Work* all the dreams as I recall are dreamed by one character, the central male character of the novel. But in *The Surface of Earth*, the dreams were a kind of a chorus dreamt by a lot of different kinds of people. I was immersed in that novel for a very long time, for nearly three years, and I kind of made it a rule that, if I used a dream at all, I'd try to use it straight, the way it had come to me or, in any case, the way I remembered it when I woke up.

In my three books of poems I have several poems, maybe as many as half a dozen, which I simply call the dream of so and so—"The Dream of a House," "The Dream of Food," "The Dream of Lee." Those are all instances when I woke up one morning and really thought, Gosh, that was an absolutely fascinating dream—not one of the usual boring kind that you know you're not supposed to tell your friends at breakfast but something that was really a wonderful story in itself, that I thought anybody could enjoy reading. So very quickly on the night after I had those dreams, I'd sit down and write them up as straightforward poems, not offering any of the details of the dream narrative. Those are instances where I was very conscious of wanting to preserve a particular story—just because the story seemed to be interesting, quite aside from whatever it might mean about me or anybody else related to my life.

Dreams are obviously the art of the artless. I mean people who don't write poetry, choreograph, paint pictures, whatever, do in fact, every night when they're asleep, construct works of art in their heads. The constructs usually turn out to be as impermanent as snowmen; but whatever dreams are about, they do seem to be everybody's attempt at, among other things, constructing storylike pieces of art.

I've never really sat down and asked any professional artist

friend of mine about his or her dreams, but I have often wondered if they're different from dreams of other people. Lots of
my nonwriting friends have told me dreams of theirs, and they
usually wind up seeming as crazy and boring and not worth
listening to as most of my own—ninety-eight percent of mine
are like that. They seem cuckoo by daylight; and yet there have
been these times when I've had dreams that were very lucid,
well-made, well-ordered. Maybe they're the result of my having
a trained narrative mind. In any case, they're the ones I want to
write down because they really do seem like good stories.
They're consistent all the way through—people don't suddenly
turn into bears and start running downhill, they enact a sort of
coherent narrative.

There was one dream in which quite clearly my brain was
perceiving that I had cancer years before the doctor ever found
it, years before I had conscious symptoms. That discovery came
in a dream I turned into a poem called "The Dream of a
House." It's in my *Vital Provisions*. In the dream I'm this mysterious solitary person and there is some kind of guide beside me.
I'm being led through this incredibly beautiful house by a man
who keeps saying, "Well, this is yours, this beautiful place; and
in it are all the pictures you've ever wanted, all the books. It's
all here; you've got this." Then I say to the guide, "Well, this is
fantastic. Am I going to be alone here?" And he says, "Oh no.
Come with me," and he opens this closet in the front hall. It's
a normal closet with nice new clothes in it and hats. Then he
pulls the clothes aside, and there's this human being who's
literally been crucified in the closet—this man who's been obviously terribly beaten and mutilated, and he's hanging on a cross.
The guide just says, "This is yours forever. This will be yours
forever."

At the end of the dream I felt very happy. I woke up and
thought, My God! What kind of weird religious fantasy is this?
That was probably in the late 1970s, around '76 or so. It was
1984 before I found out that I had this weird thing hanging up
in my spine that was ultimately going to become a torturing

companion for the rest of my life. Certainly I've looked back on this dream as some sort of premonition.

When I first had the dream it fascinated me because it seemed just like an amazing but beautiful story. And since I've basically lived alone all my life—lived alone in a house that's too big for one person, filled with things that I love and have collected over the years—I thought it was some kind of reflection on the fact that I've lived alone and haven't ever perhaps had a need of anybody sufficient to make me arrange to live in a pair. But it's hard for me to look back now, more than fifteen years, and recall what I thought about it. I certainly wrote it down immediately and published it immediately, so it didn't seem to me to be embarrassingly revealing. If I'd felt that it told the world my darkest secret I probably wouldn't have published it. But it just seemed a good story, a fascinating eerie story that would be of interest to somebody who's not interested in Reynolds Price.

Some six years later, within a matter of days after getting a diagnosis of cancer, I recognized the importance of that old dream. I don't keep a journal so I don't have a direct record of when it dawned on me, but it would've been very very soon. Then through the years, various friends of mine and various strangers have said, Wow, when did you write that poem? Because I published it long before I ever knew.

After I'd had my initial surgery and radiation, I also had a great run of dreams which were nightmares about cancer. Several of them were strong dreams in which I acted out a kind of personal refusal to die. I wrote those dreams down at the time too. I think they were very important in convincing me that my body really didn't want this thing to take over, that I shouldn't accept this. I should fight it and not just lie down and obey the doctors' prediction that I was going to die in about a month, which is what the doctors were saying eight years ago. Knock on all available wood, but I've had clear scans for eight years. The cancer's been gone for eight years now.

Over that first year after my surgery in June of '84, my legs

slowly became paralyzed. After about twelve months I had
totally lost the use of my legs. They were weak from the surgery
on, and the radiation weakened them further, but it was about
twelve months before it got so I absolutely couldn't stand up. I
couldn't use a walker, I couldn't use a walking cane and had to
be in the chair. Very near the point at which I finally had to
recognize that I couldn't use my legs, I started having a series of
really scary dreams which were about total paralysis. I didn't
write any of them down because they were so appalling. I mean
I would literally see myself, feel myself, lying in a bed so paralyzed that I couldn't even blink my eyes. My reading of that has
always been that my mind was sort of trying out the worst
possible scenarios. *Is it going to get worse?* Theoretically it
could have become that bad if the tumor really had grown up
from my upper neck, the highest point it could reach before
going into my brain. Thank God, it didn't happen; and once I
had run the worst of the scenarios the dreams stopped. I remember they lasted a period of about three weeks and then just
completely went away.

Now, in my dreams, I mostly don't seem to be in a wheelchair. I seem to be the old me who's up and walking around as
I was for my first fifty-one years. Now that I mention it, I can't
even remember a dream in which I'm living the way I presently
live—which is as an active person in a chair. I may have had
dreams where I'm in a wheelchair, but they don't immediately
come to mind.

I had great flying dreams as a child. I was always sort of
zooming around on my arms and showing the other kids what
a great pilot I was, how I could fly and they couldn't. I have
them even now occasionally. I remember, probably within the
last six months, having a wonderful flying dream: I would run
along the top of a mountain and then all of a sudden just launch
out and be gliding over these beautiful valleys. They're great,
these dreams—so effortless when they happen. They're always
so real I think, God, maybe I could do this if I really tried.

I can remember as late as my graduate student years having those scary moments when you're taking a little nap and you suddenly jolt awake and think, Oh God, I'm falling off the bed. They really stopped about that time. I've never had one since. I suspect that those falling dreams are infantile reflexes that I've gradually grown out of.

I can't think of a time in which the idea for a particular novel or short story came to me completely in a dream. I usually seem to get those while I'm awake. I think the most straightforward example of the genesis of an idea is in my first novel, *A Long and Happy Life*. When I was a student in college in 1955, I'd written a short story about a young girl whose name was Rosacoke Mustian. At Duke there was a girl who was called Rosa Coke Boyle. When I got around to writing a story I thought, Hey, that's a nice country name; and I just made it one word instead of two. My Rosacoke was about fourteen or fifteen in the story. About two years later I was living in England, in graduate school, and feeling very far away from home. It was Christmastime and someone had sent me the hometown newspaper. It had letters from children to Santa Claus in it. I was just reading and being amused by what the kids were asking for when suddenly I got this image in my head of the girl that I'd written about a couple of years earlier, Rosacoke. I suddenly thought, She's acting in a Christmas pageant at the little village church; and she's playing the part of the Virgin Mary. And, oh my God, she's pregnant! In the pageant! I just sat there and I immediately thought, Well!

I invented the story backwards. Like how did she get pregnant? Who's the father? What were the situations that led to her getting pregnant? And in about ninety seconds I had basically invented the outline of the book I spent the next four years of my life writing. That always seems to have been the case with me; it's certainly been the procedure for most of my fiction, a dreamlike state, dream-strategy.

I'm a very visual-minded person and my intuition will usually be in the form of seeing a picture. A character is doing something, and I'll say, What's that? Who is he? Why is he doing it? What leads from this? Where does it go from here? And, as is the case in *A Long and Happy Life,* what I got was the last picture in the book and from that, I invented the book backwards.

In *Blue Calhoun* I just had this tremendous compulsion to set a thirty-five-year-old man in a room with this very beautiful teenager and watch them interact, watch this lifelong love affair between them begin.

I never have been seriously blocked except immediately after my first surgery. I had written about a third of *Kate Vaiden* and then I suddenly found out I had cancer. I had surgery and five weeks of radiation and, for about five months thereafter, I just couldn't do anything but sit in a chair and gaze out the window or at the ceiling or whatever. I couldn't read, I couldn't write. While it was a normal reactive depression, it was also a very real kind of spiritual hunkering down on my part. I was really concentrating on marshaling my resources to fight this thing.

And then a friend called up and asked if she could commission me to write a play for a student group of actors at the small college in Arkansas where she teaches. I said, Well, sure. I accepted the commission and sat down and tried to start writing this play. That sort of brought my writing back to life. As soon as I finished the play, which took me about two months, I immediately went back and very rapidly finished *Kate Vaiden.* I haven't had a serious block since then.

I certainly know that there are plenty of times when I'll finish up a writing day and not quite know where I'm going the next morning, and then I'll just go to sleep. I'll have a good long night's sleep, and the next morning the answer will be there. I won't be conscious that I've worked it out in the night but obviously my mind has worked it out bypassing the dream route some way. Or maybe I dream and don't remember when I wake up. I wake up just knowing that, oh, he goes downtown. Or he goes uptown. I'll know which decision to make.

I know that from my early childhood on into my early twenties I would have these—they weren't quite nightmares, but they were very uncomfortable dreams in which I'd be trapped in this incredibly narrow tunnel. There was just about an eighth of an inch of room for me to crawl through this place. I was having to be very careful that I didn't panic and sort of edge my way through this tiny, tiny little opening to get myself wherever it was that I was going—I didn't seem to know. I've always read that as being some kind of birth-trauma dream, a response to my birth experience. I had a very difficult birth. I was a breech baby and my mother had a very hard labor with me. I was probably a teenager before I even knew what a breech birth was. But I was having those dreams in early childhood before I knew where babies came from and certainly before I understood the obstetrics of breech birth. These dreams were very important, certainly in childhood and right on into my early twenties; and then again like the total-paralysis dreams, they faded off and I don't seem to have them anymore.

I'm completely fascinated by any chance I get to read about the latest theories of sleep or dreaming or watch a "Nova" show on the subject. I'm by no means deeply read on the subject, but I haven't yet seen anything which satisfies me that we really know what the function of dreams is. I'm old-fashioned enough to think that a lot of times—not always by any means—our dreams are unquestionably attempts on the part of some deep faculty of our brain to communicate a discovery to us. Either, you'd better *stop* doing so and so; or you'd better *do* so and so. Or, my friend, you have a large tumor growing in your spine; and you don't know this, and you should prepare your mind for dealing with the upcoming trauma that this is going to subject you to.

A N N E   R I C E

ANNE RICE was born in New Orleans in 1941 and raised in an orthodox Catholic household, the second of four sisters. She turned to writing full-time after her six-year-old daughter died of a rare blood disease. Her first novel, *Interview with the Vampire*, featured, among others, a five-year-old vampire named Claudia. Rice's Vampire Chronicles, which also include *The Vampire Lestat* and *The Queen of the Damned*, have sold over 10 million copies.

Sex, death and immortality are explored in Rice's work, which include tales of mummies, witches, vampires and castratos. *The Witching Hour, Cry to Heaven* and *The Feast of All Saints* are among the titles she has produced using her own name.

Rice has also written sadomasochistic soft-core pornography under the pseudonym Anne Rampling and hard-core

S&M porn under the name A. N. Roquelaure. These tales of "discipline, love and surrender" include such titles as *The Claiming of Sleeping Beauty, Beauty's Punishment* and *Beauty's Release,* from Roquelaire, and *Exit to Eden* and *Belinda* from Rampling.

Whether explicitly sexual or not, all of Rice's work is charged with erotic energy and explores deep philosophical issues.

━━━━

I'M A VERY HEAVY daydreamer. I have been since I was a child. To me daydreaming is intimately connected with writing. Writing is like daydreaming. It's putting down in dramatic form whatever is on your mind. Daydreams are some sort of code for whatever concerns you. I really can't imagine what the minds are like of those who can't daydream or fantasize because I'm so used to doing it. So, my writing grew out of that obviously.

I don't dream too often at night. I don't always wake up knowing what the dreams are but I've had about four really startling dreams in my life. I still haven't figured out what they were about. The way they influence my writing is hard to describe logically.

When I was writing *The Queen of the Damned,* again and again I was reminded of a dream I had as a small child. In the dream I saw a woman who appeared to be made completely out of marble. She was walking on the street. I must have been five years old when I had the dream and I remember it filled me with fear. Somebody said, "That is your regis grandmother." Now, I didn't know what the word *regis* meant. I don't think I even knew how to read or had ever seen the word *regis* in print. I can remember the preliterate years when words were like shapes to me—I think it was at that time—but I don't think I found out until I was an adult that *regis* was a word you could apply to a professor in a university.

I remembered the dream as if it was some sort of vision rather than a dream. And when I was writing *The Queen of the Damned,* as I described these elders, these ancient immortals who had become so old that their skin was now completely white and they looked like moving marble, again and again I felt like I was being drawn back into the atmosphere of that dream.

In the book, the vampires have a great deal of wisdom. One of them is extremely dangerous. The wisdom of the others prevents that danger. This is a plot that's used again and again in all levels of fiction; the elder as a potentially menacing figure. How it connects to that dream I don't know except that I do remember the great fear at seeing that figure. There was a whole eerie atmosphere to the dream like a peek into something almost pre-birth.

It wasn't that I set out to write the book because of the dream. What I'm saying is, I think that dream fed me subconsciously in some way. When a dream is that intense, when it's that otherworldly, it's a little frightening. It's almost as if you saw into some other realm. You saw something that had to do with heritage or lineage that went beyond what you could see with rational eyes.

One of the things about the way I write is that I don't analyze these things. I pitch in and make a story and suddenly there are these six-thousand-year-old women and they're white as marble, they have the fate of all the others in their hands and they are discussing philosophically what is the right thing to do. At its worst it's a bit like "Star Trek" and at its best it's a novel trying to discuss the very basic questions of our lives.

I use the vampires as metaphorical figures to talk about life itself: what we don't know about it and what we must believe about it. In the absence of any revelation that I personally trust, I still believe that it is possible to live a good life. That morality is possible and that ethics are possible. I fear religion. I fear the pure idea. I fear the thing which is detached from the flesh. These elders are too detached from the flesh and they know that. And this dream figure was, perhaps, too detached from the flesh.

To my child mind it might have been a frightening religious figure even. It was like the statues in church. The sense of menace, perhaps, came from that. It was too divorced from what we are.

My writing, the whole thrust of it, has been to say, "Listen to the lessons of the flesh." Never get too far away from it, whether it's with an ideal like Communism or a religion like Catholicism. Never get too far away. If you pay attention to what people feel as fleshly beings you will have compassion for them. It's when you divorce yourself from the flesh, when you say that is not important and you repress it completely that you're capable of building systems that really hurt people, like Fascism.

A lot comes to me right before I fall asleep in that almost hypnogogic state. I remember conceiving of the twins, these two women in *Queen of the Damned*, very early. I was lying in bed when they came to me. I can't hook it to any particular day or moment, I just know that I began to think about them as I lay in bed long before I wrote the first chapters involving them.

Writers vary so much. You have people who probably are intensely conscious of everything they're writing and you have people like me who are definitely surrendering to a trancelike state in which things make sense without analysis: trusting to a sense of authenticity and intensity that's really totally intuitive.

Writing for me is being in the illusion of the novel. It's just sailing right into it. I don't sit there conscious of striking keys and making words. I'm just seeing the action. It's very much like daydreaming or dreaming. But I don't know that everybody else feels that way. My suspicion is that all these things are chemically definable and that those of us who write that way have an excess of a certain chemical in our minds.

I did literally put one dream into a novel, *Katherine and Jean*, which wasn't published. It was an extraordinarily strange dream that I had about 1972. In this dream I was a priest, a small man, fairly bald, with brown skin. It was my duty to come out before a temple and call down the rain periodically. The elders in the temple said to me, "One day you will call down the rain and the snow will come. And when the snow comes you will die." In the dream it seemed I'd been doing this forever. I was old. I went out and I raised up my arms to call down the rain and indeed the snow did come. It came in those giant crystals that you see in children's books. It was very beautiful. But I realized it meant that I was going to die. Then I looked around me and saw that the world was flooded. People were dying everywhere. Thousands of people were clustered on what looked like the tops of Greek temples. They were on the peristyle roofs. The water was coming up to the capitals of the columns. I remember one very frightening sight of an alligator or a crocodile snatching people off one of the roofs. It was chaos. It was blood. It was everything I feared from the snow coming instead of the rain.

Then I was taken by the elders into the temple. And in the bottom of the temple was a Catholic chapel. It was indeed a chapel I remember from childhood, that I saw at a convent of the Little Sisters of the Poor. In the back pew of the chapel were all the old priests. So, they hadn't died at all when they'd called down the snow. They had just been taken down here and put in the chapel. One of the things I realize now is that the Little Sisters of the Poor take care of old people. That is their job. They care for the aged.

Anyway, I remember realizing we weren't going to die. That was really the end of the dream. To this day I can get frissons from seeing certain scenes of flood or chaos or certain temples or images. It will bring on the whole atmosphere of that dream.

In these novels that deal with ancients and immortals, I seem to be writing about themes that have to do with that dream. Like right now, in the sequel to *The Witching Hour* I'm working on, I'm dealing with this character to whom something terrible happened in ancient times that had to do with worship and sacrifice and making a mistake. I know it has to do with that dream. I couldn't put it together more logically.

Now superficially one could say that that dream was just prompted by seeing *King Kong*, you know what I mean? But the dream itself was so incredibly strong, and it seemed so off the wall. Really, all that happens in *King Kong* is that the natives take the girl and tie her to the two poles and Kong comes and gets her. I had watched that movie at the time but the dream took off from there a quantum leap. Something else happened and I don't know why the snow was in it and I don't know why I was a priest and I don't know why I was a man and bald. In dreams like that you have a feeling that you're being transported someplace else.

When I write I fall into a state where I access all of that. I'm still trying to capture that feeling of standing up there and putting up my hands and calling down the rain.

In a recent dream I had that struck me with that otherworldly quality, I was one of my characters. I was the vampire Lestat, my hero. I was trying to go up the side of a castle. I threw a star-shaped thing way, way up in the air so that it held fast to the edge of the battlements. Then I climbed the rope that was attached to it. That was a very very shockingly vivid dream.

About six months later, at the Frankfurt Book Fair, my German publishers took me to Heidelberg and there I saw this castle. It was really a shock because the castle appeared to have exactly the same type of façade as the one that Lestat had climbed in the dream.

The dream of being Lestat was wonderful because he is, to me, a powerful character. That he was climbing the wall of a castle is interesting, because he can fly. Now that I say that, it brings to mind that Lestat himself complained that he didn't like *Dracula* because Dracula could demoleculize yet he crawled down the walls of his castle. The image of Dracula crawling down the wall really doesn't make any sense if you have a

character who can change into a wolf at will. I had Lestat
complain about that in one of the books. "How is one supposed
to read this preposterous novel?" Yet there in my dream I had
Lestat climbing the wall.

Two dreams I've recently had definitely worked their way into
my writing. They are dreams of flying and they have been
absolutely wonderful. The feeling of rising up out of my body,
free of it and just taking off. Those two dreams have been
incredible and I know that they were inspired by the writing.

The vampires in my later books can fly. They can't in the
early books but the older vampires have that power. I've found
that as a writer flying is a very disturbing power to work with.
But I felt it was inevitable in the story.

I prefer to work with characters who can't fly. I wrote a
whole book in which Lestat was depressed by his ability to fly.
It tends to cause the vampires to despair when they begin to be
able to fly. They really feel they've lost their humanity. It's very
disturbing for them that they can rise up and go very very high
into the atmosphere and move on the wind and come down
somewhere else. It makes it very hard for them to seek comfort.
It dehumanizes them.

I've had flying dreams for years but they're fragments. I
couldn't say what happened in the dreams. I just remember
going up out of my body, that wonderful feeling! There's
nothing like it that I've ever felt—to rise up like that in the
dream. It's so vivid. The last time I had a flying dream I knew
I was really doing it. I was aware but I was also really there. It
was fabulously real.

Dreams have not so much changed my work as deepened it.
Going a league further. But that's how writing is to me. It's like
digging deeper and deeper and deeper, and sometimes dreams
show me that my writing should go deeper.

Take the flying, as an example. Before the dream I didn't get
the real way it felt, how really great it felt; that incredible
shooting up to the ceiling like a bubble being released, then

straightening out beneath the ceiling and having no weight and moving out. That's really a deepening of the sensuous aspect of flying. And I can take that back to the typewriter or the computer and try to get that down.

I had a dream before my daughter was diagnosed as having acute granulocytic leukemia. I remember she was very sick in the dream and she was withering. She was turning blue and withering and she had a blood disease.

I keep a very good diary but this dream was so disturbing to me, so upsetting, that apparently I didn't write it down. I've gone back and searched and never found it. But it seemed to me that the dream occurred well before she got sick. Now there may have been some signs already. I may have been picking it up subconsciously. I don't know.

I have dreamed of my daughter over and over. They were dreams of disturbance. Crying. Not being able to comfort her. Kind of nightmarish dreams. They did not bring solace.

There was one dream in which I realized a friendship I had was a bad friendship. It was a dream in which I saw that the type of solace and comfort and attention this friend gave was basically not for my best growth and strength. The dream was crazy. It would sound insane. I saw images in the dream of my friend performing actions that seemed menial and debasing, performing lowly tasks like bathing my feet, things that were very distasteful. And I thought this is not good. This is not what we want. There was very much that feeling of being shocked into a strong awareness of something that had been disturbing me for a long time. But loyalty and love of the friend hadn't allowed these feelings to surface.

The dream caused me to reconsider the friendship and I realized it brought out the victim in me, and comforted me as victim repeatedly in a way that was not dignified or healthy or desirable. I think the dream resulted from wanting to get free of that friendship, free of the role of playing the victim for that person. It subsequently proved to be a friendship that would not allow me to become successful. This person had been a wonderful friend to me whenever I was distressed or upset. But my friend was having an enormous amount of trouble with the success of my first book and was becoming agitated and disturbed; not at all supportive or cheerful or happy with my success.

Six years after the publication of *Interview with the Vampire* I decided to write a second vampire novel. I wanted to go back to the supernatural theme, to write about the vampires and their concerns, and I remember having a very frightening dream. I saw the typewriter that I'd written *Interview* on fly off the table onto the floor and crash. The dream filled me with fear. I hadn't used that typewriter in years. I had written *Interview with the Vampire* on it and that had brought me enough money that I was able to get better typewriters. But I saved that typewriter, I still have it. Anyway, in the dream it flew off the table. It started going and going and going and typing and typing and typing and wouldn't stop, like some sort of crazy thing. It flew off the table, *crash!* onto the floor, and then I was on St. Charles Avenue in New Orleans. It was a pitch black night and I was with Claudia, the child vampire. She was looking up the avenue. I was terrified. I woke up from that dream really determined to go on and write the book. I thought it was very exciting to have seen those images. Those were images of intensity and runaway energy and it was absolutely right to go into that darkness. But it was very very frightening. There I was, in a dream, back there in New Orleans, in pitch blackness with Claudia. And there was that image of the typewriter somewhere, God knows where, exploding practically, and I thought "That's it. Go with it!"

I thought that was a dream that said, "Go where the pain

and the intensity and the fear is." Because what I fear in writing is the safe decision. I want each book to be a risk. I think it's very dangerous to tell people how to interpret dreams. Somebody else might've said, "Anne, don't write that book. The dream is telling you darkness lies ahead." But only you really know. You've got to interpret your dreams yourself.

JOHN SAYLES

ALTHOUGH most people know John Sayles as a film-maker, he has been writing novels since the 1970s. His first novel, *Pride of the Bimbos*, was published in 1975. His second, *Union Dues*, was nominated for the National Book Award as well as the National Book Critics Circle Award. Sayles published a collection of short stories, *The Anarchists' Convention*, in 1979 and the novel *Los Gusanos* in 1991.

Sayles began his career as a screenwriter working for Roger Corman's New World Pictures. He made his directorial debut in 1980 with *Return of the Secaucus Seven*, produced from his own script for a mere $60,000. This was followed by *Lianna, Baby It's You, Brother from Another Planet, Matewan, Eight Men Out* and *City of Hope*.

Sayles has also produced three music videos for Bruce Springsteen and the screenplay for an award-winning made-for-television film about agent orange called *Unnatural Causes*.

Born in 1950 in Schenectady, New York, John Sayles worked as a meatpacker, day laborer and hospital orderly before becoming a successful writer and director. He is the recipient of a MacArthur Foundation "genius" award and currently makes his home in New Jersey.

———

I WAS WORKING on the music and sound mixing of *Baby It's You,* and under a lot of pressure—because that's a part of the movie-making process that really costs a lot of money per minute—and I started to have these dreams.

The first dream was that I had been hired to do a very short, quick rewrite of a movie that Joe Dante was going to direct. In the dream Dante just said, "John, you've got to write this movie. I've shot a little of it but now what we really need is a script." The name of the movie was *Assholes from Outer Space.* I saw the title coming at me in 3-D—streaking at me like in a fifties science fiction movie—*Assholes from Outer Space!* With tinny music. And then a really lame fifties scene from something like *Reefer Madness.* It was about these people who look just like us—with kind of fifties suits on—but they had antennas in their heads. They were like bureaucrats who worked in motor vehicle departments and banks. And they were assholes.

I woke up from that dream and felt like, Well, that was a weird dream but I can't do anything with that. That's like a skit.

Then a couple nights later I had a second dream—which was that I was actually hired to direct a movie. I had come in somewhere halfway through the movie to finish it. It was called *Bigfoot in the City* and it took place in Seattle. There was a lot of rain and so there were a lot of wet-down cobblestone streets. It was about a Bigfoot, a yeti, who had somehow wandered into the city. The movie was very much like this Carol Reed movie where there's an IRA guy who's on the run because he was in a shootout and the cops are after him—except he's a Bigfoot instead of a real person. The only scene I remember from the dream was a kind of sympathetic but tough cop with two detectives and a couple of cops in blue behind him, walking down this alley where the Bigfoot has been cornered, wounded and bleeding. They stand over the guy in the rain and the detective looks down at the Bigfoot and says "Book him."

I woke up from that dream and I felt like, Oh, that was even weirder but it's still kind of like a skit. You could do maybe a good half hour of this thing.

Then, finally, a couple nights later, I had a dream that was even shorter. It was a kind of sunny day and I was on a street in Harlem. It was a black neighborhood and I said to myself, Oh, this is Harlem, I recognize the buildings. I was watching this black man walk down the street. He was obviously a little bit frightened and he looked really lost. Then I realized—the way you realize things in dreams without seeing anything dramatized, or anybody saying anything—that, Oh, he's from another planet. No wonder he feels lost. He can't talk. How alienating, literally, that must be. How lonely he must be.

I woke up and I said, Yeah! I had this wild dream and, you know, that really could turn into something. What an interesting guide into a neighborhood, into a life a lot of people have never been able, or wouldn't be able, to go to.

And then, as I started percolating the idea, the first two dreams came back to me.

As a result, my film *Brother from Another Planet* has the science fiction aspect of *Assholes from Outer Space,* plus some of the comedy aspect. It also has the fugitive aspect, that *Odd Man Out* kind of idea. And it has the black man who's lost in Harlem, who can't speak, who's from another planet and who is alienated.

It's one of the very few times that I've actually gotten any decent ideas from dreams.

* * *

I have a lot of nightmares. They wake me up. And then I go back to sleep and hope they aren't so bad that I have a hangover from them. I can get a bad dream hangover and really feel bad the next day.

I played sports when I was in high school. That was certainly what kept me interested in coming in every day. My attendance was very high, not because I wanted to go to school, but because I had practice. You just weren't supposed to miss practice. An awful lot of dreams are frustration dreams so I continue to have dreams where the game is going to start in a few minutes and I can't find my locker. Or I don't know the combination. Or I'm getting on the bus and I don't have my spikes. I have the rest of my football uniform on but I don't have my spikes. They're back in the locker and I can't even find the lockerroom. There's always that feeling of, Oh my God! You almost break out into a sweat saying, How many possible numbers could this be? With the locks we had you can always feel the last number—because if you pulled on it and twisted the dial it would give a little click on the last one—but it was still sixty times sixty possibilities, which is an awful lot of combinations to try. Plus, then you didn't know—is it one of those ones where you have to go around three times and then around once and then around twice to get to it?

I have that dream probably once a month.

I really don't know that my dreams are triggered in a very specific way. Very often when things are fine I have awful dreams. And sometimes, when things are awful, I have dreams that are okay. But it doesn't necessarily stack up that way.

One of the things that's interesting to me about dreams is that they have their own power. They don't always seem to be corresponding to what is going on in my life. There are some that really seem to have their own life. And when they're bad I'm not too happy about it.

My dreams are very graphic. It may be *because* I write and

do other things that they're so graphic. Or it may be that I write and do other things because of whatever it is that makes my dreams graphic. I remember having a dream when I was in high school where somehow I was an Arab with a few other Arabs on a caravan. And a bunch of other Arabs attacked the caravan and were killing everybody.

I fell off my camel and lay down in the sand with a couple of these other people who were my friends. I remember that after the raiders shot at everybody they went around with these spears and stuck a spear through each person to make sure they were dead. I remember the people near me started to cry out as they got speared. And the sound that the spear made when it went through their skin was a sound that a fork makes when it goes through a sausage at breakfast—that kind of wet popping sound. The dream was really that graphic! I also recall feeling the sand in my nose because my face was pressed in it—you know how when you breathe sand, trying not to cough—hoping that somehow they'd think they had already speared me and go back. And feeling the thump of feet going by. That graphic.

So, that kind of dream can be the most powerful thing, the most upsetting thing that happened to you that whole day. Or that whole week. But although you rationally wake up—you say, That was only a dream, I'm not in the desert, I don't have to learn how to ride a camel—that dream still may effect your mood. You may be freaked out for a day or more because of that dream. That's what I mean by saying they have their own life. They have their own power. At least sometimes for me.

I was a psychology major in college. We talked about dream stuff and we talked about various interpretations of dreams. I grew up around people who would buy dream books in order to figure out what numbers they should bet. I remember those little books—friends' aunts or mothers or uncles would buy them. They'd read them and say, Oh, I had a rabbit dream the other night! I guess there's a three in the number somewhere.

I don't live that violent a life and I'd say, of the bad dreams

I have, in half of them I'm the victim and half I'm not. I often have dreams where I'm with somebody else, or I'm alone, breaking out of something and really, very graphically, killing people. Cutting people with knives while running down the backstairs of some big stone building; killing so many people that I'm slipping on the blood while I'm doing it. And the blood is hot. All those details. So if that dream is speaking to me, I don't want to know what it's saying.

I'm not sure which comes first, is it the ability to supply details? Or maybe being awake to those details, and noticing them in real life, means that those neurons, or whatever it is that feeds your dreams, can be active and embellish when you're having a dream. Or maybe whatever it is about a person that notices details is already there in their dreams.

I don't generally write down my dreams. Usually I don't take notes even when I have an idea for a story until I actually sit down to do it. Because I always have felt that I have so many ideas that the ones that are important to me, that really are good, will stay. And the other stuff will fade. That's kind of a filing system. If it was not that interesting, or not that good an idea, if it had a germ of something good in it, that part will come back. It'll be in there somewhere.

One of the reasons that I like to swim is that I get good ideas then. Or when I'm running. With that physical activity and lack of other input, I can put myself in kind of a trance. I fall into a state that's not totally conscious fairly easily. And I think that physical exercise usually helps you to do that, especially swimming. It's almost like having your eyes closed but it's not so tiring. You're not likely to fall asleep.

I used to have factory dreams. I would get them when I'd go to work in a new factory. Those are terrible because you put in your eight hours and you've got to move your fingers right or you'll burn them; or you'll chop them; or you'll squash them. I worked in a plastic factory for a long time. We were on piece work. We made 180 pieces and we could barely get those 180 pieces made. It was the same fifty-three actions over and over again to make a piece and you probably did them twice within a two-minute period. So you really were like a machine. For the first week or so that I worked in that factory I would go to sleep and I would have the factory dream. I'd be doing the same motions. The parts would be coming down the belt at me one after another. I'd wake up and I'd feel exhausted. I'd feel like I'd had no rest from the job.

I used to have very bad insomnia. Sometimes I would put myself to sleep remembering the name of every kid in my second-grade class. Or in my third-grade class. I can't do that any more. I can remember thousands of names but those have been filed somewhere else.

I had it worse when I was a kid but I had it up all the way through college and a few years later. I think some of it was true insomnia and some of it was that I wasn't necessarily on a twenty-four-hour schedule. I may have been getting forty hours of sleep a week but it was like two, six, ten and twelve—two, six, ten, twelve. The cycle may have been off. Also, because I didn't like school much, I got into the habit of sleeping through the whole morning, waking up a little bit at lunch and then coming alive the last two classes before practice when I had to be awake. That meant that each night I would kind of be up. Sometimes I'd just lay in bed and ask, When is this going to end? When am I going to get to sleep?

I've written dreams that I've put in some of my books. There's a dream that I used to have when I was a kid, I was raised Catholic and at school we had a nun who always tried to gross us out. I remember this nun telling us that people's hair and fingernails kept growing after they died. I had a friend who was working one summer mowing the lawns in a cemetery for the local parish, and I had this dream that in fact what he was mowing was the hair of the people who were dead. The hair was coming up in all these different colored patches. He had to be really careful because when there was a bump he would bring up pus if the blades scraped the scalp. He really hated it. They had to go with a machete where the fingernails grew up in these little stubbly rootlike things. I wrote that into a story.

I think that dream is in "Fission." There are a couple other semierotic, semihorrible dreams in that story. A character has them while he's been unknowingly dosed with LSD. He's not sure if he's dreaming or seeing things for real.

There's a dream I used in *Los Gusanos* about walking on the backs of sheep. Walking on a carpet of wool, barefoot, and realizing it's the backs of sheep. It's a dream that I had when I was very young. There's a lot of Catholic imagery about sheep and flocks. You'd rather get one stray back then the other ninety-nine who don't stray. A lot of pictures in kids' books for Catholics are Jesus shepherding these sheep. There's kind of a nice golden sun and pretty fleeces, things like that.

Once I put a dream on paper, then I start to feel like, Okay, now there are some other dots I connect here. I usually fictionalize the dream a little bit to tie in more with the character. Because it's not my dream any more. I try to actually give it a little more metaphorical meaning than it probably had to begin with. I really don't psyche my dreams out that much after I have them because they're so visceral.

Sometimes the combination of horror and attraction is what's interesting to me. In some of my erotic horror dreams there's this kind of come-on, maybe bees, or something awful, and flowing honey. Beehives are always interesting: there's the idea of this reward but there are also these things that are close to you that can sting you.

The dream in *Los Gusanos* about a woman whose "bollo" is oozing with honey was based on one of my own dreams. In the original dream the whole woman was full of honey so that if you touched her cheek, honey would ooze out of anything that

it could ooze out of. It wasn't quite as sticky as honey usually
is and it was warmer than honey usually is, like it had been
heated. The dream was just this strange feeling of knowing this
person who was very attractive, who you couldn't really touch,
or squeeze, or anything, because there was just so much of this
stuff in her. When she opened her mouth there would be a
bubble of honey in there. She couldn't really speak because she
was constantly running with this stuff. So the original dream
wasn't as organ specific; it wasn't as simply sexual as what I
finally used in the fiction.

In *Los Gusanos* this man gets involved with this young
prostitute. At first he really is just kind of brutalizing her and
then gradually—as his life starts to fall apart and the power that
he thought he had starts to crumble and he starts to get
scared—he actually starts to fall in love with her. And he
realizes somewhere that if he's going to survive he has to kill
those feelings in himself. Eventually he literally kills her.

In the book I changed the dream from something just
visceral to something that a reader could read and say, Oh I see
what's happening. Here's something that's very attractive to
this man—feelings—but at the same time he knows that it could
be the death of him. It could have a sting. There's the liquidity
and the softness of this woman and the fact that, even though
she's fallen into being a prostitute, she always cries. There's
something really attractive about the life of feeling to him. But
there are these bees. And the bees are what he knows about the
world, what he knows about how hard the world is.

When I was a kid I used to free dive a lot. I'd take a big rock
and jump into the water and that would take me down to the
bottom. There had been a TVA-like place that had been flooded
so there were still some old fences and things underneath to look
at. Sometimes I would stay under too long and push myself back
up and get worried about coming back to the surface. I have lots
of drowning dreams. They all are being underwater and not
getting back to the surface. This was compounded by seeing the

Houdini story with Tony Curtis where he gets stuck under the ice. That was a horrible thing. I've actually had dreams where I'm stuck under the ice—except it's not cold, it's warm—and I'd say, What the fuck is the ice doing here? I wish Tony Curtis was here.

In this dream I am swimming underwater with no real problem. Holding my breath and realizing, Gee, I can hold it for a long time. I have this bad eardrum so I can't go deep any more. But in this dream the eardrum was good and I realized, Ah ha, I can go deeper than I usually can. I see a car underwater and I go down to it. There's a woman in the front seat of the car who's dead. The window is rolled down and her head is half out of the window. She has very, very fine blond hair. I realize the door is jammed. I want to bring her body up. She's very pale and I realize if I take her by the hair—there's all this blond very cornsilk hair—it's going to tear out of her head like the cornsilk tears out of corn. I don't want to do that. That would be too gross. And I can't really reach in to get any other part of her body. Except her mouth is like this perfect O. In fact it's been nibbled away a little bit by fishes. There are little fish darting in and out of it. I realize, Well, I guess I have to do this to get the body up. I have to reach my hand in her mouth and pull her up by that. And at that moment I realize, Oh! It's Mary Jo Kopechne. And I really want to help her. In some way I feel like it's important to get her to the top. And then, when I put my hand in her mouth, her mouth closes around my wrist and her eyes open. I can't move my arm. I'm stuck there. And that's where I wake up.

MAURICE SENDAK

MAURICE SENDAK'S portrayal of the painful
emotions of childhood—the anxieties, loneliness, jealousy,
rage and sensuality ignored by most children's book writers—
gives his work a powerful appeal to both children and adults.

Sendak was born in Brooklyn in 1928, the son of Polish
Jewish immigrants. He was working as a window decorator
at FAO Schwartz when, in 1951, children's book editor
Ursula Nordstrom invited him to illustrate *The Wonderful
Farm*. His second book, *A Hole Is to Dig*, became a
children's classic and launched a career which has earned
Sendak eighteen *New York Times* awards for illustration.

In 1956 Sendak began writing text to accompany his
drawings. Dreams figured prominently in his first writing
venture, *Kenny's Window*. *Where the Wild Things Are*,
published in 1963, provoked heated debate over the nature

of children's literature and won a Caldecott Medal in 1964.
Higglety Pigglety Pop, written in honor of Sendak's beloved
dog, Jennie, was nominated for an American Book Award in
1980. *In the Night Kitchen* again sparked controversy, this
time over the frontal nudity displayed by its young hero
Mickey. In 1982 Sendak won an American Book Award for
Outside Over There, a darkly illustrated book in which
sibling jealousy and fear of death were prominent themes.

In the 1980s Sendak began designing sets and costumes
for ballet and opera, including Mozart's *Magic Flute* and
Tchaikovsky's *Nutcracker*. In 1991 he formed the Night
Kitchen Theater to produce live performances for children.

Sendak lives in Ridgefield, Connecticut, with his German
shepherd, Runge.

—————

DREAMS DON'T ever directly influence my work in terms
of plot, movement or even idea. Never. What they do is raise the
emotional level of what I'm doing at the moment. They add
color or counterpoint to the work, acting as an almost sym-
phonic accompaniment to what I'm doing.

When I was working on designs for the opera *Hansel and
Gretel*, I had seemingly endless dreams where I saw other people's designs. They didn't look at all like what I was working on.
I also saw rehearsals and felt that extraordinary excitement at
seeing the production occur. Yet the dreams didn't match at all
with what I had done. My only sense of it is that they matched
emotionally, not literally, my own work. When I'm working,
something is cooking so desperately that the dreams just mani-
fest themselves. But they don't act as harbingers of ideas for me.
Or, if they do, I'm not aware of it.

What I suspect is that I dream something but don't remember it. And then it resurrects itself. It becomes part of my conscious equipment when I try to pull drawings out of my head.

It's not so specifically dreams I'm using in my work as

unconscious motifs: dream patternings which now become part of whatever in the brain is used for creative labor. After a certain age—I'm a middle-aged man, I'm starting to be an elderly man actually—there's so much packing and casing and overlaying that I have systems that now function for me. Like my studio. So dream patternings, which I don't even recollect I had, or childhood events, or whatever, just simply come to me. But that's part of long rehearsal, long experience and long exposure to the creative process. And of the seriousness with which I take the creative process.

There's a sequential order in one's unconscious life as an artist and you just follow the order. You don't question it. You could question it. You could resist it. But I don't. It's the only thing I trust.

I've leaned on these things so heavily all through my life that they now respond to my leaning. You know what I mean? Just a mere touch and I can get those things because I've honed them. It's like developing any specific set of muscles.

There's only one time in my entire experience that I saw an image in a dream and I later tried to re-create it. The image was a very vivid one of a mother and a child. It was as if I was looking at a drawing, like when I used to travel when I was young in France. I'd go to these wonderful print shops and just sit there and look at these wonderful engravings. You could just pore over them. The dream was like that. Kind of a European setting. I was looking at pictures and I came upon this one. I was absolutely stunned. It was in black and white and in the background was a woman looking out over a balcony. Her face was turned away from us. And in the foreground was a little girl, partly hidden by a curtain. Her face was absolutely furious and her hair was wild. She was staring at her mother who was staring away from her and looking out onto a landscape of some kind. All very shadowy. That was it.

I had the dream years before I started *Outside Over There.* I tried to copy the picture, I have it somewhere. I remember using it when I started to do the book. I was trying to figure a way to use it because it made sense. My brain then started to assemble a story which had to include a baby. The baby had not been in the original image.

The specific image from my dream is not in the book. Except that it is, in a series of images of the mother looking away and the little girl being furious. It is closest to the original dream in the image in the book where the mother is seated in an arbor, looking fixedly away and the little girl is standing next to her in a rage holding her baby sister. Her mother seems to be oblivious.

It's sort of like there are rude images that the brain conjures. And then the creative process is a refinement of those images. They come up from the gut and then you have to smooth them out. The brain is like a computer and shoots up the image raw. It has a FAX look to it. Your job is to be extremely stimulated by the image. The training and craft then become the moderator and the image goes through a transformation.

That book, *Outside Over There* was, to use an overabused word, traumatic for me. The whole doing of that book from its conception to its publication was a ferocious experience. It was a very, very complicated part of my life. But then, I'd taken on a very complicated subject. And you always pay for that.

For weeks before I delivered the manuscript to my publisher I had dreams of someone trying to take my baby away from me. The dreams I had around the book were terrifying. But they were also reassuring—confirming that this was a very serious trip, but it was one that I had to take.

Herman Melville was always using the image of the artist as diver. He loved that word. Having to dive from some height, meaning, of course, taking a serious risk. Because if you dive and you're lucky, you'll come up with gold from the bottom of yourself. You dive deep into the self. But you can also drown, you can smash your head upon the rocks—there are terrible risks in diving from a great height. But if you didn't dive, then you were not an artist in his terms. Without risk you were just a middle-of-the-road type guy. I have dived in my life, but the deepest dive was *Outside Over There*.

I think dreams are important in terms of how they assist you creatively. They can help clarify an emotional condition. Say you're ambivalent about a project—which happens frequently— you might have a dream where your true emotional state is revealed. Either for or against the project. Something in the dream occurs and you wake up and say, Oh, so that's how I feel about that. I really do want to do it. Or, it's clear I know how to do it. Not that the dream tells you anything. There are no mysterioso clues, it's just the way you wake up and feel.

Or you might wake up and feel dejected. Some inner sense is uncertain about this thing you're about to embark on. You want so much to do this project but something balks inwardly. And if that happens then you've got to resign yourself that you ain't gonna do it.

It's like you have all these quickie pregnancies—lots of miscarriages. You may want this project to go to full term for all kinds of reasons, but if it doesn't satisfy something inwardly then you ain't gonna have the baby. No matter how you prepare the nursery.

Kenny's Window, about a little boy's dreams, was the first book I ever actually wrote. That book was a child of therapy. I had only been in therapy for a short time so I was very concerned with the business of using dreams. I was only twenty-seven. Kenny is definitely a product of that time, and of the excitement and scariness of being analyzed.

This is why I approve of analysis so much: it begins to give you a certain creative power over your inner workings. Lots of artists are frightened of therapy. The creative process is such a secret thing that they see discussing it in analysis as a form of castration. But my feeling always has been that if that's your anxiety maybe you shouldn't be an artist. Being an artist is your life, it isn't some secret thing. It's what you are. And you can't be that easily destroyed. You can't be that vulnerable. I never ever worried about that.

The greatest thing therapy can do is put you in contact with some element of the creative process which then you begin to develop. Therapy may not solve your life's problems, but then nothing does.

Freud gave us real tools. Freud is kicked around all over the place, but there are basic tenets now which most of us have accepted. I have. I simply believe them. I recently read a paper by a therapist which was immensely amusing about the sexual puns in Herman Melville. There are those who don't think the puns are there. They think it's ridiculous or vaguely obscene or undercuts the story to admit the idea of sexual metaphor. "How can you enjoy the story ever after if you think it means that?" Well, I don't think if a thing means penis or vagina that it undercuts the story. I think it envelops the story in yet another layer of interest. We live very close to our genitals and those people who wish to forget them, that's their problem.

I didn't mind the sexual interpretations critics had of *In the Night Kitchen*. I somehow made it easy for everybody. There were no metaphors for a penis in that book. It was just there. You didn't have to say, Hmm, I wonder if he meant that? You don't have to get Freudian over that book, I think.

A lot of my dreams are actually infantile dreams of playing with Mickey Mouse toys. In these dreams I'm a grown-up who's collecting the toys as I do in real life. I often recollect dreams of finding stationary stores, or what we called candy stores when I was a kid. They're excavating and they find a Brooklyn candy store intact behind ancient brick walls. It's opened up and there it is—the whole ambience of a thirties store. The women working in it are all thirties dressed and hair do-ed, looking like Myrna Loy. Everything is just as it was when I was a child.

All the beautiful toys in their original boxes. There's this overwhelming joy at finding them.

I have this dream fairly often actually. Once every few months. It's strange.

Quite recently, on a tour to sell my latest book, I went to an event where there were new people that I met. And on the surface it seemed very successful. It *was* successful from a worldly point of view. Everyone congratulated me. I didn't think they were flattering me. But I was really unhappy and I didn't know why. And then I had a dream. It was a very funny dream because it put me in a position of such discomfort. It was an irritating dream. I despised the situation in the dream, it was so bad. I woke up and really had to laugh because it told me that however well things seemed to go on the surface, emotionally I was distressed and uneasy and angry at the situation. The dream just confirmed my real condition, my real state of mind. Everybody saying, "Everything is great, Maurice," didn't console me because deeply I didn't believe it. The dream made up a little story—like a homily to tell me what instinctually I knew all the time.

You could not, in the worldly sense, have expected the occasion to go better. But that isn't what you care about emotionally. That never is what you care about. That's like saying "I can't trust him," and everybody saying, "No reason not to." But you can't shake the feeling of mistrust even though it flies in the face of logic.

My dog had no problem with that, you know, he just barks and the fur flies. I look at him and I say, You're out of your mind! Why are you carrying on about this person? Well, nothing in the world will make him like that person. And he doesn't have to stay up all night thinking why. Whereas we stupid humans endlessly question our instinctual takes on people and situations.

The dream was all about how I should've changed the

circumstances. I could've, but I didn't. I was lazy and, rather than reconcile myself to it, I was just furious. It was a very good dream. Very good.

I have since made a decision to never attend an event like that again. I won't put myself in a position like that again. That's what my dream taught me.

ANNE RIVERS SIDDONS

"SHE BREAKS your heart, knocks your socks off and writes with such lyrical beauty that you want to read her aloud to anyone you ever loved," wrote Pat Conroy of Anne Rivers Siddons. Described by the *Atlanta Journal and Constitution* as "the Jane Austen of modern Atlanta," Siddons has allowed her characters to travel North but the Southern sensibility travels with them.

Anne Rivers Siddons was born in 1936 into a family that has lived in the same Georgia town for six generations. In 1964, after years in advertising, she became one of *Atlanta* magazine's first senior editors. She thought it was a prank when a note arrived from a Doubleday editor suggesting she should write a book. She ignored the letter but he followed up, offering her a two-book contract under which *John Chancellor Makes Me Cry*, a collection of essays, and *Heartbreak*

Hotel, her first novel, were produced. Siddons went on
to write *The House Next Door* and *Fox's Earth* and
Homeplace. Peachtree Road became a national best-seller,
as have her more recent novels, *King's Oak, Outer Banks*
and *Colony.*

Siddons lives with her husband, Heyward, dividing her
time between Atlanta and Maine.

———

I THINK every creative impulse that a working writer, or artist
of any sort has, comes out of that dark old country where
dreams come from. I don't know how it would be possible to
use that side of yourself, to write or create, without recognizing
your dreams or drawing from them.

There have been times when I was stuck, when I couldn't
work something out in a book, and quite literally it would work
itself out in dreams. In *Peachtree Road* I was not sure what to
do with the main character of Lucy Bondurant. She was a very
troublesome, beautiful and charismatic woman who had caused
great pain and destruction for herself and other people. I felt
that some resolution, some closure, was going to be necessary
for Lucy at the end of the book but I didn't know what. I
literally dreamed a scene from start to finish and woke up
thinking, Of course, it just has to be that way. Why didn't *I*
think of that? I suppose I may have had it all along but dreams
are the channel that bring the good part of us, the free part of
us, out into the open.

It's happened before that some small thing about a book
will work itself out while I'm asleep. *If* I get out of my own way
and let it happen.

My first book, called *Heartbreak Hotel,* was an autobiographical book about coming of age at a Southern college cam-
pus in 1957 on the fringes of the Civil Rights movement. There
was to be a climax where I felt it would be necessary for this
young woman to confront a black person in a totally new

environment, to make her really see the blacks around her as people instead of what they had been to her all her life, loved servants but diminished people. I couldn't think of a way to do that without being out of character with the Civil Rights movement because at that very early time we were not marching in the streets or firebombing. It was a very delicate "one heart at a time" awakening. One night in a dream an old memory returned: I had been over to visit friends in Mississippi and while we were at the local jail, visiting the deputy sheriff, there was a jailbreak. Someone shoved me into a little room and said, "Don't come out of this office." But through the glass pane I saw the escaped prisoner run by the door. He looked in at me and I looked at him. It seemed as if we held that look forever.

I had more or less buried that memory. And then one night I dreamed that that's how it would happen for my protagonist: she would see a man in the middle of a jailbreak and, by his eyes, know him totally. Know his fear and his terror and know that they were her own. The whole thing became alive and real to her then.

I'd had that experience and I could've thought of it but I wasn't using it. It took the dream to call it out. If we will let them, dreams will give great order to our lives.

I don't dream that specifically in my personal life. I wish I knew a way to put that kind of a problem-solving mechanism to work. I suppose I work out a lot in my dreams. It seems to be that, as in my fiction, I'm continually trying to work out the same thing. I think that all writers have one thing that sticks with them, one sticking point, and they write their books over and over again until they've solved it.

I seem to be working out the issue of a woman becoming strong enough, literally, to stand alone. All of my women seem to be on their way from a situation in which they have depended on too many other things to finding a way toward becoming autonomous people. It took an editor to point this out to me—we rarely see what we are doing.

I find that I have conflict dreams a great deal. And dreams about being totally alone. I realize that's my own greatest fear. I think that by listening to my dreams I can at least isolate what it is that I fear most, what keeps me off balance and nervous. Dreams give me some insight into what I need to work on. That's one of their great values. I don't think dreams solve problems for you; very overtly, very often, I think what they do is clarify the areas of pain and conflict. Or adjust the areas of focus. They help you look at things that are just too frightening or too painful to look at in reality. You can trust your subconscious to supply you with truly horrendous, wonderful dreams if you're in the middle of something that's disturbing you badly. And I think it pays to pay attention to that.

You know it's funny, Scratch, a black character in *King's Oak,* showed up in one of my dreams.

When I was very small we used to cook outside in the back. I lived in a very small house that backed up onto the woods. I dreamed we were cooking hamburgers out at the barbeque grill and one of the people there was Scratch. He was just sitting on a chair in the circle. We always sat in a circle and told family stories after those dinners. And in the dream he was part of my family. Part of my family when I was a little girl. I loved that. I felt so happy to have him in my family.

At the time of the dream I was actually writing about Scratch. I have no strong fatherly black figure in my life. As a Southerner I have, of course, a strong black woman—many Southern women my age had a black woman who cared for them—but no strong black man. I don't know what Scratch represents to me. I think some sort of warm, wise earth father, an earth figure of some kind. I felt so comfortable and content and serene when he was around me I conceived the idea that that's what he should be to Andy, my heroine, and her daughter Hillary: a figure to drive away fear.

*   *   *

King's Oak was born on a speaking trip to a little Southern town in the hunt country of South Georgia. It's the country of the enormous private hunting plantations that we have in the South. I suppose there are such places in other parts of the country, but not so many very old, very secret and very strange ones. Anyway, the young woman who was driving me around was telling me about her husband. She said, "He's an Ivy League lawyer—he's well thought of in the town, he has lots of friends, he's a member of the symphony guild—the thing is, he just won't come out of the woods." She said, "He has a house up the creek in the river swamp and if you're going to live with him you have to live there. He just simply will not give the woods up. He hunts, he tracks, he just disappears into the woods for weeks at a time." And I thought, Well, what a neat thing! He's found a way to make his life really work for him in all ways. Later I met him. For just about five minutes. That was all I ever saw of him and I found him a fascinating man. Very captivating, very charismatic. He was the nucleus, the seed for the man Tom Dabney became.

I think it was inevitable that my heroine, Andy, in flight from everything, seeking only safety, would run headlong into this man who asked everything of her and needed to explore her dark side, her wild side. And she sure got it.

When my mother read *King's Oak,* bless her heart, she said, "You know it's not too late to get your teaching certificate." My mother is not wild about sex scenes in books. It's not her favorite thing. But it would almost be impossible to have a man so in love with everything natural and exuberant, so in love with life, who was not a very sexual being. He simply would be. And I think, if you're going to have him, you might as well show it. It's not fair not to.

I felt it was necessary for Andy to come to the love of Tom Dabney very slowly. She was a very damaged woman. She had lived all her life under the thumb of one man or another. The realization that she was alone was a great start, but it took more than that. I have a psychiatrist friend who says, "Insight by itself is just worth zip." You can be the most insightful depressive in history and you're still depressed. It's finding a way then to work through it. But it has to start with the insight. So though Andy, alone in the woods, had the insight, what she had to do for the next one or two hundred pages was find a way to cut the moorings and let go.

When we do finally commit, it takes a conscious decision. If we waited until we felt like it none of us would ever do it. You have to make commitment a policy. Personally I'm afraid of risk. I'm getting less afraid of it, but I realize that I work my own fear out through the women in my books.

My husband says I have very tough, strict little rituals, especially when I'm just getting started to write a book. Once I'm under way the ritual is just repetition. I need to do it exactly the way I did it before to keep writing. He says, "Have you ever noticed that first you make a nest of papers, like a mouse getting ready for the winter, then you have nests of paper all over the house, and then you start walking into walls?" I once put my kitten in the refrigerator and put the orange juice carton out the back door. I found the kitten immediately, but that's the state I'm in. And then all of a sudden the day comes when it's time to write. My husband says, "You will fix a big breakfast and clean up the house and go out to your little writing studio. I know I have seen the end of you for two or three days until the book is under way." He says I do it every single time I start to write a book.

Ritual is one of the deepest parts of any human being. Joseph Campbell showed me how important mythology, which comes almost directly out of dreams, is. All the mythologies of all the cultures in the world have three or four central myths to them. You will find the dream of the hunter and the hunted animal—whether it's induced by a substance like a mushroom or by fasting or by a trance state—somewhere in there. Before the actual hunt begins, a dream is at the heart of it. This is where the hunting man finds the most real part of himself and is, literally, in communion with the animal he is going to hunt. I find mythology has so much to say to us today. Because in days when there was a strong body of belief in myth, we had a way through life. We had a pattern to follow and things to show us how we were connected to the wild and to the natural world. When you lose your myths, and Campbell pointed this out, when you hit a society that has no mythology, no dreams, you have anarchy. You have crack houses, you have gangs attacking people in Central Park, you have alcoholic wards. And one of the things that we are suffering now in our times, these sad, beat-up times of ours, is a lack of contemporary mythology. One thing I wanted to do with *King's Oak* was to see if you could create a myth for the last decade of the twentieth century. And, if you could, who the hero would be.

The central message in all mythology, in all portions of history, in all the world, is that there are ways, such as dreaming, to tap into the wild side of us, which is where all the richness and all the healing and all the creativity comes from. We've managed to shut it off completely, most of us, in this modern day, and it can cripple us badly. Very, very badly.

I came to realize in the writing of *King's Oak* that perhaps the most important thing we can ever do in our lives is find a way to keep the wild—both the wild inside us and the wild outside us—and to tap into it. It's very rich.

ART SPIEGELMAN

As the son of Auschwitz survivors, Art Spiegelman set out to document his family history using the medium he knew best, adult comic books. The result was *Maus,* a two-volume memoir in pictures—*Maus I: A Survivor's Tale* and *Maus II: And Here My Troubles Began.* Spiegelman based the book on taped conversations with his father, Vladek. He drew the Jews as mice, the Nazis as cats, the Poles as pigs and the Americans as dogs. Spiegelman wove his father's memories of the Holocaust into a complex narrative exploring the painful relationship between father and son.

Born in Stockholm, Sweden, in 1948, and raised in New York, Art Spiegelman began drawing for the school newspaper at the age of thirteen. By fourteen, he was selling sports and political cartoons to the *Long Island Post.* In the

1960s he became part of the underground comic movement, producing titles such as *Young Lust, Real Pulp. Bizarre Sex* and *Sleazy Scandals of the Silver Screen.*

In 1980, with his wife, Françoise Mouly, Spiegelman co-founded *Raw,* an annual magazine of avant-garde comics and graphics. In 1992 he was given a one-man show on "The Making of *Maus*" at New York's Museum of Modern Art. He was awarded a special Pulitzer Prize for *Maus* that same year.

━━━

I WOULD SAY the thing that's uncanny to me is how rarely I remember my dreams unless I really go out of my way to do so. I went for a brief period, a few months, deciding to remember them and I'd write them down every day. Then it worked. But I have to make that kind of concerted effort. Otherwise, it's rare that I remember them.

On the other hand, I know that the dream lab is very active. Often I'll find that if I go to sleep laying the day's problem out to myself, and get a fairly clear fix on the various strands and bits of what I was working on right before going to sleep, letting those be my last conscious thoughts, I'll more or less consistently wake up with a solution.

With *Maus* this happened on an almost ongoing basis. There would just be the daily snag and the daily snag would have to wait overnight for me to come up with the answer. The kind of problems that I'm thinking about were narrative problems in construction.

One problem was where to enter things. Although there was a present and a past, I took liberties with when something in the present happened. Like a conversation with my father about his feelings about African Americans may not have happened at the exact moment that he was telling me about the liberation of Dachau, but it happened within that general time frame. There were ongoing problems of when to enter things and how to make them echo back into the rest of the text without being too blatant or obvious, turning them into just some kind of cheap symbolism.

There were also things I just couldn't visualize. I remember in the first book I had a lot of trouble visualizing this garbage pit that some friends of my father were hiding in. I had about ten different scenarios, none of which seemed to be very logical to me. They didn't look right in my head. That would be the kind of thing where I would go to sleep and wake up with a pretty fair image of what I had to draw.

While I was working on *Maus* I dreamt about the Holocaust a lot. Everytime I'd finish a section of *Maus* I would take some time off, do some other kinds of drawing, other kinds of writing and then I'd have to "reenter." Part of reentry was rereading the transcripts of my conversations with my father, listening to the tapes of our talks and reading Holocaust history more concertedly. Or reading survivors' testaments. And, until I would get inured again—which was actually a necessary part of working on *Maus*—I'd have a lot of really fitful and horrible dreams about being in the camps.

My father didn't tell me his nightmares per se, but it was clear from the fact that he would wake up in a sweat, screaming, that there were things that kept coming up.

In *Maus I* there is one dream that I incorporate, his prophetic dream. This was a dream in which my father's grandfather came to him and told him what day he would be released from the prisoner of war camp. It's a true story, a story he always remembered because that date became his magical date. It's the date on which he had been married, which was before he had gone to the prisoner of war camp and before he had that dream. Now I shouldn't say "date" as in January 3rd 19—whatever. It was a date that would change every year but it was the date on which a certain fragment of the Torah called Parshas Trumah would be read. I even looked it up and read it but, in and of itself, it didn't have much resonance. It was just some minor point of Talmudic Law. On your Bar Mitzvah you're supposed to read a piece of the Torah out loud as the confirmation that you've gone through this tribal ritual. And it turned out that mine was Parshas Trumah. Without anybody rigging anything. And so for him that became a magical date.

I recorded my dreams for a while because I was frustrated with not remembering them. I wanted to see if this was like a congenital problem or just prioritizing what my brain was going to be busy with during the day. It was kind of gratifying to know I could remember. I mean it was interesting to remember them, and occasionally I'd bring one to the shrink and we'd talk about it. A dream would trigger off conversation. There'd be an image that might send me down a path of unearthing buried dilemmas. But, on the other hand, looking long enough at a Dewar's scotch ad could do the same thing. For the most part, the dreams per se weren't that useful for analyzing myself.

Now, for me there's another kind of waking dreaming, which I call doodling. I mean, on occasion, I'll sit down and make a picture not knowing what I'm making and then I'll literally write around the image, covering every crevice around the square that has the picture. I find that often becomes a crystalization and a clarification of a lot of what's going on in my head. The process seems very much like what one would go through dreaming. A lot of random stuff sticks together, coalesces to make something that has its own logic.

I actually trust that kind of waking dream more, in terms of bringing me in touch with psychological issues, than the kind I do at night. Because I know that on some level or other that's what I'm doing. Once I've started ranging with the pen, I figure I'll start making images that have other connections.

Because they deal in essences, rather than nuance description, comics move into the way, I believe, the brain works, which is in encoded, simplified images and concentrated verbal clusters. One not only thinks in words, but in images as well. Yet those images are very stripped down. We don't even think photographically, which is already a simplification of reality, but in terms of high-definition imagery. Not necessarily with the humorous notion that a caricature would bring up, but in kind of a set of caricatures. In other words, if you are thinking about a friend, you will remember their gait, let's say, or a pronounced brow or a specific kind of clothes they often wear, or a specific body gesture. These are very highlighted and exaggerated visuals that you conjure up. This is a description of how the brain recalls things and also a description of what comics are.

I had one dream about comics, incidentally. It took place a long time ago. This guy, who was very important in helping me get started as a cartoonist, had one of the world's greatest collections of paper ephemera and old comic strips in his basement. I would stay in his basement and occasionally just fall asleep there, drift off. I had a dream that consisted of drifting off in his basement looking at "Happy Hooligan," a turn-of-the-century comic strip about a kind of tramp character, who wore a tin can on his head. In the dream I have a tin can on my head. I'm trying to get the can off and it won't come off. It's permanently there. The dream has several episodes of me trying to get this can off by having people pull at it, by knocking it against something. Nothing works. Finally I sit under a tree and start sobbing. Then this other character kind of lopes in and says, "Don't worry, Buddy Boy, it's just the style you're drawn in."

This was a dream with a punch line!

The other interesting thing that happened in this dream was that there were these occasional and very rhythmic moments that were rather painful. These were the moments where I disappeared and reappeared again. And they would happen rhythmically. I realized those were the little white spaces between panels.

There's nothing like drawing a comic strip of your dream to help remember it twenty-five years later!

I remember when I was very, very young—I guess when I'd first been exposed to television—all of a sudden my dreams started having titles and credits. Even though I couldn't read! I was like five or six, so I couldn't really read the titles as they were going by, even on the cartoons, but my dreams would start with the same format that I had seen looking at TV.

Something that's referred to in *Maus* was actually a childhood dream image: all the kids in my class being separated out—Jewish kids, not-Jewish kids—and the Jewish kids being led away. That was something that happened in a dream. But it's not as though it was a recurring dream. It was just a strong image that stayed with me.

My wet dreams I remember. Like certain very strong erotic images that I first had when I was about twelve: a naked woman writhing in a net. Very erotic to me. Especially having her breasts and her vagina up against the netting. That was really hot for me. But explain why? I can't. I'll leave that to an analyst somewhere.

In the Sunday *New York Times* recently there was an article about how dreams move through your brain, positing not that what was charging through your head was random, but that it's a problem-solving machine. Kind of continuing the thoughts that weren't worked through during the day. In that sense it's not totally distant from the Freudian model. I can relate to this idea. It seems to me that part of what happens in your dream life is totally random. And some of the images are clearly your riddle for the week. You know, the things you're supposed to chew on.

I think some of what happens is just neurons firing, just random imagery. But there are bits of dreams that are also very specifically related to interpersonal problem solving.

I can think of various times where there were people who I consciously thought were just A-okay but my dream life told me they weren't. And that made me wary. Then I would discover all this other stuff that justified the wariness. That's happened to me several times actually. Though all it really means is that I'm an incredibly poor judge of character.

Dreams have helped me understand people who were troubling me. Like being unable to articulate consciously that a good friend was very jealous of what was happening to me. Having the fantasy episode in a dream was not just like an alarm bell going off, saying, Go away, but a way of empathizing and understanding what somebody else was seeing without having talked to him about it. Having that articulated to me in dream life helped me work things through to get our friendship into a new equilibrium.

One kind of dream I've had a number of times is seeing a work of art, usually a drawing or a comic strip, in my sleep. Like discovering a comic book that I'd never seen before. It would be just the best thing I'd ever seen. Ever. I'd be feeling incredibly jealous of this work. And then I'd wake up and not be able to remember anything except the feeling that I'd seen it. And then realizing, Hey, it's mine, I can do that. But by then the dream would've evaporated.

For a while I was actually doing work very specifically based on my dreams. I had three or four comic strips that were called "Real Dreams" and I was trying to make these rational narrative comic strips out of my irrational subconscious.

I pretended the dreams were totally narrative. Sometimes I had to add a few words to get them to be less disjointed, trying to turn them into one-page strips. The most interesting one for me was one where I ran an interpretation of the dream at the bottom of the strip. It was all done as a gag. I reinterpreted what was so blatantly and obviously a Freudian dream as having to do with Jews and Nazis.

One "Real Dream" starts with a quote from Macbeth

saying: "Infected minds, to their deep pillows, discharge their secrets." Then there's me, describing the dream:

> I was at a party. I don't know what we were celebrating. The hostess weaved through the room holding a large sausage to her groin. Every few minutes she would shake the sausage vigorously and vomit. The guests enjoyed the revolting display, applauding, except me. Ech! I figured I might feel better if I washed my face. But when I looked in the mirror, good God, my mustache washed off.

And below the strip, Dr. Shpiegelmann's dream interpretation:

> The party is obviously the Nazi party. The hostess bears an uncanny resemblance to Odilo Globocnik, head of the Polish SS. The sausage, a Polish sausage, is roughly the same shape as the map of occupied Poland. The "revolting" display symbolizes the tragic uprising of the Jews of the Warsaw Ghetto. And when the dreamer attempts to wipe away the horrors of World War II (his mustache) he is nevertheless left face to face with the naked truth of his own guilt.

I did about three or four "Real Dreams" and then I invited people to send me their dreams. As they came in I realized I was much more interested in my own dreams than I was in other people's. I know exactly how to dream up the imagery that will make my short hairs stand up and get the various parts of me to light up and jangle. It's not as easy with other people's imagery.

Occasionally I've drawn a dream and occasionally I just allow an image to stay conscious, allowing it to come back so I can have it more concretely present.

I only remember the dreams I've drawn. The other ones I

can kind of conjure up if I look back over my dream notebook. Let's see, here's one. How's this?

> I'm taking care of [my daughter] Nadja. I pick her up by the head. She slips in my hands. I think she's okay at first. She's crying. I look again and see I've pulled part of her ear off by mistake. She's howling. Françoise and a friend of ours are aghast but put the ear back into position and it sticks. They've fixed her. The feeling of pulling the ear off is like pulling on an old kneaded eraser.

It took me a while to get used to having the idea of being a father and having a kid, finding a way to do that that wasn't recapitulating my father's and my relationship.

I tried to include a dream section in *Maus* that I ended up kicking out. It would've been in the section in *Maus* where I'm with the therapist. I'm talking to him about a dream that I'd had that had to do with the skittishness about having a kid. So this is all from the same period:

> My downstairs neighbor, George, tells me he's going to the doctor or dentist. Next time I see him he points out that his hands have been removed. His arms are shortened and narrowed in circumference. Somehow they're attached to wires in his mouth. He's quite casual about it, says it's temporary. In the next few days I meet George at the mailbox and we enter into a mail competition: who gets more. I'm winning.

George, the person in the dream, had a child a month before I did. So that's the topic of this dream. His hands being cut off by having a kid seems to me like a real limitation of freedom. And then I dream of this "male" competition with him about having kids.

That's what my dreams are like. You know, the usual muck.

* * *

I find that I can't work right after waking up, like some of my friends do. That's because whatever is going on in the dream life has to clear out before I can start making the conscious dream.

The most comfortable time for me to work is in the afternoons and into the evenings. When life patterns allowed, it would be working through the night.

In the morning I usually do errands. You know, like telephone calls, letters. The early part of the day is just taking care of stuff where the genie doesn't have to come out of the bottle.

When I'm writing any sound just jangles, but when I'm drawing I start by listening to music. On occasion I use music consciously. In fact I have four tapes, ninety minutes each, of the complete works of the Comedian Harmonists, which was a German popular group in the twenties. I listen to a lot of twenties' and thirties' music in general—the kind of stuff that was used for the sound track in Betty Boop films. The history of the people in the Comedian Harmonists resonated so deeply into the stories of *Maus* that it was the best and most appropriate music I could find.

I would listen to these fourteen hours over and over and over again until Françoise was ready to drive me out of the house with my tape recorder, never to darken the door again. That music conjured up a lot for me. Yet, after a certain point, I wasn't hearing music. Or I would just be listening and not working. So I'd just get involved in talk radio.

I listen to whatever drivel talk radio I can find. Good talk radio, if I can find it. But even if it's just some kind of right-wing rant, I figure the left brain can kind of get occupied there and leave my right brain alone to draw. It has to be conversation, if it's music then it really starts seeping in to right brain activity.

I'll actually engage with the radio. Part of me will be going, "That son of a bitch, he can't say that! What about, you know, Nixon? What about, you know, whatever?" See, if

I wasn't doing that, if I was working quietly, my mind would be moving around useless circles. Like thinking about somebody who had slighted me in some minor way. So my "That son of a bitch, he can't get away with that" takes all that and puts it somewhere in the air waves and leaves me alone so I can get my work done.

ROBERT STONE

Praised as heir to the tradition of Herman Melville and Joseph Conrad, Robert Stone writes about the contemporary struggle between good and evil, life and death. In novels filled with violence, drugs and obsession, Stone's characters seek transcendence while often facing the consequences of regrettable decisions. Robert Stone questions the nature and existance of God while evoking images of suffering and redemption.

Stone's *Hall of Mirrors* won the Faulkner Award for Best First Novel of 1967. His second novel, *Dog Soldiers,* won the National Book Award in 1974. This was followed by the critically acclaimed *A Flag for Sunrise* in 1981, *Children of Light* in 1986 and *Outerbridge Reach* in 1992.

Born in Brooklyn in 1937, Stone was raised in Manhattan by his mother and the Catholic Order of Marist Brothers.

Joining the Navy at the age of seventeen, he earned his high school equivalency degree at sea. In 1967 he attended the writing program at Stanford University on a Wallace Stegner Fellowship. There he became involved with Ken Kesey's Merry Pranksters and explored states of altered consciousness.

Despite never having completed either high school or college, Stone has taught at Harvard, Princeton, Amherst, University of California at Irvine and Stanford. He has been married for over thirty-three years to Janice Stone, with whom he has two children.

——

THERE'S A similarity between what I dream and what I write in as much as there are basic instincts and attitudes that my dreams and my writing reflect. It's not so much that I'll have a narrative or actual story material come from a dream but it seems that the same thing that's going on in my work is often going on in my dreams.

I dream a lot of the ocean. I spent a lot of time at sea when I was young and was in a number of institutions of different kinds. When I was very small I was in a kind of quasiorphanage boarding school. And I lived in small, cheap hotels with my mother for a long time. I never really had a bathroom of my own until my early twenties when I was married. I grew up basically with one parent and no siblings so a lot of my dream material is solitary and a lot of it is institutional—at sea or in the military or in situations like that.

I have a lot of recurring dreams and a lot of dreams that turn out, after some superficial differences, to be the same dream. Many of these dreams are about dereliction: not having done something that I was supposed to do or having done something that I wasn't supposed to do—failing to discharge responsibilities and being hauled on the carpet for it or about to be punished for having done something that's gotten me in trouble. I guess everybody dreams this kind of stuff, but I'm almost always in some authoritarian structure.

When I wasn't with my mother, who was a schizophrenic, I was in these sort of institutionalized Catholic settings which were very strict and male. Not nuns in my case, but brothers who used corporal punishment and were very strict. So, to be in trouble was very frightening. And you were always in trouble. If you were raised like that you kind of go on feeling that you're in trouble. Or about to be in trouble. Or about to find out that you're in trouble. It's a bit corrupting because it gets the notion of conscience and guilt a little scrambled.

The Navy, when I was in it, was also very demanding in exactly the same way, having your clothes folded just right and all that. So I have a huge amount of that kind of stuff: Is my locker in order? Is everything in my sea bag in order? Are my shoes shined? Freud writes about the examination dream, for me very often it's the inspection dream.

For example, when I was in boot camp in the Navy—this was the late 1950s—you had to wash your own clothes. You got a bar of ivory soap and a scrub brush. You couldn't iron your clothes, you had to fold them in such a way that they kept a certain crease. Your uniform had to be absolutely spotless. And if it was summer, you were wearing whites. Every morning you'd go out on the parade ground and you would get the command "uncover." At the command "uncover" you had to take your hat off and hold it out. It had to be completely spotless inside and out. The guy would go and look you up and down. They don't do that anymore, but they did in those days. You do enough of that kind of stuff at an early stage and that's going to keep you in dreams for the rest of your life.

I have quite a lot of ocean in my dreams. Sometimes I'm in the water and sometimes I'm on ship. There's a kind of quality of life at sea that's very different from life ashore. It has its rhythms. I can get back into that in dreams.

* * *

I can tell you the essence of my most commonly recurring dream. I'll give you two versions of it. One of them happens on a ship and one of them happens in a New York subway. They're essentially the same dream. The New York subway also occurs fairly often in my dreams still, being the kind of very special place it is.

In its nautical version the dream goes like this: I'm on a ship, it's a civilian ship, not a Navy ship. It's a freighter. Last time I had it we were going from the South of France to Corsica. We can see the coast of Corsica and I'm with somebody. I'm not quite sure who. A woman. She is there for a while and then not there. Increasingly the prospect of landing seems fraught and menacing. I begin to realize that I'm guilty of something. And when I figure out what it is; it's always about having some kind of dope. I've got all this marijuana which I can't possibly conceal and I'm about to be caught by the officials ashore. I discover that the crew of the ship, who I haven't seen before, are entirely Chinese. And they have no sympathy for my predicament. On the contrary, they're amused by it. So I'm getting deeper and deeper into trouble. I'm about to be found out carrying all this stuff and nobody cares. Nobody's on my side.

I have exactly the same dream in the New York subway: I'm in a subway car which at first seems to be empty. The cops get on the train. They're on the train and they're searching everybody. I've got dope on me. Then suddenly the car is full of people. They're all black. I'm the only white person in the car and everybody's laughing at me. Nobody's on my side. Everybody's very amused by my predicament. I'm about to be busted and I can't escape.

That dream in various forms is one of my recurring dreams. I'm among people who are other than me and I'm something other than what everybody else is. I have something to conceal and I'm about to be found out. That's the structure. I have that dream a lot.

I think the dream still occurs because this is an imprinted

way of thinking that I can't control. I really came to feel unsupported, unprotected, except by myself. And that's really insufficient, finally. At least it is when you're dreaming and you have to surrender control. I know where it comes from because, in a way, life is like that. Life is like that for everybody some of the time and for a lot of people a whole lot of the time. I don't think I walk around with this when I'm awake, but when I'm asleep and primary process takes over I see that again and again.

Although I wasn't there long, Vietnam does occur in my dreams. I worked there for a couple of months as press in 1971. In this dream I always find out that I'm in Vietnam when I thought I was somewhere else. There's this kind of deception involved and I'm back. I used to dream again and again that I'd reenlisted, that I was back in the Navy for some reason. The idea that I'd been out was a mistake somehow and it had to be explained to me by what crazy chain of circumstances I was back in. The same sort of thing happens with the Vietnam experience.

In some of my dreams, if they're particularly frightening, I apparently manage to construct some kind of favorable chain of circumstances that gets me off the spot. Not in the dreams where I'm being accused. In those I wake up just at the point of being found out. But sometimes it's almost as though I'm consciously working out a narrative in which I get off the hook.

When I remember these dreams it's plain to me that I was making things come out right. Sometimes I'm unpleasantly surprised and sometimes I'm irrationally relieved when things that really were dangerous are somehow explained away as nonthreatening. It feels as though it's something that I do, as if I'm controlling things in the dream.

Volition in dreams is funny. Sometimes you get it when you keep waking up and falling back to sleep, drifting back into dreams. You really feel like you're doing it at some point.

I've had a dream like Rheinhardt's dream in *Hall of Mirrors* of everything being entirely wrong. Nothing is where it should be. It's the dream of being just entirely in the wrong place—maybe someplace that you really don't belong, that you didn't think you were going. You don't know why you're there, people don't want you there.

One of the things I think that this dream reflects is going from seaport to seaport, going ashore in different countries. My first foreign liberty port was Havana under Batista. I was sort of initiated into all the mysteries of adulthood in Havana. We were always going to a different Mediterranean port. Those experiences were mainly pretty pleasant so I don't know why things go wrong. I don't know what exactly that means except that obviously life lets you down sometimes.

It seems to me as though both anxieties and hopes are what's in dreams. There are things that I want at a given time and I dream of getting them or not getting them. Those are the two principal things going on in everybody's dreams, what you're afraid of and what you want.

I really feel that as a writer I haven't done enough. I haven't done enough work. I don't take a lot of comfort in what I've done and I'm really quite anxious to try and do more. I feel kind of guilty about not working hard enough.

I often feel like I'm not measuring up, or that I'm getting it wrong. That's my basic attitude. It's an underlying attitude and I'm rather stuck with it, though it's not without its positive side. If you work for yourself and you have to get yourself started and you're as lazy as I am, you really require some kind of internal mechanism to get you going. If you have to torture yourself with images of primitive authority, well, you have to get yourself to work somehow.

People in the world may have an exaggerated opinion of how much I actually drink. My characters drink a lot. They do my drinking for me. I haven't stopped drinking, but I never drink that much alcohol.

I can't use alcohol when I write at all. If I start drinking alcohol I'm through. I'll either go on and on and it'll be three times too long or else I just wander off and party.

They say F. Scott Fitzgerald wrote a lot of his stories while he was drinking alcohol and I think there are writers who do. Paul Scott, who wrote *The Raj Quartet,* according to his biographer, used to drink all day. He finally killed himself, but he seems to somehow have been able to sit there and drink and write. I can't do it. I just can't.

I think everybody who's quit smoking dreams about it. The one I used to get all the time was: I find myself smoking, which horrifies me because I've wasted all that time and suffering quitting and I'm smoking again. Then I get some screwy explanation like, It's the second Thursday of the month. You always get to smoke the second Thursday of the month! I wake up with great relief to find out that I'm not really smoking again. But I haven't had that one in awhile. It's been going on ten years now since I quit. I'm getting free of that one.

I have had various dreams involving rejection or disapproval that undoubtedly reflect anxiety about the book that I'm working on. Not so much critics, but people who really know the difference between a good book and a bad book, find it a bad book. I'll dream that I've really blown it, that I've just indulged in some illusion that has caused me to write a book that isn't nearly as good as I think it is.

The people in these dreams aren't real. I don't know quite who they are. They are critical, criticlike figures. They're vaguely professorial, teacherlike figures. There's a feeling of being ridiculed. I don't specifically hear or even see anything. I'm just aware of a situation in which I have, in attempting to be serious, actually made myself ridiculous at something I do.

It isn't pleasant to get bad reviews but you can't rely on critics for your feedback because very few critics are that good that they can give you the feedback that you want. Sometimes the praise isn't convincing and sometimes the condemnation is obviously from nowhere.

Very often critics don't read the books they review very closely. Sometimes they don't read them at all. It's not uncommon. It's more common in England, especially if the book is American, that they'll write a review off the blurb. When Americans are dishonest they copy each other's reviews. The English tend not to read the book and say they did. Or they'll read just a little of it.

I've had dreams in which I could hear music and I could also see the notation. I studied music for two years when I was six or seven and I learned the F clefs. "All good boys deserve fun," you know, the scale notation. I will sometimes see notation and hear music and the notation may not correspond because I've forgotten how it goes.

Music is important to me. I spend a lot of time listening to it and I often refer to it in my writing. When I'm making words, when I'm composing, I can't listen to music because the music just crowds me out. I have to have one thing or the other. There's no music really quite bland enough for me. Sound is important to me when I write. I mean, I take a lot of trouble with sound. I really have to hear, I have to have my ear for the language and for the dialogue so I can't have music on while I'm actually writing. Sometimes, if I want to sort of play something down and dream, I'll turn the radio back on.

I sometimes get dreams where colors are tremendously bright. Also, like everybody who took a fair amount of acid back in the sixties, I'll dream about being stoned. The last time I took acid was about 1971, so it's been twenty years, but I used to dream that I was stoned fairly often.

Some of my dreams are rather complicated. It's very hard to hold on to the fragments of narrative. Some of them have a lot of plot, a lot of story to them. But very often the underlying things are really few and simple. And primary, basic. But those primary things, the anxieties—which is what they mainly are—just appear under a whole lot of different guises, different forms. It's a funny way to live your life, to be constantly inventing incidents. You go on doing that when you dream. If you're a writer of fiction and you're elaborating incidents—and you do it all day long—this has its effect on your dreaming life.

Sometimes I have the feeling that since some of my dreams have such complications—both the scenes and the people in them undergo so many changes—that this may reflect the process of invention that goes on during the day. It is a chicken-egg question. The writing condition is a strange one. As somebody once said, people only write when they have to. People who write fiction are really, for some reason, driven to it. It is something that you discover you have to do. Not everybody who has to do it actually does it. I mean an absolute necessity of imposing the order of structure and narrative on raw phenomenology. That's a very basic necessity, coherence. And in a way, when you invent character and incident, when you invent a narrative line, what you're doing is making sense of raw reality. And to do that is to reassure one's self. Making sense of things is a way of making the world amenable. It's a way of reducing things to a form in which they can be handled.

I'm sure there are people who really, as a primary need in their lives, require some kind of expression for the things that oppress them inside. And language is wonderful. But language isn't the only way of dealing with it. Language was the vehicle that served me. Language was my primary way of coping and of rationalizing the world. And language is probably my principle pleasure as far as the pleasures of the mind go. I rely on language tremendously and so it's the medium that I choose when I have to act.

The practice of art, the practice of writing fiction is an act against solitude. It's ironic because one of the great difficulties of the writing life is its solitude. You do so much alone. You end up being much more autonomous than you want to be because, not only have you got to start yourself, but you end up having tremendously strong experiences in solitude. Anyone who's ever written anything he cares about has found himself in a deeply emotional state and all alone. All by yourself. You get yourself worked up into states that are quite intense. I think this is necessary and it's not a bad thing. It's tough on the psyche to have to be enduring all that emotion with no one else to take it to, but there's something about the way the emotional buildup progresses and resolves itself that makes me think there's a really primary need being served in this process. That this is a response that is necessary. And that I might be in real trouble if I wasn't able to do it. Because the drive to do it, if it's not satisfied, becomes eventually destructive, something that turns against itself.

This is one of the things that's going on in *Hall of Mirrors*, and Rheinhardt actually says this: he believes in his talent as a musician as a kind of God-given thing and he really believes that it's going to destroy him if he doesn't use it. But out of a kind of spite he's not using it. He's going through enormous amounts of trouble in order to not be an artist. In order to not be a musician. Out of a spite that he can't even understand.

Spite is a great anger at the imperfections of the world. It's a tremendous refusal to accept the limitations of reality and of life. Camus's *Caligula* is not a great play but it has a wonderful idea behind it. Caligula becomes a murderous tyrant out of revenge against the world for being such a murderous, bad place. To revenge himself on things, he imitates life itself. I know that the spite that's in Rhinehart, the spite that's in a lot of my characters and that's in me, is a kind of fundamentally childish rage against things for being so imperfect. For being so unsatisfactory. This brings forth a tremendous anger. And when you're making up stories, perhaps you're doing it when you're dreaming too, you're trying to make things come out right. Which doesn't mean that you're writing happy stories or giving them happy endings—obviously I don't do that—but to spin narratives, to daydream, that's a way of making things come out right.

Writing is strong medicine. It takes a certain amount of discipline and handling. It's like the old image of the goddess Kundalini going up your spinal column. Whether it's meditation or whether it's writing fiction, you bring this strong stuff forth, you surrender to it. You've got to really work out some kind of discipline to get it going and then to get it settled down.

Frederick Exley, really a rather good writer who wrote a book called *A Fan's Notes,* talks about "the terrible exhilaration at the end of a day's writing." I mean the exhilaration not as something good, although you feel good—you're bouncing off the walls, you're manic. But one of the reasons writers drink is to get themselves settled down again. It's very hard to handle all this stuff. You get yourself in extremely emotional states. You get very wrought up. Even when you're feeling good you get to kind of dread that manic, exhilarated feeling because it keeps you awake, it keeps you from settling down. You're walking around, you're talking to yourself, you know you're unpresentable and you can't make the transition. It's very hard to make these transitions from the functioning, walking-around, breakfast level of things to the intense emotional states that you get into when you're writing. It's very hard on the self—on the frame and on the interior.

The process of creating is related to the process of dreaming although when you are writing you're doing it and when you're dreaming it's doing you.

I'm in control because I'm using language. Any artist who's using a tool, whether it's paint or sounds, is controlling it. I'm experiencing something that maybe is below the level of language, or prelinguistic, but I'm giving it an expression that is language. So I am controlling it. When I'm dreaming I'm being acted upon in a way. One can't be too literal about these images—because a metaphor is only a metaphor—but it is as though it was a thing, a basic thing and dreams and making fiction are two ways of relating to something that is, in fact, out there. I suppose it's that part of the universe that isn't you, which is most of it.

I think of my characters really as though they were people, especially the ones in the book I've just finished because I've been with them so long. I'll spend a lot of time just sitting around running these characters through my mind. In fact, I probably know them in a way better than real people because one's principal characters are aspects of one's self. You create projections out of yourself. What can you make characters out of if not out of yourself essentially? But I can't recall ever dreaming about a character.

Every writer will put something into their work at one time or another that they don't altogether understand. It's good to take those things and somehow use them, to give your work the proper contour, something that you don't understand. My latest novel is called *Outerbridge Reach*. Outerbridge Reach is a little stretch of water between Staten Island and New Jersey. There's a tank farm there. It's a very desolate stretch of outer New York harbor. It's the kind of scene which I often dream about because it's the kind of thing that I used to see from the rail of the ship coming into a seaport. This image means something to me that I don't altogether understand but I love the words "Outerbridge Reach," which I saw on a chart going through this passage. The words themselves suggest limits and extending and trying for something. So what's informing this book in a way is an image of a place, a very desolate place that I really don't understand, that has certainly appeared to me in dreams. And the words that go with it, the words on the chart, they're more evocative than literally meaningful. That's a good example of how the dream state and the level of language and conscious creation and unconscious reaction are linked together.

I used to spend a lot of time in the Museum of Natural History when I was young. I grew up on the West Side of New York. I can remember one of the most frightening dreams I ever had was finding myself in a setting that was like the African Hall of the Museum. I must've been about eleven. There were glass cases and some kind of dioramic display inside the cases. The hall was dark. The cases were lit. There was room after room of dark hallway with lighted cases displaying something, I don't know what.

I remember some kind of bright mineral object that was on display. It was like an enormous jewel or a quartz, something like that. I really don't remember what, except that it wasn't good.

The place was empty and I was completely lost in it. When I'd come to the end of one hall I would just go into another and it was more of the same. It was a very frightening dream, a real lolapalooza of a nightmare. I can remember it to this day and it must be forty years ago that I had it.

The first time I remember being scared in a dream I must've been pretty small. I'm in a tunnel down in Riverside Park on the West Side and I'm throwing a ball against the wall of the tunnel. I don't know why it's so frightening but it is. There's nothing in the visual content of the dream that is of itself frightening. It's just utterly terrifying. I do not understand the reason why. There was nothing in it but me—and I'm very small—and a rubber ball in the tunnel in the park. That's all. And it's enormously frightening.

Very often in my dreams I'm solitary or I'm alienated. In quite a few of my dreams I'm alone. I'm not sure what the significance of that is but very often, certainly in most of the childhood dreams I can remember, I'm alone.

I can remember childhood dreams in which there was some religious content or Catholic ceremonies taking place but without any particular religious feeling. Just ceremonies with which I was familiar from going to church. I can remember someone's eye filling the whole frame of the dream. The eye was suddenly divided into three panels. It was like a door and you could push it. That was not at all frightening. It was generally agreeable.

Another recurring dream I've had is that I'm flying something and it's disassembling. What's going on is I'm realizing there's nothing keeping me up. I feel like I'm in an airplane and I begin to realize more and more that there's nothing to this airplane, that I'm just sort of riding a broom or something and finally riding nothing. I don't fall but I get very scared. Suddenly I'm up in the air without anything holding me up. I've had that dream a lot.

I think that in writing, or anything else where you're performing, you really do require enormous amounts of confidence, reserves of it. Very often people who write are inclined to doubt themselves to start with so you really have to balance the self-doubt and the confidence. You've got to be able to relax. And when you're making yourself not worry about reactions, and what you can and can't do, you build up a tremendous amount of tension that gets reflected in your dreams. Having just finished *Outerbridge Reach* there were times when I really felt certain that I had bit off far more than I could chew, that I was really going to blow it. And I'm sure that a lot of the anxiety-provoking dreams that I had were just reflecting that tension.

The only real way to keep yourself up, outside of trying to keep in some kind of training and take a little care of yourself, is to keep yourself entertained. Because, although it's hard, it should also be fun. You've got to beguile yourself. The same way that you make a child feel better by telling a story. The basic storytelling process has got to be a resolving literary one. What you're trying to work on a reader is an altered state of consciousness. You're basically trying to occupy the reader's space with your narrative, with your story, in order to provoke insight, emotion, catharsis. Stuff that's basically good for people. And that process is an ineffable one. It's a slightly mysterious one. It's that altering of the consciousness to a different state in order to resolve and to heal. And you've got to work this process first on yourself. You relax into the story and you beguile yourself. You start by doing for yourself what you hope you're going to be doing for the reader. And you get into the pleasure of language and the constructing of the page at hand, the thing at hand, and it liberates you. It liberates you from not only your anxieties about what you're doing, but your anxieties about yourself and who you are and what's going to happen next.

You've got to get into the process. The process is liberating. The process is good. You have to take it by the day. You just can't find yourself sitting there saying, What am I going to write next? Ultimately that is what you're saying but you just can't obsess over that. You take it word by word. You take it day by day. And you have to not worry too much.

It's very difficult because the whole object is to eliminate self-consciousness. The more consciously you do it, the more difficult it is. So I do a lot of walking. I really like walking and I do a lot of thinking when I walk.

It's all about letting the story take over. It's surrendering to the process, letting yourself become involved in the process, that is necessary. You can't be outside your own story, as it were. You can't be just constructing it consciously, self-consciously, moment by moment. You've got to let your imagination go. And begin to hear voices, figuratively speaking. Get into it and do it. Beguile yourself. Entertain yourself. And keep yourself inside it.

WILLIAM STYRON

I THOUGHT I'd definitely blown it when I opened my radio interview, "My guest today is William Styron, author of *Darkness Revisited* . . ." Yet it may have been that Freudian slip that broke the ice between us. I was nervous being in the presence of one of my literary idols. The slip allowed Styron the excuse to reassure me. It was, he said, a natural mistake since his first book was *Lie Down in Darkness* and his new book, *Darkness Visible*, was revisiting the darkness that led heroine Peyton Loftis to kill herself. In fact depression, alcoholism and madness are present in all of Styron's rich, multilayered novels.

William Styron was born in 1925 in Newport News, Virginia. When he was thirteen he lost his mother to cancer. In 1951, at the age of twenty-six, William Styron stunned the literary world with the publication of his first novel, *Lie*

Down in Darkness, for which he was awarded the American
Academy of Arts and Letters' Prix du Rome. Six years later
The Long March, a novella, was published, followed in 1960
by *Set This House on Fire. The Confessions of Nat Turner*
(1967) generated enormous controversy as many questioned
the right of a white Southerner to speak from the viewpoint
of a black rebel slave. The power of the book won Styron
a Pulitzer Prize in 1968 and the Howells Medal in 1970.
Sophie's Choice, which won an American Book Award in
1980, generated further controversy when Styron chose as his
heroine a gentile survivor of the Holocaust.

In 1985, at the age of sixty, Styron found his body unable
to absorb the alcohol to which he had become habituated.
This, combined with the effects of sleeping pills, plunged
Styron into a profound depression. Hospitalized for seven
weeks, he began the slow process of recovery. Styron chronicled his experience in *Darkness Visible,* a book which has
helped bring new understanding to the nature of clinical
depression.

In 1987 Styron was awarded the title of Commandeur,
Ordre des Arts et Lettres in France. He is married to poet
and human-rights activist Rose Styron. They have four
grown children.

———

M Y ASSUMPTION is that dreams serve some very useful
psychological function, so they're important to me as they are
to, I suspect, most people.

I have to stress, emphasize to myself and to you, that I don't
know what dreams mean. Some do seem to have a kind of
profound significance. But one is constantly questioning the
natural process that makes most people, myself included, forget
a great number, if not most, of their dreams. I've had dreams in
recent years that were so astonishing that immediately when I
woke up I told my wife, I had this remarkable dream. But, even

now, I've forgotten what those dreams were. It's as if they were on a computer printout which is not really clear. I don't think dreams print on the memory like memory itself does. So, with some exceptions, I've tended to ignore dreams as a setting-off point for my fiction because often they've just never lingered long enough for me to retrieve them.

I do not believe that every dream is significant. I'm convinced of that. I believe that dreams are psychobiologically necessary and functional in the sense that dreams are our protective mechanism. We dream of a slamming door when indeed the door has slammed nearby. It protects us from waking up. I think it's often overlooked that one of the most useful functions of dreams is to keep us environmentally stable while we're asleep. A most common phenomenon, if I may be slightly indelicate, is urination dreams. We dream we're urinating to prevent ourselves from waking up to actually do the act. And this is very common. So plainly the dream mechanism has that important protective function.

I do think a small minority, but a significant minority, of dreams are meaningful. Whenever I am impressed by this significant minority of dreams, they seem important enough to want to put them in my work as a descriptive factor. They relate to the reality of my own sleeping imagination.

The whole concept of *Sophie's Choice* was the result, if not of a dream, of a kind of waking vision which occurred when I woke up one spring morning in the mid-seventies. I think it was 1974. I'd been working on a book that was not coming together for me at all. I had been slaving away at it and was getting very upset over the fact that it wasn't proceeding well. And one morning I woke up with this lingering vision. I don't like to characterize it as a dream, although I think it had the aspects of the remnant of a dream. I think there was a merging from the dream to a conscious vision and memory of this girl named Sophie. And it was powerful because I lay there in bed with the abrupt knowledge that I was going to deal with this as a work of fiction. That I had to abandon the other book I was trying to do and, because of her, because of all of the resonance surrounding her story, I was suddenly going to have to write the book which later became *Sophie's Choice*. That very morning, I remember I walked over to my studio and wrote down the first words just as they are in the book, and went from there to the end without any deviation to speak of. So, in a sense, you could say that the whole concept of the book was, if not the product of a dream itself, the product of some resonance that a dream had given me.

The kernel of my character, Sophie, was a real person, a person who looked and walked and talked very much like the Sophie I created. She was a young woman who disappeared from my life almost as quickly as she came. The story itself is really an improvisation. It's an elaboration on an idea in which she is the central figure, but her real destiny—I don't know what it really was at all.

It may be that I recalled her as I first saw her in the book, entering the hallway of this humble boarding house in Flatbush with a book under her arm, looking very beautiful in the middle of summer with a sort of summer dress on and her arm bared and the tattoo visible. That was the image I think I had but I can't really say for sure. I was seized by this absolute sense of necessity—I had to write the book. I realized then that it would end as it did in the book, at Auschwitz, with her sacrificing her children. In other words, I had the various germs of the story just at my fingertips. The choice was part of my imaginative ploy, so to speak.

I remember when I was living in Brooklyn in this Pink Palace, as I called it. I was only there five or six weeks before I left. It was a flimsy place and I was very frustrated. There was this shadow figure, he used to go and visit the woman upstairs and, as in the book, I would hear this rumpus of lovemaking right above me. A few feet above me. It was like a sort of auditory voyeurism. I was listening to this mad, passionate fornication, morning, noon and night. And it was very very upsetting to someone who, like myself, like Stingo, was very frustrated. But the true nature of her lover never became apparent to me because I never saw him in reality. He'd walk in and out. He was a rather inoffensive-looking fellow, but of course I was writing a work of fiction. I merely elaborated on this impression to create Nathan.

The so-called magic of fiction is to lure the reader into a state of believing. Believing that all this unbelievable stuff actually happened. And it's more or less a tribute or not to the writer's ability to imaginatively re-create that he convinces the reader that this indeed is a real piece of life.

In *Sophie's Choice* I needed to give Stingo as much credibility as possible in order to give the story credibility. If I could expose him more or less to the scrutiny of my imagination, make him real as a twenty-two-year-old kid who was going to learn these extraordinary things about a woman named Sophie and in the process explore what to me is a major event of the twentieth century, namely the Holocaust, I had to make him credible. And part of a young man's being, especially when twenty-two, is his erotic life. A kind of sniping criticism I got was about the fact that he masturbates. Well, a twenty-two-year-old boy, if he's not getting sex, masturbates. Constantly. I mean that's his life. It's part of his fantasy life and it's nothing that anyone in the world should be shocked about. So I wanted to include that and also to do it perhaps with a little humor. Because I think sex has elements of humor—is humorous—in its more humane manifestations. I wanted to give that undercurrent of eroticism which was pervasive in this young man's life in order to validate the rest of his experience, including his attempted seduction of this Jewish girl, which came to naught, of course. That was there because I wanted to render the texture of his experience of that particular summer many years ago.

I think erotic dreams are very troubling and probably very useful too. I used to have very intense erotic dreams. I don't have them too much any longer. It's not because I'm not still interested in erotic matters, it's just, I guess, that Eros is absorbed into the rest of my experience. So I'm not troubled by them. But certainly I used to have extremely severe erotic dreams from which I would wake sort of shaken in the same way I would waken from the dreams of death. Like the ones about my mother.

I recall, after my mother died, having a rather ghastly dream of her coming alive in the coffin. I don't believe it was a recurrent dream. It happened to be very vivid—her ravaged face twisting toward me from the satin vault. My mother died when I was thirteen, so this dream must have happened in the year or two after her death. I remember being just shaken by it. That's why I put the dream in *Sophie's Choice*.

One of the fascinating things about my own creative process in writing *Sophie's Choice* was the fact that I really believed Sophie, both as a writer and as a kind of alterego of Stingo, when she presented her father as this noble fellow. When she started talking to Stingo, she talked about her experience as a child and how she had this marvelous father who was a Polish intellectual and how she was so devoted to him intellectually, among other reasons, because of his sacrifice to save Jews during the war. When I put that down, and it's in the book just as I wrote it, I believed what she was saying. But it began to dawn on me later on as I was writing the book that what she was saying was a lie. That she was deceiving Stingo for her own self-protection, her own self-image, to prevent her from having to tell the truth. Which was the fact that instead of being a man who helped save Jews, he was in fact a rabid anti-Semite. Of course I reveal that later, but it's one of the interesting aspects of the creative process that I really believed her in the beginning.

Somewhere along the line I began to realize, as a writer, that one of her character defects, or quirks at least, was this obsessive need to lie. And it was interesting because that way I could discover her both lying and telling the truth at will.

Whenever I wanted her to tell the truth she'd tell the truth. It seemed to me a splendid way of revealing a story, to make both the narrator and the reader puzzle over whether she was telling the truth or not.

When I'm writing at my best I'm aware that I'm tapping subconscious sources. Certainly dreams well up from that particular source too. There is a kind of interweaving of the dream life even though I can't, as I say, remember specific dreams too vividly.

I know for sure that one of the most amazing aspects of the depressive illness I suffered from was my awareness that I had inserted this depressive mood into the characters of my fiction throughout my career. From Peyton Loftis to Sophie. Why did all these people commit suicide? It must've had the same wellspring as that which sent me into my near-suicidal depression.

As I said in *Darkness Visible,* after I'd recovered from this illness, I was aware, for the first time in my life, that it was an illness which had more or less been in the suburbs of my existence all my life. Ever since my mother died. I still believe that her death was a traumatic event for me. That I was living that trauma and trying to re-create aspects of it throughout most of my creative life. And that I was in effect—I don't like the word but I will use it—a depressive, for most of my life. I kept most of the malignant aspects of depression at bay, at arm's length, by drinking alcohol, which prevented the true depression from taking hold. And when I abandoned alcohol, the cataclysm came down on me.

In the old days, when I drank much too heavily for my own good, even then, I never wrote a word while I was under the influence of alcohol. It was always after. Or long, long before. I could never set down a word if I was boozed up. You simply have to be sober when you write. There's just no getting around that.

I think that there was a subconscious need and a subconscious welling up of depression throughout my entire creative life. I wrote vividly about, for instance, Sophie's suffering depression. You may recall there's a place in the book where she's on a subway and she is digitally raped. This traumatizes her and she goes back to her room in the rooming house and she lies there contemplating suicide. Now I wrote that without knowing anything at the time about the pathological effects of depression. I wrote it out of intuition. What I'm trying to say is that this is evidence to me of the fact that I was always linked to the depressive mood throughout my writing life.

One of the desperately painful aspects of many depressions is sleep disruption. It seems to be the biological key to a lot of serious depressions. And in this disruption of sleep often—at least it was in my case—there is a total absence of dreams. Which causes me to say that the absence of dreams is a sign of psychic unhealth. And the presence of dreams is, contrarily, a sign of psychic health, or at least of psychic balance. I think one has to have dreams in order to fulfill the function of sleep. And so to have an absence of dreams was an almost intolerable aspect of my illness. I was quite conscious of the fact that when I woke from a kind of synthetic, pill-induced sleep (I was taking tranquilizers at the time in order to sleep) that there were no dreams that I registered in my mind during that period. Whether it's the cart before the horse I don't know, but the point is that the absence of dreams was very much bound up with my illness.

Depression is a serious disorder of the brain. All your juices dry up—your creative juices, your procreative juices—everything is withered. There's nothing there. That's one of the characteristics of depression, all the life, the vital, biological processors are dust.

Not everyone experiences an absence of dreams while in a deep depression, I've been told. But it certainly was my experience and I know that by contrast the sudden appearance of dreams was an announcement to me that I was getting well.

On the first pass I had from the hospital—after over seven

weeks, I was allowed to go home—that particular night I remember being unbelievably exhausted for some reason, from the cumulative effect of the illness, even though I was getting well. I remember falling into bed at about nine o'clock in the evening and just dreaming a marathon dream all night. It was like *Raiders of the Lost Ark*. It was my first truly nonstop dream in many many months. It was as if the absence of dreams was being compensated for by this one marathon, very boisterous and quite wonderful dream where I dreamt over and over again I was in some sort of wily action-adventure movie. I was in various kinds of machines, sort of cross-country all-purpose machines, and I was being chased. And I was chasing. There was no menace about this, it was more like a kid's game. It went on for hour after hour. It was quite extraordinary and incredibly therapeutic. It was as if my brain was announcing the return to well-being through this kind of amazing nonstop dream. It was quite an experience.

For me the cure was time and a kind of process of letting this illness, whatever it was—this mind storm, brain storm—just dissipate, evaporate. It took time. It took two months, but it disappeared finally.

For years when I was younger I had a kind of seminightmare. I say seminightmare because it wasn't one of those shattering nightmares that just leave you broken and distressed, but it was troubling anyway. It was a dream of water spouts: being in a cellar or heading for a cellar like one flees to from a tornado, being terrified that the tornado was going to overtake and destroy me.

I was always saved. Or I'd wake up before they overwhelmed the house or wherever I was fleeing from.

I lived near the James River when I grew up and we did actually have water spouts. They were usually quite harmless but in my dreams they appeared as figures of terrible menace. They recurred for a number of years. And then, for some reason, disappeared. That's the only experience I ever had of recurrent dreams.

Perhaps my work was troubling me and they represented the threat of uncompleted work or something. I'm not really sure. Plainly they represented some sort of threat. And they probably were therapeutic.

I think that music has been central, in a curious way, to all my work. Had it not been for music I doubt if I would have ever been a writer. It's been an inspiration to me in the same way that, for other writers, the plastic arts or nature can be an inspiration. It just happens to be music that has often created the wellspring out of which my imaginative efforts have sprung.

I could never be distracted at the moment of writing but surrounding my writing—before, after—the pleasure and the kind of aesthetic bliss that one gets from music has been very central to my imaginative process.

My creative process is slow, laborious, very painful. I wish it were not so, I wish I were more fecund but I'm not. I've had finally to deal with that and just to accept it.

I have to have an overwhelming need to write a work. This was true for virtually everything I've ever written. A kind of sense of knowing that, when I've finished it, I will have said something—to me at least—very important, something of overwhelming necessity. I don't mean to say I can't sit down and write a nice article about something which is not going to shake the world by its ears, but I mean that when I'm trying to write a book of some weight and substance it really has to seize me. By my ears so to speak. It has to tap into all my emotional and intellectual needs. And I have to get it down or else. I have to be consumed by it, in effect.

I mean Sophie was to me so—when I had that apparition that morning in the mid-seventies. I knew that I was onto something that for me was absolutely essential to deliver myself of. I knew that I would be creating a very important effect if, on the last page, I could move the reader in the way I was moved by the sight of a woman condemning one of her children to death. I wanted it to be almost a metaphor for this ghastliest event of human history. If I could achieve that then I would say I'm satisfied. I've done the best I can. I'm sorry I haven't written twenty-eight more books like Joyce Carol Oates, but I've done my best and that to me is enough to satisfy my needs as an artist.

AMY TAN

AMY TAN was born in Oakland, California, in 1952, two and a half years after her parents immigrated to the United States from China. She began writing at an early age, winning her first literary contest at the age of eight.

Tan's first novel, *The Joy Luck Club,* was an instant best-seller. This tale of four Chinese mothers, their American-born daughters and the secrets between them became a finalist for the National Book Award and the National Book Critics Circle Award.

Tan's second novel, *The Kitchen God's Wife,* is based on a series of conversations she had with her mother, Daisy, after the latter complained that too many people thought *The Joy Luck Club* was her true story.

Amy Tan lives in San Francisco with her husband, Lou DeMattei.

▬▬▬

FIFTEEN YEARS ago I realized how important dreams were in my life. They weren't just flotsam and jetsam, I could actually change the way that I felt about myself through dreams. The most significant dreams came to me shortly after my friend Pete died. He was actually murdered. One night I entered into a dream and Pete was there. He said, "I want to take you to this place where I live." I thought, Well, that's interesting. When we arrived, I saw it was a wonderful idyllic setting with a lot of creatures flying around: elephants, camels, people. I said, "I'd like to try flying myself." And he said, "Sure, but since you're not dead, you have to go over to that booth there and rent some wings. They're only a quarter." I said, "Great," and I went and rented the wings.

I took off, and I was flying around with all the other people, having a wonderful time. All of a sudden, I realized, "This is ridiculous. How can I fly with these twenty-five-cent wings?" Immediately I started to fall. I was terrified I was going to die. Then I thought, Wait a minute, I was just flying a minute ago, and I started flying again. I went back and forth with this— falling and flying, falling and flying—until it finally dawned on me what this was about. I said to myself: It is not these wings that enable you to fly, it's your own confidence.

I realized there were many things in my life that I was not allowing myself to do because I lacked the confidence. I needed the props. I could see all the props that I'd been using, and they were just like those twenty-five-cent wings. I could see how ridiculous it was.

Even though it was a dream, I felt it on a gut level of experience—the fear of failing, falling, and the elation of fly- ing—and without the dream, it probably would have taken me much longer to come to such a very simple realization about myself.

I also had dreams about my fears. I think we all have dreams of being chased by something so horrible that we become paralyzed. The harder you run, the more difficult it is to get away. I had a dream in which Pete said, "Turn around and look at what's chasing you. Turn around and look." And I said, "No, it'll kill me." And Pete said, "No, turn around." And I turned around, and I looked, and it was this version of Old Mr. Chou.

Old Mr. Chou is a character that I had heard about when I was a child. He is the mythical guardian of dreams who lets you in a door and gives you your dreams for the evening. The Old Mr. Chou archetype showed up in my dreams over and over in different incarnations—a sort of mythical being who's supposed to be benevolent but suddenly becomes evil. He becomes very strong and malevolent and chases you.

When I turned around in the dream, Old Mr. Chou looked so surprised to see me looking at him that he disappeared. The instant realization I had from that dream was this: You give these Old Mr. Chous, these phantoms, their power through your fear, and if you turn around and face them—confront what's chasing you—they will disappear.

All during the nine months of the trial for Pete's murder, I had dreams like this. Every single night, I would be taken to a place and given lessons: the lesson with the wings, the lesson about my fears chasing me. The dreams were incredible. At the end of the nine months, when the trial was finally over, Pete came to me and said, "Now I have to go, and you have to go on with your life. We're not going to be doing these things together any more in the dreams." I had really enjoyed that period of learning. I said, "Who are you to decide? You are not the one who decides. These are *my* dreams." I was so angry. I remember yelling and saying, "You have no right! You have no right! This is *my* dream!" And he said, "No, this is the way it is. I'm sorry. But I will leave you with a friend you'll get to know in the future. I think you'll like her." Well, I did meet the person he talked about, a fiction writer, and we've become good friends. She was one of the first people to encourage me to write fiction.

Those dreams with Pete were very clear. But since the last dream, I have never had a dream where I was able to talk directly to him. The dreams I have about Pete now are more surrealistic. They're bizarre and sometimes violent and distressing, often having to do with his death, but none of them have conversation. It could be that at that point in my life, when the trial was over, I too realized I needed to move on to other things, and this is the way I had to learn that lesson.

The kind of writing I do is very dreamlike. The process I go through is similar to what happens when I dream. I have found in dreams that I can change the setting by simply looking down at my feet then looking up again. I'll be following my feet for a while and, if I don't like what I see in front of me, I will just look down at my feet. I'll start walking, and when I look up, I'll be in a different place.

I do a similar thing when I'm writing. I focus on a specific image, and that image takes me into a scene. Then I begin to see the scene and I ask myself, "What's to your right? What's to your left?" and I open up into this fictional world. I often play music as a way of blocking out the rest of my consciousness, so I can enter into this world and let it go where it wants to go, wherever the characters want to go. It takes me into some surprising places.

The kind of imagination I use in writing, when I try to lose control of consciousness, works very much like dreams. The subconscious takes over and it's fun. I discover things I could never pull up if I were really trying to. When I get into a dream world I can create fiction by going down surprising pathways.

That's the magic that comes through fiction, through not knowing things completely. I've heard psychologists say that the kind of brain waves operating when you are creating are similar to the kind of patterns that you have in deep relaxation and sleep. Things that come from your subconscious in a dreamlike state can be a lot more honest than they would be if your consciousness was turned on or if your defenses were completely in place. When you lose that sense of protecting your ego, richer symbols appear.

Sometimes, if I'm stuck on the ending of a story, I'll just take the story with me to bed. I'll let it become part of a dream and see if something surfaces.

I did this once with a story in *The Joy Luck Club*, the one about a woman trying to get out of an arranged marriage. As I was writing it, I felt as though I was blocking myself into a corner. I was like a little rat running around a maze and I didn't know how to get out. This woman in the story was in a complicated situation. She couldn't break her promise, yet she needed to get out of the marriage. So I took that story problem to bed with me, along with some other information, and I dreamed an ending that turned out to be quite workable and funny.

I don't normally see my characters in dreams exactly as they appear in a book, but I do experience a similar kind of feeling or emotion, something that gives me new insight into the questions that I'm asking of those characters.

My mother believes that my dreams have always been powerful. I don't know what to make of this. She's always believed that, coupled with my imagination, I've had this ability to make contact with the other world. She thinks that I do this sometimes in my sleep, sometimes when I write fiction.

I've had remarkable coincidences happen to me both in waking life and in dreams. They had to do with somebody nudging me and saying, Pay attention to your writing. There was all this stuff going on in my life and I didn't really know what to pay attention to. But around 1987, before *The Joy Luck Club* was sold, I remember saying to my husband, "Every time I forget about writing fiction, something happens, like this reminder to write, to keep it up, to keep it in mind." I said, "Remember this conversation because something is going to happen."

* * *

I've had dreams in which I'm at a slot machine or a telephone and all of a sudden the return change slot goes crazy. It keeps pouring out money. Only when I reach for the money, something happens—I can't quite get to the money, although it's right there. Well, I've learned to control the dream so I can make the money keep coming out and I can get to it. If it's a slot machine, I'll say to myself, Wait a minute, this is a dream. I have control over this, I can make all the cherries come up. The key is realizing that it is a dream and that there's a part of me that can control what is happening in the dream. Just like I look down at my shoes and look up and control the setting. If I can recognize these little cues, they actually work.

If something is interesting to me in a dream I'll tell myself, Pay attention and take a closer look, especially with things having to do with violence. I used to worry because a lot of my dreams are very violent. But I read recently that if you have a lot of dreams about violence, it's an indication that you are a creative person.

The childhood dreams that I remember are very frightening. I remember one that relates to mothers and daughters. I was six years old and I was running away from my mother. I escaped, but then someone else caught me and held me under a faucet of hot water—until I turned into a bunch of linked sausages. That was the most frightening dream of my childhood. I have never forgotten that dream. I don't know what it means, but I suppose the message was, if you disobey your mother, it's instant hot-dog death.

My mother once told me that in Chinese culture to dream of your teeth falling out means that you're going to lose something. So of course now when I have dreams of losing my teeth, I get really nervous. I find myself hoping to lose something inconsequential, like a pencil. I think these dreams happen when I'm not really paying attention to more important things in life.

If I dream about something very realistic, like losing a friend or my purse, my first interpretation would be that this might happen in real life. But then I realize that these are not premonitions, but a warning that comes through the subconscious and it's saying, "Be careful, don't lose yourself, be a little more careful." In other words, go ahead and lose a pencil, but realize that there are some things that are worth hanging on to.

The most difficult parts of my life certainly have been integrated into my dreams—like the deaths of my father and brother. I sometimes dream that they really didn't die and that I am now responsible for making sure that they get well. In these dreams, they're always changed a little bit. They have this sad look that seems to say, "I want to go home now." Those are my most difficult dreams. I've never been able to tell myself, "Oh, this is just a dream, I can cure them," or "This is a dream, I can send them off to the other world happily." Those dreams are disturbing and they just keep coming back. I suppose they represent moments of unresolved grief in my life, a wish that I'd like to take them home and feel a sense of security and comfort again.

The success of *The Joy Luck Club* was the kind of experience where one could say, "You have absolutely nothing to complain about. This is all so wonderful." That's true. But there was a part of me that was very angry, and I didn't understand why at first. Well, I have a lot of dreams that have to do with shoes, and one night I had a dream that my husband and I were walking somewhere when I suddenly realized that I had lost my shoes. I said to him, "I have to go back and get my shoes, they're my favorite, my most comfortable shoes. I can't go on without them." He had also lost his shoes and there were snakes in the grass. It was dangerous to go on. We retraced our steps and he found his shoes right away. But mine were gone and I was upset that I knew I would never find these comfortable old shoes again. At that point, a shoe salesman pointed to a rack of shoes nearby and said to me, "Here, you can buy these shoes instead." They were all high heels, all fancy things, and I said, "I don't want those, I want the same old shoes." I had such a sense of loss. When I woke up, I realized what I had lost: this old feeling of comfort. And that my husband could still enjoy it.

I remember my dreams every morning, but if I don't write them down, they flit away. They go back to their own world again. They're still out there as I'm waking up, but if I don't write them down, they retreat and the door closes and I don't remember them anymore.

There was a period in my life when I tried to record my dreams. I could recall them in so much detail that I'd end up spending half the morning writing them down. Pretty soon it would get really confusing because I couldn't distinguish between things that had actually happened—good feelings that I'd had or emotional upsets during the day—and the things that were simply dreams. So I stopped recording them. But I do feel if ever I was looking for a source of material, all I would have to do is go back to my dreams.

INDEX